OFF THE BEATEN PATH®
WASHINGTON →

Help Us Keep This Guide Up to Date

We've made every effort to make this guide as accurate and useful as possible. However, many changes occur after a guide is published—establishments close, phone numbers change, hiking trails are rerouted, facilities come under new management, etc.

We would love to hear about your experiences with this guide and how you feel it could be improved. While we may not be able to respond to all comments and suggestions, we'll take them to heart, and we'll make certain to share them with the authors. Please send your comments and suggestions to the following address:

The Globe Pequot Press
Reader Response/Editorial Departmen
P.O. Box 480
Guilford, CT 06437

Or you may e-mail us at: editorial@GlobePequot.com.

Thanks for your input, and happy travels!

OFF THE BEATEN PATH® SERIES

EIGHTH EDITION

OFF THE BEATEN PATH®
WASHINGTON →

A GUIDE TO UNIQUE PLACES

SHARON WOOTTON AND MAGGIE SAVAGE

gpp®
travel

Guilford, Connecticut

The prices, rates, and hours listed in this guidebook were confirmed at press time. We recommend, however, that you call establishments to obtain current information before traveling.

To buy books in quantity for corporate use
or incentives, call **(800) 962-0973**
or e-mail **premiums@GlobePequot.com.**

Text design by Linda R. Loiewski
Maps by Equator Graphics © Morris Book Publishing, LLC
Illustrations by Carole Drong
Spot photography throughout © Mike Norton/Shutterstock

ISSN 1540-8442
ISBN 978-0-7627-4882-2

Printed in the United States of America
10 9 8 7 6 5 4 3 2 1

Contents

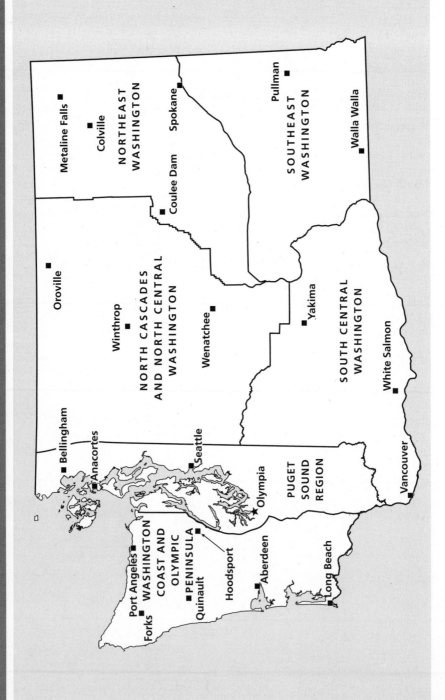

WASHINGTON

Metaline Falls ■

Colville ■

NORTHEAST
WASHINGTON

Spokane ■

Coulee Dam ■

Pullman ■

SOUTHEAST
WASHINGTON

Walla Walla ■

Oroville ■

Winthrop ■

NORTH CASCADES
AND NORTH CENTRAL
WASHINGTON

Wenatchee ■

Yakima ■

SOUTH CENTRAL
WASHINGTON

White Salmon ■

Bellingham ■

Anacortes ■

Seattle ■

Olympia ★

PUGET
SOUND
REGION

Vancouver ■

Port Angeles ■

WASHINGTON
COAST AND
OLYMPIC
PENINSULA

Forks ■

Quinault ■

Hoodsport ■

Aberdeen ■

Long Beach ■

Acknowledgments

Our many thanks to the dozens of folks who were very helpful in updating the information in this edition. No one knows an area best like local residents: the restaurants, cafes, bakeries, and coffee shop owners; museum and park staffs and volunteers; shopkeepers and innkeepers; visitor information centers' staffs and volunteers; regional history gurus; and the men and women on the street who gave us information and opinions. Our special thanks to Myrna Oakley, who after writing several editions of *Washington Off the Beaten Path*, has put the book in our hands.

Introduction

The Space Needle, Mount Rainier, Seattle, and the Olympic Mountains are well-known tourist destinations in Washington but the real fun begins when you explore off the beaten path. Washington's attractions are diverse and scattered across the state, mixed in with dense evergreen forests, fertile farmlands, and foggy islands as well as secluded windblown beaches, rivers, small-town cafes, and tiny hamlets, particularly in the southeast and northeast corners. Because of our interest in cozy bed-and-breakfast inns, great public gardens, historic downtowns, and outdoor activities, readers will find these subjects expanded in this, the eighth edition of *Washington Off the Beaten Path*.

Using This Guide to Plan Great Trips

Although it sometimes seems that there are only two seasons in Washington—the Rainy Season and the Dry Season, we do have four seasons to consider when planning your trips. The busiest times for most destinations west of the Cascade Mountains, particularly around Puget Sound waters and the San Juan Islands, will be during June, July, and August. Major freeways and all ferries will carry more traffic and waiting lines at ferry terminals will be considerably longer. If you want less traffic and fewer crowds, plan to travel midweek or travel in the shoulder seasons, April and May or September and October. Autumn in the Northwest is usually sunny and mild, with fall colors especially fine in October.

If you enjoy snow and winter sports, plan treks to the Cascade Mountains from late November through February. Be prepared with all-weather tires and chains, layers of warm clothing, emergency kits, and plenty of snacks and beverages. To start your winter research you'll find helpful telephone numbers and Web sites in the Skiing Washington sidebar in the "Mountain Passes, Valleys, and Canyons" section of the North Cascades and North Central Washington chapter.

The eastern two-thirds of the Evergreen State offer crisp, cold winters and hot, dry summers. Travel early spring and fall for some of the best weather east of the Cascade Mountains. Eastern Washington also offers fewer crowds, quieter byways, and many pleasant, undiscovered destinations. You'll encounter friendly locals who are glad to help travelers with directions. Note: Plan for long distances between services in the eastern regions—gas up often and load up on picnic foods, snacks, beverages, and ice for the cooler.

To help plan your accommodations, within each chapter we've offered lodging suggestions including telephone numbers and, usually, a Web site. Nearly all establishments are smoke free and do not allow pets. Call ahead to ask specific questions 'and to make reservations. See Places to Eat at the end of each chapter for cafes, coffee shops, and casual restaurants in selected towns and cities. You will also find dining suggestions within each chapter.

A Few More Ideas

We suggest maintaining a flexible schedule. Allow plenty of time to stop for unexpected sights. Even with the best research, a place or attraction may be closed or hours or telephone numbers changed. If this occurs, stop at the nearest visitor information center or chamber of commerce (often the same) where staff and volunteers can offer current information and suggestions. Often these centers are open on weekdays as well as weekends during summer months. Additionally, locals around town are usually willing to offer travelers information, ideas, and directions.

If you're traveling with youngsters, encourage them to write notes to new folks they meet and to collect information on historic sights, attractions, geology, natural history, and whatever else tickles their fancies. In this way you can help them become savvy travelers who appreciate making new friends and who care for preserving towns and cities as well as respecting the great outdoors.

Travel Styles and Interests

Your family is the rugged outdoors type? You want four-season recreation information? Go to the chapter on North Cascades and North Central Washington.

A word about . . .

Pets: Except for state campgrounds and RV parks, where leashed pets are usually allowed, assume that most places do not allow pets.

Eateries: Hours tend to range from longer in the summer to shorter in the winter, especially in the San Juan Islands and the farther off the beaten path that you travel. If in doubt, stop at visitor information centers to check on the local cafes and restaurants.

Web sites: Not all Web sites are regularly updated and outdated information can languish on these sites for years. If you're unsure, call for the latest information.

To pass through Canadian customs: U.S. citizens age 19 or older need proof of citizenship, such as a birth certificate or naturalization certificate or passport; and government-issue ID such as a driver's license to prove identity. An alternative to a passport is an enhanced Washington state driver's license and identification card. Children 18 and younger need proof of citizenship, such as a birth certificate. Pets need proof of an up-to-date rabies vaccination.

For assistance with serious backcountry and wilderness trip planning, contact the Outdoor Recreation Information Center in the REI flagship store in Seattle (206-470-4060). National park or Forest Service rangers are there 10:00 a.m. to 6:00 p.m. daily at 222 Yale Avenue North. Or perhaps you and your family are water-loving types, fond of salt water, surf sounds, and watching the tides change. Go to the chapters on the Washington Coast and Olympic Peninsula and on Puget Sound and the Islands.

If you have a hankerin' to pull on the Levi's, cowboy or cowgirl boots, and a wide-brimmed hat or you want to see a rodeo or ride a horse, browse Northeast Washington, Southeast Washington, and the Okanogan Valley region in the North Cascades and North Central Washington chapter. If you want to explore the routes taken by the *Lewis and Clark expedition* go to the chapters on the Washington Coast and Olympic Peninsula, South Central Washington, and Southeast Washington.

A Final Word

May your travels in the Pacific Northwest be filled with great adventures, much serendipity, many new vistas, and new friends from the diverse cultures that live and work in this vast region of waters, islands, mountains, rolling farmlands, deep gorges, and high deserts. Please tell us about places that you'd recommend for the next edition of *Washington Off the Beaten Path*. Send your suggestions to songandword@rockisland.com.

FAST FACTS ABOUT WASHINGTON

- **Population:** 6.5 million
- **Area:** 66,582 square miles
- **Capital:** Olympia, located in Thurston County south of Seattle at the southernmost tip of Puget Sound
- **Number of counties:** thirty-nine
- **County names, from west to east:** Wahkiakum, Pacific, Grays Harbor, Jefferson, Clallam, Mason, Thurston, Lewis, Cowlitz, Clark, Skamania, Pierce, King, Kitsap, Snohomish, Island, San Juan, Skagit, Whatcom, Okanogan, Chelan, Kittitas, Yakima, Klickitat, Benton, Grant, Douglas, Ferry, Lincoln, Adams, Franklin, Walla Walla, Columbia, Asotin, Garfield, Whitman, Spokane, Stevens, Pend Oreille
- **Highest point:** Mount Rainier (14,410 feet), located southeast of Tacoma
- **Largest county:** Okanogan; 5,268 square miles
- **Least populated county:** Garfield; 2,223 people

- **Major body of water:** Puget Sound, which carves deep into the northwest section of the state from the Strait of Juan de Fuca south to Olympia
- **Major rivers:** Columbia River east of the Cascade Mountain Range flows south and west to the Pacific Ocean; Snake River flows west from the Idaho border and empties into the Columbia River at the Tri-Cities; and the Skagit River flows west from the Cascades to Puget Sound.
- **Largest natural lake:** Fifty-five-mile-long Lake Chelan in central Washington, fed by streams from the North Cascades at Stehekin and east to the town of Chelan.
- **Nickname:** Evergreen State
- **State bird:** goldfinch
- **State fish:** steelhead trout
- **State flower:** coastal rhododendron
- **State gem/rock:** petrified wood
- **State tree:** Western hemlock
- **State folk song:** "Roll on Columbia, Roll On"
- **State grass:** bluebunch wheatgrass
- **State insect:** blue darner dragonfly
- **State fossil:** Columbian mammoth
- **State fruit:** apple
- **State marine mammal:** orca
- **State amphibian:** Pacific chorus frog

Washington Coast and Olympic Peninsula

Washington's Pacific Ocean coastline is a stretch of contrasts from the **Strait of Juan de Fuca** in the north to the mouth of the Columbia River in the south. The Olympic Peninsula's ocean shoreline is rugged, with steep cliffs and rocky formations sculpted by wave and wind. Farther south are gentle, sandy beaches lined with summer cottages and tourist communities. **Grays Harbor** and **Willapa Bay** break up the coastline and create extensive wetlands that are important wildlife habitats, especially during bird migrations. The Olympic Peninsula rain forest has the highest annual rainfall on the continental United States, yet the Dungeness Valley on the Strait of Juan de Fuca—near the community of Sequim—has the lowest precipitation on the coast north of Los Angeles.

The snow-covered peaks of the Olympic Mountains provide a stunning backdrop to beaches, forests, and valleys in the region. Most of the Olympic Peninsula is thickly forested and includes some of the world's largest trees. Many local families have been loggers, fishermen, or mill workers for three or four generations, although logging is now a shadow of its former self. Several small Indian reservations are on the Olympic Peninsula including the Makah, the Jamestown S'Klallam,

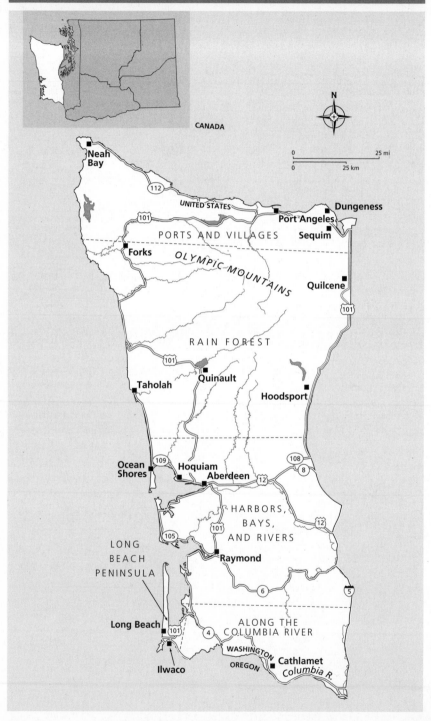

WASHINGTON COAST AND OLYMPIC PENINSULA

CANADA

0   25 mi

0   25 km

N

Neah
Bay

112

UNITED STATES

101

Dungeness

Port Angeles

PORTS AND VILLAGES   Sequim

Forks

OLYMPIC MOUNTAINS

Quilcene

101

RAIN FOREST

101

Quinault

Taholah

Hoodsport

109

108

Ocean
Shores

8

Hoquiam

12

Aberdeen

HARBORS,

BAYS,

105

AND RIVERS

12

LONG

101

BEACH

PENINSULA

Raymond

6

5

ALONG THE

Long Beach   COLUMBIA RIVER

101

4

WASHINGTON   Cathlamet

OREGON   Columbia R.

Ilwaco

the Lower Elwah, the Quileute, the Hoh, the Quinault, the Shoalwater, and the Skokomish.

Outdoor activities include hiking, bicycling, kite-flying, kayaking, fishing, birding, and beachcombing. Bring along rain gear and good walking shoes or boots so that you and the kids can take advantage of the trails and beaches that are accessible most of the year.

Ports and Villages

Fifteen miles west and north of *Olympia* on U.S. Highway 101, as you enter the Hood Canal area, the craggy Olympic Mountains will come into view on the northern horizon. The first stop is the lumber town of *Shelton,* dominated by a lumber mill that sprawls along the waterfront; its entire complex can be seen from the hilltop viewpoint adjacent to the huge sawmill wheel, a monument to the lumber industry. The Shelton-Mason County Chamber of Commerce (800-576-2021) is at 221 West Railroad Avenue. The visitor center (same telephone) is across the street in the red caboose at 230 West Railroad

WASHINGTON COAST'S TOP ATTRACTIONS

Aberdeen Museum of History
Aberdeen

Arthur D. Feiro Marine Life Center
Port Angeles

Cape Disappointment State Park
Mouth of the Columbia River

Columbia Pacific Heritage Museum
Ilwaco

Dungeness National Wildlife Refuge
Sequim

Grays Harbor Historical Seaport
Aberdeen

Hoh Rainforest
Forks

Hurricane Ridge
Port Angeles

Lake Quinault Resort
Lake Quinault

Leadbetter Point State Park
Oysterville

Lewis and Clark Interpretive Center
Ilwaco

Makah Museum
Neah Bay

Northwest Carriage Museum
Raymond

Pacific County Historical Museum
South Bend

Tokeland Hotel
Tokeland

Westport Maritime Museum
Westport

Whale-watching
Westport

World Kite Museum & Hall of Fame
Long Beach

Lavender Town U.S.A.

Sequim's rich soil, low rainfall, and warm temperatures have spawned a booming agricultural industry. Waves of lavender plants from pale violet to deep purple grow on farms in the Dungeness Valley. To see and sniff hundreds of varieties such as Provence, Grosso, and Munstead, plan to attend the annual Lavender Festival the third weekend of July. Enjoy activities that include farm tours, a street fair, great food, art shows, and live music. See www.lavenderfestival.com for details, then enjoy visiting lavender farms and finding lavender plants for your gardens while stocking up on lavender soaps, bath oils, and lotions for your senses.

Cedarbrook Herb & Lavender Farm
(800) 470-8423
www.lavenderfarms.com/cedarbrook

The Cutting Garden and Farmhouse Gallery
(360) 681-3099
www.cuttinggarden.com

Jardin du Soleil Lavender
(877) 527-3461
www.jardindusoleil.com

Lost Mountain Lavender
(888) 507-7481
www.lostmountainlavender.com

Olympic Lavender Farm
(360) 683-4475
www.olympiclavender.com

Purple Haze Lavender Farm
(360) 683-1714
www.purplehazelavender.com

Sequim Lavender
Growers Association
www.lavendergrowers.org

Avenue. Nearby, you can order a juicy hamburger or fresh seafood at **Big E's** (324 West Railroad Avenue; 360-426-2186). For quick snacks and great coffee and espresso, check out **Urraco Coffee Roaster Company** (628 South Cota Street; 360-462-5282), and **Riverside Espresso** (332 South First Street; 360-426-3300).

At the corner of Railroad Avenue and Fifth Street, the **Mason County Historical Society Museum** (360-426-1020) offers exhibits of the region's logging and frontier past. Located in a library building constructed in 1914, the museum features family photographs, pioneer tools and artifacts, and a nineteenth-century schoolroom. The museum is open from 11:00 a.m. to 5:00 p.m. Tuesday through Friday, and 11:00 a.m. to 4:00 p.m. Saturday. Stroll down Railroad Avenue and Cota Street to get a feel for the town and its antiques and secondhand shops.

From Shelton continue north on US 101 along the salty tidal waters of Hood Canal, passing through the waterside communities of Hoodsport, Lilliwaup, Brinnon, and Quilcene on your way to Port Townsend, Sequim, and

Port Angeles in the northern section of the Olympic Peninsula. A scenic spot that may entice an overnight stay is the ***Glen Ayr Hood Canal Waterfront Resort*** at 25381 North U.S. Highway 101 (866-877-9522; www.glenayr.com) located about 1 mile north of Hoodsport. Glen Ayr is part RV park, part motel, part one-bedroom suites, and a two-bedroom townhouse. The Hoodsport Visitors Center (150 N. Cushman Road; 360-877-2021) can offer a wealth of information on Hood Canal attractions, recreation, lodging, and dining. Or, continue north on winding US 101 for 1½ miles and check out waterside RV sites at ***Rest-a-While RV Park*** (360-877-9474; www.restawhile.com). It was homesteaded in 1889 and turned into a resort in the early 1900s.

The towering peaks of the Olympic Mountains shelter the northernmost Dungeness Valley from the copious rainfall of the rest of the peninsula, making it the "banana belt" of the Northwest coast. ***Sequim*** is the commercial center of the valley and a good base from which to explore this scenic region. For an overnight stay on a secluded hilltop, call the ***Greywolf Inn*** vacation rental (395 Keeler Road; 800-914-9653), which offers a whole-house rental. For those who would like to be closer to the water, check out ***Juan de Fuca Cottages*** at 182 Marine Drive (866-683-4433; www.juandefuca.com) where there are five cozy cottages with kitchens and wide-angle views of the strait, as well as two suites and a three-bedroom house 1 mile away. Or call Dungeness Bay Cottages at 140 Marine Drive (888-683-3013; www.dungenessbay.com) and ask about its six comfy units with great water views and private beach. For a more historical stay, try one of the six cabooses from the golden age of rail at the Red Caboose Getaway at 24 Old Coyote Way (360-683-7350; www .caboosegetaway.com). A stay includes a queen-size feather bed and a Jacuzzi for two. Look forward to a gourmet breakfast on white linen tablecloth with crystal glassware in a 1937 Zephyr dining car (ask about lunch, too).

Just west of the city limits at the end of Hendrickson Road is the ***Dungeness River Railroad Bridge Park,*** a scenic spot with nature trails to the river and an Audubon center near the parking lot. On another excursion take Taylor Cut-off Road south from US 101 toward the mountains to reach ***Lost Mountain Winery*** at 3174 Lost Mountain Road (888-683-5229; www.lostmountain

Sleep with History

Looking for unusual places to sleep? Washington offers U.S. Forest Service fire lookouts (long on views, short on square footage), lighthouse keepers' residences at Cape Disappointment State Park, and a former Victorian home and a "castle" at Fort Worden State Park in Port Townsend.

.com). Since 1981 award-winning red dinner wines without added sulfites have been hand-crafted in limited bottles at this secluded winery high in the Olympic foothills. The small facility currently produces approximately 1,500 cases per year of hearty Italian-style reds. Also in the area is Lost Mountain Lavender Farm at 1541 Taylor Cutoff Road (888-507-7481), a three-acre farm with more than 120 varieties of lavender.

Find a delightful place to eat lunch at **Cedarbrook Lavender & Herb Farm** at 1345 South Sequim Avenue (800-470-8423), a twelve-acre farm planted in aromatic herbs and native plants that's open year-round except for January and February. You can purchase fresh flowers, lavender plants, dried herbs, herb vinegars, dried flower bouquets and wreaths, garlic ropes, and herb sachets. Lavender lovers can stop at **Purple Haze Lavender Farm** (180 Bell Bottom Lane; 888-852-6560) to inspect a colorful display garden, collect a bouquet from the U-pick field of organic lavender plants, and browse a nice selection of lavender products during the summer season.

rainshadow

It might rain 140 inches in the **Hoh Rainforest** on the Olympic Peninsula's west side but Sequim's average rainfall is 17 inches, the driest Pacific Coast climate north of Los Angeles. It's in the rain shadow of the Olympic Mountains on the peninsula's northeast corner. The mountains block most of the rain.

To explore the historic community of **Dungeness,** head north from US 101 on Sequim–Dungeness Way from downtown Sequim. Dungeness is old by Washington standards, named in 1792 by British explorer Captain George Vancouver. Charles Seal established the Dungeness Trading Company in the 1890s and built a large country farmhouse with the proceeds. Simone Nichols has renovated Seal's home into **Groveland Cottage Bed and Breakfast Inn** at 4861 Sequim–Dungeness Way (800-879-8859; www.grovelandcottage.com). Guests sleep in cozy rooms on the second floor and wake up to views of the Olympic Mountains and the gardens, plus a delicious breakfast. There's also the historic **Dungeness Schoolhouse,** built in 1892 and used to educate local children until 1955, as well as several turn-of-the-century homes. Sequim–Dungeness Way ends near Cline Spit.

In the downtown Sequim area, try **Oak Table Cafe** at 292 West Bell Street (360-683-2179) for waist-bulging breakfasts, or the Buzz Coffee Shop at 128 North Sequim Avenue (360-683-2503). At 2 p.m. Sunday, bring your Scrabble board for a game, or enjoy an open mic Wednesday night. Other options include Alder Wood Bistro for wood-fired coastal cuisine (139 West Alder Street; 360-683-4321), Dockside Grill (888-640-7226) at John Wayne Marina (yes, that John Wayne!), and Seven Cedars Casino at 270756 Highway 101 (800-458-2597; www.7cedarscasino.com).

A fun place to visit near Dungeness is the ***Olympic Game Farm*** at 1423 Ward Road (800-778-4295; www.olygamefarm.com). Year-round drive-through tours will put you in the company of four-legged stars. Walt Disney Studios has employed farm residents, including grizzlies and wolves, in more than eighty wildlife productions. Many animals you'll see there are endangered species. Enjoy Siberian and Bengal tigers, African lions, timber wolves, and a small herd of bison.

The ***Dungeness National Wildlife Refuge,*** located west of the game farm, offers an exhilarating immersion in wildlife in the spring and fall when thousands of migrating waterfowl stop here. From the parking lot, take an easy ¼-mile walk to a viewpoint overlooking ***Dungeness Spit,*** one of the nation's largest natural sand hooks. For slightly hardier walkers, follow all or part of the 5½-mile trail through the forest and down the beach. Allow enough time to walk the whole distance and come back during low tide, or just meander a section. There's a $3 per family fee for refuge exploration.

See Washington by Following the Flocks

Dancing sandhill cranes can inspire superlatives, the cry of an eagle a shiver, the hoot of an owl an ear tuned to an answering call, a songbird a smile. This year, go where the birds are: Join experienced birders and listen to expert presenters at one of the Washington birding festivals, then explore the area on your own.

Bird Fest & Bluegrass
October, Ridgefield
www.ridgefieldfriends.org

Grand Coulee Balde Eagle Festival
February
www.eaglefestival.com

Grays Harbor Shorebird Festival
May, Hoquiam
www.shorebirdfestival.com

Leavenworth Bird Festival
May, Leavenworth
www.leavenworthspringbirdfest.com

Olympic Peninsula BirdFest
April, Sequim
www.olympicbirdfest.org

Othello Sandhill Crane Festival
March, Othello
www.othellosandhillcranefestival.org

Port Susan Snow Goose & Birding Festival
February, Camano Island and Stanwood
www.snowgoosefest.org

Puget Sound Bird Fest
September, Edmonds
www.pugetsoundbirdfest.org

Upper Skagit Bald Eagle Festival
January, Rockport
www.skagiteagle.org

Watch out for harbor seals bobbing about as they fish and frolic offshore. The last half-mile of the spit beyond the *New Dungeness Lighthouse* and the south shore is closed to ensure protection of the seals. The lighthouse, built in 1857 and automated in 1937, is the oldest one north of the Columbia River. For information about exploring, touring the lighthouse, or becoming a volunteer lighthouse keeper, call (360) 457-8451 or check www.fws.gov/washingtonmaritime/dungeness.

The best way to go through the Dungeness Valley between Sequim and Port Angeles is on the *Old Olympic Highway.* This pleasant, less-traveled route through green farmlands offers great views of the mountains rising to the south. Those yearning for luxurious lodgings and a five-course gourmet breakfast featuring locally grown fare could stay at *Domaine Madeleine Bed & Breakfast Inn* at 146 Wildflower Lane (360-457-4174; www.domainemadeleine.com), a contemporary home on a bluff above the Strait of Juan de Fuca. Four of the five guest rooms have whirlpool tubs. Guests can wander five acres of grounds and gardens or cozy up in the living room near the huge basalt fireplace. Each room has a fireplace and panoramic views. The inn is about 5½ miles west of Sequim and a mile off the Old Olympic Highway.

For a different and adventuresome perspective, drive about 3 miles east of Port Angeles on Deer Park Road and turn right on a narrow, winding 18-mile drive over the forest-covered slopes of Blue Mountain to Deer Park in *Olympic National Park* (www.nps.gov/olym). Since the last nine miles is graveled and also the steepest section, don't bring RVs or trailers. You'll find an alpine campground, a summer-only ranger station, and scenic hikes that provide views of the interior Olympics, Dungeness Valley, Port Angeles, and the Strait of Juan de Fuca.

A less adventurous but still stunning ride is to take paved Hurricane Ridge Road uphill for 17 miles out of Port Angeles to *Hurricane Ridge* and several easier trails, wildflowers in early summer, and great views of Olympic peaks. Please don't feed the deer in the parking lot! If there's a question about snow conditions, call (360) 565-3131. During the summer park rangers lead nature walks, and campfire programs are given nightly in the Heart o' the Hills Campground amphitheater located about five miles away from July 1 through Labor Day. The panoramic views on the way down are of the strait and its Canadian islands to the north. The visitor center is a good place to start. It has a museum, deli, and gift shop. Restrooms are open year-round. For more information stop by the Olympic National Park Visitor Center in Port Angeles at 600 East Park Avenue (360-565-3130).

Port Angeles (www.portangeles.org), the largest city on the Olympic Peninsula, is dominated by its busy waterfront. This deepwater harbor is a port of call for international shipping, a base for ocean fishing and a major Coast Guard station, and terminus for Black Ball's Coho ferry for walk-on passengers and vehicles (360-457-4491; www.cohoferry.com). The ferry makes daily trips to Victoria, British Columbia, a city with a British flavor nestled at the southern tip of Vancouver Island. Before starting out, review the customs' regulations on page vii.

The City Pier, 1 block east of the ferry terminal, is a good starting point for your explorations. You'll find a small park, a viewing tower, a berth for the 110-foot Coast Guard cutter *Cuttyhunk,* a public marine laboratory, and plenty of nearby restaurants and shops. The Feiro Marine Life Center (360-417-6254) on the City Pier is the place to see and touch some of the remarkable sea creatures that live on Washington's coast. Watch the graceful movements of an octopus, stroke a stuffed sea lion, and handle a variety of marine life in the touch-tanks. Volunteers answer questions and tell visitors about the Northwest region's marine ecology. The laboratory is open for a small admission fee; call for hours or go to www.olypen.com/feirolab.

To explore along the lively Port Angeles waterfront, pick up a walking-tour brochure at the visitor center (located next to the City Pier). The Olympic Discovery Trail, which follows the harbor shore east along Hollywood Beach to Sequim, is ideal for walking or bicycling. You can also bicycle west to *Ediz Hook,* the natural sand spit that forms the Port Angeles harbor. Bikes are available for rent at *Sound Bikes and Kayaks* at 120 East Front Street

olympic discoverytrail

The partially completed Olympic Discovery Trail, a non-motorized multiple-use path, will one day stretch 100 miles from Port Townsend to La Push on the Pacific coast.

(360-457-1240). Not into biking today? Pop into *Captain T's,* located at 124 West Railroad Avenue (360-452-6549) for railroad-related T-shirts; or *Pacific Rim Hobby,* 138 West Railroad Avenue (800-994-6229), for more railroad souvenirs.

For good eats in Port Angeles, try a local breakfast favorite, *First Street Haven Café* (107 East First Street; 360-457-0352); *Itty Bitty Buzz* (110 East First Street; 360-565-8080); or *Olympic Bagel Company* (802 East First Street; 360-452-9100). Other places include Joy's Wine Bistro (1135 East Front Street; 360-452-9449) and the Plunkin' Shack for breakfast or lunch (704 Marine Drive; 360-417-6961), a brief drive from downtown.

The downtown has benefited from a facelift the past several years. For information on activities such as art walks, outdoor sculptures, an underground

Quick Guide to Victoria and Vancouver Island, British Columbia

Getting to Victoria from Port Angeles is easy. Park at the Port Angeles ferry terminal and either hop aboard the *Victoria Express* (800-633-1589; www.victoriaexpress .com) as a foot passenger, or take your car aboard the *M.V.* **Coho** *ferry* for its ninety-five-minute cruise across the Strait of Juan de Fuca (360-457-4491; www .ferrytovictoria.com).

It's easy walking in Victoria's scenic *Inner Harbor area* to see the ivy-covered Empress Hotel, stately Parliament buildings and landscaped grounds that sparkle with thousands of lights after dark, and the don't-miss Provincial Museum, and harbor activities from Inner Harbor walkways. Sample a plethora of cafes, coffeehouses, boutiques, and tea houses. For information contact *Victoria Travel Info-Centre* (250-953-2003) and *Tourism British Columbia* (800-435-5622; www.hellobc.com).

Other places to explore near Victoria include spectacular *Butchart Gardens* north of Victoria (plan late spring and summer visits during midweek to avoid the crowds); *Brentwood Bay and Saanich Inlet* (try Seahorses Café near Mill Bay ferry landing); *Sooke* (good hiking, eateries, and shops); and *Port Alberni* (fishing and forestry village). Drive north to the seaside community of *Sidney.* For eats on the waterfront at Port Sidney Marina, try *Rum Runner Pub* at 9881 Seaport Place (250-656-5643); *Boondocks Cafe & Pub* at 9732 First Street (250-656-4088); and *Fish on Fifth Cafe* at 9812 Fifth Street (250-656-4022). For overnight lodging check *Best Western Emerald Isle Inn* (800-315-3377; www.bwemeraldisle.com).

From Sidney you can visit the San Juan Islands via international ferry sailing on *Washington State Ferries* (www.wsdot.wa.gov/ferries). Check with San Juan Island Visitor Information (800-468-3701; www.guidetosanjuans.com).

For border crossing requirements go to the *U.S.–Canadian Border Crossing* Web site at www.cbp.gov or call (206) 553-0770.

tour, a five-acre outdoor gallery, and events. Check out www.portangeles downtown.com.

If you enjoy watching the waterfront activities, consider **Ocean Crest Bed & Breakfast** at 402 South M Street (877-413-2169; www.oceancrestbnb.com), a large, comfortable home that offers panoramic views of the harbor, the strait, and Vancouver Island. Romantics might enjoy the old-world ambience of the 1910 **Tudor Inn Bed & Breakfast** at 1108 South Oak Street (360-452-3138; www.tudorinn.com), located a few blocks from the ferry terminal. Or contact the innkeepers at **Five SeaSuns Bed & Breakfast** at 1006 South Lincoln Street (360-452-8248; www.seasuns.com). Guests find sumptuous accommodations and grounds that feature a pond, an elegant pergola, and garden beds and planters overflowing with colorful flowers.

There is still much to see on the north end of the Olympic Peninsula. Stop at the Elwha Ranger Station (3911 Olympic Hot Springs Road; 360-452-9191) for information on hiking trails and the Olympic Hot Springs, or take a raft trip down the scenic Elwha River. Contact **Olympic Raft and Kayak** (360-452-1443; www.raftandkayak.com) or Adventures through Kayaking in Port Angeles (888-900-3015; www.atkayaking.com). Ask about kayaking on Lake Aldwell or sea kayaking Fresh Water Bay.

Continuing west of Port Angeles, follow US 101 inland or take Highway 112 along the coastline. If you opt for the inland route, you'll find **Lake Crescent** set in the forest. The lake is 12 miles long and more than a mile wide. Much of the area around the lake is part of Olympic National Park. A right turn onto East Beach Road at Lake Crescent's eastern edge takes you along a scenic, winding lakeside road to Log Cabin Resort at 3183 East Beach Road (360-928-3325; www.logcabinresort.net). Established in 1895 on the lake's isolated north shore, the "sunny side of the lake," its unpretentious cabins, RV sites, ten camping spots, general store, and Log Cabin Restaurant provide a secluded, friendly atmosphere. Be sure to stop by the **Soda Jerk Cafe** between 11:00 a.m. and 2:00 p.m. for pizzas. Guests can rent rowboats or canoes. Hike among giant old-growth cedars and firs or rent mountain bikes to explore forest trails. Take the 4-mile Spruce Division Railroad Trail, originally a railroad grade built during World War I to help extract spruce logs for airplane production.

A visitor information center is located on the lake's south shore, just off US 101, in a log cabin built in 1905. From the cabin a ¾-mile trail follows a level, gravel path through the forest and ends with an uphill climb through the rain forest to 90-foot **Marymere Falls. Lake Crescent Lodge** at 416 Lake Crescent Road (360-928-3211; www.lakecrescentlodge.com), just west of the visitor center, is a classic old resort that has changed little since it was built on the lakeshore in 1916. While staying here in 1937, President Franklin Roosevelt decided to create Olympic National Park to preserve this area's beauty for future generations. Visitors enjoy lodge rooms or cottages, boating, fishing, and nature hikes. Reservations are recommended for the resort's restaurant; watch the sunset over the lake while savoring a fine dinner.

You'll find forested campgrounds, boat rentals, and groceries at Fairholm on the western edge of Lake Crescent. Farther west on US 101, a 12-mile drive south on Sol Duc Road takes you to **Sol Duc Hot Springs Resort** (360-327-3583; www.visitsolduck.com). **Sol Duc** means "sparkling water" in the Quileute language. Visitors have been flocking to these mineral waters since a magnificent spa was built at the site in 1912 (which, sadly, burned in 1916). The resort, open April through October, offers three large outdoor hot mineral pools, a freshwater heated swimming pool, dining, massage therapy, a gift

Lake Crescent Lodge sunroom

shop, groceries, RV hookups, and cabins. Camping, hiking trails, and naturalist programs are available at nearby **Sol Duc Campground.**

An alternative route is to leave US 101 at the junction west of Port Angeles and take Highway 112, a National Scenic Byway, for close-up views of the Olympic Peninsula's rugged northern coastline. Ten miles west of Port Angeles, turn on Camp Hayden Road to reach **Salt Creek Recreation Area,** a marine sanctuary with tidal pools full of waving sea anemones, gooseneck barnacles, coal-black mussels, and colorful starfish, as well as kelp beds and small rocky islands. The adjacent Clallam County Park offers campsites, showers, and beach. Continuing west on Highway 112, you may see a gray whale spouting or a pod of orcas or a California sea lion. Watch for crowds of harbor seals relaxing on the small offshore islands. A great place to take a break is at Pillar Point County Park (360-417-2291). Try beachcombing along a beautiful estuary, admire the views and birding opportunities, and have a picnic.

Clallam Bay and Sekiu are two fishing villages along the Juan de Fuca Strait, just the right size for finding a seafood-oriented meal, poking about the marinas, renting a boat, or catching a fishing charter. Contact the Clallam Bay-Sekiu Chamber of Commerce (877-694-9433; www.sekiu.com) for more information. The Web site has many dining and lodging options, most of them low-key.

Continue west to **Neah Bay** or take the turnoff on Hoko-Ozette Road, just past the fishing village of Sekiu on Clallam Bay, to **Lake Ozette,** one of the largest natural bodies of freshwater in Washington State. The 10-mile loop trail to the lake and ocean beach makes a very long day hike, or pack for an overnighter at secluded oceanside campsites. The Ozette ranger station (360-963-2725) at the lake can provide tide tables and other important information. The park offers interpretive programs in the summer as well as a pleasant twenty-two-site campground at the lake's north end.

Or contact Lost Resort at 20860 Hoko-Ozette Road (800-950-2829; www .lostresort.net) in Clallam Bay, about ¼-mile from the ranger station. It offers a campground, cabins, and store. For more civilized accommodations in Clallam Bay, contact **Winter Summer Inn** overlooking the Strait of Juan de Fuca at 16651 Highway 112 (360-963-2264; www.wintersummerinn.com), open year-round.

one beak
two beak

Every year volunteers gather at Sand Creek County Park west of Port Angeles to count migrating turkey vultures between Sept. 24 and Oct. 6. The birds stage at the southern tip of Vancouver Island before flying across the Strait of Juan de Fuca in groups as large as 400 birds on their way to California and South America.

For an easy day hike from Ozette, walk along the 3-mile boardwalk over coastal wetlands to Cape Alava, the site of an ancient Makah Indian fishing village that was buried by a mud slide 500 years ago and partially excavated in the 1980s. The well-preserved contents of the village, exposed by tidal action in the 1970s, are housed at the **Makah Museum** (360-645-2711; www.makah .com), which is part of the Makah Cultural and Research Center in Neah Bay on the **Makah Indian Reservation,** about 60 miles west of Port Angeles. Owned and operated by the Makah Tribe, this first-class museum tells the story of people who lived a rigorous life hunting whales, seals, and fish.

Neah Bay holds its Makah Days celebration the last weekend in August, featuring traditional salmon bakes along with traditional dancing, singing, and canoe races. There are several modest motels and RV parks.

Olympic National Park

Olympic National Park was designated as a World Heritage Site by UNESCO in 1981. It contains the largest virgin temperate rain forest in the Western Hemisphere, the largest intact stand of coniferous forest in the U.S. mainland, and the largest wild herd of Roosevelt elk. The park contains more than 1,200 types of plants, more than 300 species of birds, and more than seventy species of mammals. At least eight kinds of plants and eighteen kinds of animals are found only on the Olympic Peninsula, including the Olympic marmot and snow mole; Flett's violet, Piper's bellflower, and Olympic Mountain daisy; and Beardslee and Crescenti trout.

Byways off the beaten path

The Cape Flattery Tribal Scenic Byway that runs from Neah Bay to Cape Flattery is the first Tribal Scenic Byway in the state. The 36-mile loop route, designated in 2002, starts at the Makah Cultural and Resource Center. Highlights include the Makah National Salmon Hatchery, Neah Bay and marina, Olympic Coast National Marine Sanctuary, Shi Shi Beach, Tatoosh Island and lighthouse, and the Cape Flattery Trail, which leads to the most northwestern point on the U.S. mainland.

The state has six nationally designated routes: two All-American Roads, Chinook Pass Scenic Byway (S.R. 310) and International Selkirk Loop (S.R. 31, 20); and four National Scenic Byways: Mountains to Sound Greenway (I-90), Strait of Juan de Fuca Highway (S.R. 112), Coulee Corridor (S.R. 17, 155), and Stevens Pass Greenway (U.S. 2). There are also dozens of state-designated byways and scenic drives.

For more information or to obtain a Washington State Scenic Byways Map, call 800-544-1800.

Follow signs to the Makah Air Force Station west of Neah Bay and take the right-hand fork to reach the ¾-mile trail to **Cape Flattery,** a trail totally improved by the Makahs to include better footing, some wooden walkways, and fences. This gem is the northwestern most point of the United States mainland and includes several observation decks and picnic tables. At the end and high above the ocean, experience great views of Tatoosh Island, a half-mile-long volcanic outcropping that was once a favorite Makah retreat, and is now home to a century-old lighthouse and nesting seabirds. From here you may see gray whales during their spring and fall migrations. Cape Flattery is well known for its high winds and extremely high rainfall.

To reach additional scenic ocean beaches, take the south fork at the Air Force Station. **Hobuck** and **Sooes Beaches** are located on the outer coast a few miles south of Neah Bay. From Makah Bay south the beaches are mostly undisturbed by humans. Remember, a reservation and operates by tribal rules and fees. Check www.makah.com or call (360) 645-2201 for specifics.

Rain Forest

When you're ready to continue your peninsula journey, return on Highway 112 and take the turnoff south on Burnt Mountain Road, located 6 miles south of Clallam Bay, which connects to US 101 at Sappho. A mile farther west you can take Pavel Road 2 miles to the **Sol Duc Salmon Hatchery** and a small interpretive center with colorful dioramas illustrating the life cycle of the salmon and the challenges facing fisheries industries. Just north of **Forks,** La

Push Road connects US 101 with **Rialto Beach, Mora Campground** (part of Olympic National Park), and the Quileute community of **La Push.**

A short distance from the beach is **Manitou Lodge** at 813 Kilmer Road in Forks (360-374-6295; www.manitoulodge.com). Take advantage of its proximity to rain forests, rivers, and unspoiled beaches. To spend a night closer to the ocean, try **Quileute Oceanside Resort** at 320 Ocean Drive; (800-487-1267; www.ocean-park.org) in La Push, a Quileute tribal enterprise. Guests enjoy ocean views and access to miles of sandy and rocky beaches.

Back on US 101, explore Forks, historically a logging town although logging is down to a shadow of its former self. The **Forks Timber Museum** (360-374-9663) south of town offers a comprehensive introduction to the history, economy, and culture of logging. Photographs, old logging equipment, and dioramas give a glimpse of what life was like in old logging camps and pioneer homes and how simple tools and hard work were employed to fell, transport, and saw timber into commercial lumber. The old-fashioned Fourth of July celebration in Forks highlights traditional logging skill competitions. For more information contact the Forks Chamber of Commerce at (800) 443-6757 or www.forkswa.com.

For good eats along US 101 in Forks, and to meet local folks, try **Forks Coffee Shop Cafe** at 241 South Forks Avenue (360-374-6769). You'll see old Forks newspapers and a couple of stuffed elk heads. Or stop by another local favorite, the espresso bar at **Forks Outfitters** (360-374-6161) at the south end of town. The **Smokehouse Restaurant** at 193161 US 101 (360-374-6258) offers excellent smoked salmon and fresh seafood. Others suggest two Chinese restaurants, the **Golden Gate** (111 South Forks Avenue; 360-374-5528) or South North Gardens (140 Sol Duc Way; 360-374-9779).

For a stay in Forks call the **Miller Tree Inn Bed & Breakfast** (800-943-6563; www.millertreeinn.com), a 1917 homestead on three park-like acres at 654 East Division Street. At **Misty Valley Inn Bed & Breakfast** at 194894 US 101 North (877-374-9389; www.mistyvalleyinn.com), enjoy pastoral views and gourmet breakfasts. For a cozy cottage in town, contact **Shady Nook Cottages** at 81 Ash Avenue (360-374-5497; www.shadynookcottage.com) or Mill Creek Inn at 1061 Forks Avenue South (360-374-5873; www.forksbnb .com). Unless you are camping or driving a self-contained RV, be sure to arrange your summer overnight accommodations well ahead of visiting the Forks–Neah Bay area.

Twelve miles south of Forks, Upper Hoh Road follows the Hoh River Valley 18 miles east into one of the thickest parts of the rain forest. At the end of the road are the Olympic National Park's **Hoh Rainforest Visitor Center** (360-374-6925; www.nps.gov/olym), campground, and eye-opening nature trails. More than 120 inches of rain fall annually, creating a lush multilayered environment highlighted with every shade of green imaginable. Even a quick excursion through the Hall of Mosses Trail or along the Spruce Nature Trail offers an opportunity to experience the grandeur of the old-growth hemlock/ spruce forests that once covered much of Western Washington. To reach more secluded areas, walk a few miles toward the Blue Glacier. Backpackers can take longer hikes to camp sites such as Olympus (9 miles from the visitor center) or Glacier Meadows (an additional 8 miles).

lonelystoplight

Forks, on the far north section of the Olympic Peninsula and the westernmost incorporated town in the mainland United States, is so far off the beaten path that it has the only stoplight for 60 miles in either direction.

Located 7 miles south of Upper Hoh Road near milepost 172 is the *Hoh Humm Ranch B&B* (171763 US 101; 360-374-5337), a working farm owned by the Huelsdonk family and situated on the banks of the Hoh River along with llamas, deer, goats, and cattle, plus the resident ranch cats. Six ranch-house guest rooms share two baths.

The *Rain Forest Hostel* (360-374-2270; www.rainforesthostel.com), located 23 miles south of Forks on US 101, offers basic accommodations at a minimal price; reservations are required. It's a popular base for young adult travelers exploring the Olympic Peninsula, so part of the fun is meeting visitors from around the world.

US 101 curves west to follow the cliffs above *Ruby* and *Kalaloch* (pronounced CLAY-lock) *Beaches,* offering magnificent views of the Pacific Ocean. It's a rugged coastline punctured with sea stacks and rock pillars where waves leap, foam, and crash against rocks, driftwood, and offshore islands. At night you'll see flashes from the lighthouse, which has provided a warning to coastal mariners since it was built in 1891 on distant Destruction Island.

Olympic National Park's only oceanfront lodging is the Kalaloch Lodge (866-525-2562; www.visitkalaloch.com) south of Forks at 157151 US 101. It's rustic, cedar-shingled, and perched on a bluff looking across a wide beach to the Pacific Ocean; the much-in-demand bluff cabins have views. Make reservations many months in advance, or consider this as a winter storm-watching destination. Bring your raincoat. Kalaloch gets more than 150 inches of rain a year.

At Queets the highway turns inland to *Lake Quinault,* one of the densest parts of the rain forest. To experience this lush green place with its giant cedar, hemlock, and spruce, stay at *Lochaerie Resort Cabins* at 638 North Shore Road, Amanda Park (360-288-2215; www.lochaerie.com), located 4 miles east of US 101 on the lake's north shore. The six rustic cabins with kitchens have changed little since they were built on the cliffs above the lake in the 1920s and 1930s. Information about day hikes can be obtained from the Quinault Ranger Station (360-288-2525).

Good eateries suggested by locals include **Salmon House Restaurant** at **Rain Forest Resort Village** at 516 South Shore Road (800-255-6936; www .rainforestresort.com) and the **Shake Mill Restaurant,** at 6080 Highway 101 in Amanda Park (360-288-2377). Rain Forest Resort also offers lake-view cabins.

On the south side of the lake 2 miles east of the highway at 345 South Shore Road sits **Lake Quinault Lodge** (800-562-6672; www.visitlakequinault .com), a ninety-two-room waterfront resort built in 1926. Guests can rent boats and canoes, play badminton on the grass, soak in the pool, and enjoy gourmet dining in the Roosevelt Room. For more rustic accommodations ask about the 1923 **Boathouse Annex** where pets are allowed. There are no TVs or telephones in the room.

If you'd like to explore the Quinault Valley rain forest and scenic Lake Quinault from the sunny side of the lake and stay in a more intimate lodg-ing, contact the folks at the newer **Lake Quinault Resort** at 314 North Shore Road (800-650-2362; www.lakequinault.com). In this quiet spot relax in your Adirondack chair amid a flotilla of flowers and savor views of the lake, which can be seen from all the guest rooms. Choose from units with kitchenettes or townhouse suites.

This section of the Olympic Peninsula also can be reached from Olympia by heading west on U.S. Highway 12 to Aberdeen and then north on US 101 for about 40 miles to Quinault and Amanda Park.

Harbors, Bays, and Rivers

The twin port cities of Hoquiam and **Aberdeen** on Grays Harbor are hardwork-ing communities where logging, fishing, and shipping are nearly everybody's business. On a hillside above residential Hoquiam at 515 Chenault Avenue sits the splendid **Hoquiam's Castle Bed and Breakfast** (360-533-2005; www .hoquiamcastle.com), built in 1897 by a lumber baron and now listed on the State and National Registers of Historic Places. The restored twenty-room mansion is filled with opulent antiques, lovely cut-glass windows, a turn-of-the-century saloon, and four spacious guest rooms outfitted with antique furnishings and finery. For other comfortable accommodations, try **Aberdeen Mansion Bed & Breakfast** (807 North M Street, Aberdeen; 360-533-7079; www.aberdeenmansionbb.com) or **Abel House Bed & Breakfast** at 117 Fleet Street South in nearby Montesano (360-249-6002; www.abelhouse.com).

Hoquiam's Castle

Downtown Hoquiam has a waterfront park where you can watch work and pleasure boats on the river. Or climb the viewing tower at the end of Twenty-eighth Street on Grays Harbor to see the ocean-going cargo ships. Continue west past Hoquiam to follow the coast north on Highway 109 past a number of small communities. Along the way you'll find windswept beaches, art galleries, antiques, gift shops, and resorts. For more information on places to stay in the area, contact Grays Harbor Tourism, (800) 621-9625 or www .graysharbortourism.com.

The **_Aberdeen Museum of History_** (111 East Third Street; 360-533-1976), a few miles east of Hoquiam, includes an eclectic variety of curiosities and displays from Grays Harbor's past. Enjoy old logging and farming equipment, period clothing, toys, and a one-room schoolhouse. The museum is open 10:00 a.m. to 5:00 p.m. Tuesday through Saturday and noon to 4:00 p.m. Sunday.

Grays Harbor was a major shipbuilding center during the days of sail when locally milled lumber was in great demand for hulls, masts, and spars. Three- and four-masted schooners, wooden steamships, and tugboats were constructed along the bay, and they

elwhaecosystem

Nine miles west of Port Angeles, you can turn south on Olympic Hot Springs Road to explore the scenic **_Elwha River Valley._** The Elwha ecosystem was the most productive stream system on the Olympic Peninsula until two dams were built. Both are scheduled to be removed in 2012 to restore the ecosystem, which would allow five species of Pacific salmon, steelhead, and other fish to swim seventy miles of river habitat and spawn.

crowded the harbor's docks. At the **Grays Harbor Historical Seaport** (712 Hagara Street; 360–532–8611), absorb marine history aboard a full-scale reproduction of the *Lady Washington,* one of the ships used by explorer Robert Gray to sail into the harbor in 1792. The state's official ship was built in 1989 as part of the state's centennial celebration and now sails regularly along the West Coast. The Web site www.ladywashington.com provides information about dockside tours, educational programs, adventure sail training, and the current sailing schedule. The seaport also owns the 161-foot *Hawaiian Chieftain,* also available for tours. For additional information, contact the Grays Harbor Visitor Information Center (800-321-1924; www .graysharbor.org).

Westport, where maritime life abounds, is twenty miles west of Aberdeen, just off Highway 105. At the bustling marina the fishing and charter boats prepare for offshore tours or return loaded with fish and crabs. Check out the boardwalk, an ideal place to stroll and watch the waterfront activity, or climb the viewing tower for a bird's-eye view of Grays Harbor.

cranberrycoast

The semicircle of Aberdeen, Westport, and Raymond includes the Cranberry Coast State Scenic Byway that focuses on the historical tribal culture of the Shoalwater Bay Native Americans and the community industries built around harvesting salmon, oysters, clams, timber, and cranberries. Inhabited by Native Americans and hardy settlers, the flavor of the history is in the salt sea air and the uses of the lands and water including the rich natural resources of Willapa Bay.

The colonial-revival structure located at 2201 Westhaven Drive was built in 1939 to house the Coast Guard's Lifeboat Station at Grays Harbor but now houses the **Westport Maritime Museum** (360-268-0078; www.westportwa .com/museum). Tour the **Grays Harbor Lighthouse** at nearby Point Chehalis or see the lighthouse from a roadside viewing platform. The 107-foot-tall structure is more than a hundred years old, and its automated light, at 123 feet above the water, ranks as the highest light on the Washington coast.

For a long look at the Pacific just before you turn in for the night, choose an ocean-view room at Chateau Westport, 104 rooms at 710 Hancock (800-255-9101; www.chateauwestport.com). Enjoy a continental breakfast and a morning swim in a heated pool before heading to the beach.

March and April area peak times to catch sight of gray whale families migrating from their breeding lagoons in Baja, California, to the krill-rich waters of the Bering Sea. To find out about whale-watching cruises, contact the Westport–Grayland Chamber of Commerce (800-345-6223; www.westport grayland-chamber.org).

TOP ANNUAL EVENTS ON THE WASHINGTON COAST AND OLYMPIC PENINSULA

Clallam County Fair
Port Angeles, August
(360) 417-2551

Country Music Jam
Ocean Shores, May
(800) 762-3224

Crab Races, Crab Feed & Crab Derby
Westport, April
(800) 345-6223

Cranberry Harvest Festival
Grayland, October
(800) 473-6018

**Grays Harbor
Shorebird Festival**
Hoquiam, late April/early May
(800) 303-8498

International Kite Festival
Long Beach, August
(800) 451-2542

Lavender Festival
Sequim, July
(360) 683-6197

Makah Days
Neah Bay, August
(360) 645-2201

Olympic Peninsula BirdFest
Sequim, April
(360) 681-4076

**Oysterfest:
West Coast Shucking Championships
& Seafood Festival**
Shelton, October
(800) 576-2021

Rainfest
Forks, April
(800) 443-6757

Whale Fest
Westport, March–May
(800) 345-6223

Explore *Ocean Shores* and the scenic north coast area, including Ocean City, Copalis Beach, Pacific Beach, *Moclips,* and at the far northern end of Highway 109, Taholah. You'll find coffee shops, funky cafes, cozy bookstores, and warm places to hole up for the night. Check out *Ocean Shores B&B* (360-289-7960; www.thegibsonsbandb.com), with a soda fountain and an art deco–style movie theater. An excellent place to stay along the canal is Floating Feathers Inn (888-257-0894; www.floatingfeathersinn.com), right along the freshwater Grand Canal at 982 Point Brown Avenue Southeast. Enjoy one of the non-smoking suites with feather beds as well as feathered friends outside and a gourmet breakfast.

Following the coast south on US 101, enjoy wide views of the Pacific Ocean before turning east at Willapa Bay on Highway 109. This long, shallow bay is rich with wildlife and shellfish. You can sample this bounty by following the turnoff at the Shoalwater Indian Reservation to the *Tokeland Hotel & Restaurant,* located at 100 Hotel Road in Tokeland (360) 267-7006. The hotel's dining room offers a panoramic view of Willapa Bay as well as hearty food. Established in 1889 as the Kindred Inn, this is the oldest operating hotel in Washington State, offering simple but satisfying accommodations. There is concern, however, over the ever-encroaching bay waters reclaiming property along the coast.

Raymond, located just south of the junction of US 101 and Highway 105, is on the Willapa River. The old *Dennis Company* building at Blake and Fifth Streets offers a glimpse of the region's history in an 85-foot-long mural depicting shipping and logging activity in 1905. Pop into *Ugly Ed's & Deb's* (360-942-2345), located behind Dennis Company, for antiques, garage-sale-type items and collectibles. Then visit the *Northwest Carriage Museum,* at 314 Alder Street (360-942-4150), open 10:00 a.m. to 4:00 p.m. Monday through Saturday; noon to 4 p.m. Sunday. Inspect twenty horse-drawn carriages, buggies, and sleighs dating from the late 1800s. In summer, browse for goodies at the *Willapa Public Market.* The 5-mile-long Willapa River Trail is part of a long-term 57-mile project called the Willapa Hills State Trail. It runs along the western part of Highway 6 in Raymond and on US 101 as it follows the river to *South Bend.*

Continuing on US 101, the roadsides are dotted with steel sculptures (loggers, Native Americans, bears, shorebirds) on the Raymond Wildlife Heritage Sculpture Corridor. Then pass through the picturesque village of South Bend, also located on the Willapa River. The town's shoreline is worth a leisurely stroll to view the fishing docks, piles of empty oyster shells, and oyster- and crab-processing plants. Plan to stay overnight at *Russell House Bed & Breakfast* at 902 East Water Street (888-484-6907; www.russellhousebb.com), an 1891 Victorian mansion that offers cozy rooms and wide-angle views of the river and town.

Summerhouse, located at 931 Cole Avenue in Raymond (360-942-2843), has a comfy guest house and two full RV hookups. The *Pacific County Historical Museum,* on the highway at 1008 West Robert Bush Drive in South Bend (360-875-5224; www.pacificcohistory.org), offers glimpses of the area's colorful past. The museum is open daily 11:00 a.m. to 4:00 p.m. Walk up the

A Coffin Goes West

Willie Keil, a 19-year-old anxious to lead his father's commune's wagon train west to Washington Territory in 1855, died of malaria just before departure but his father kept his son's dream alive. Willie, in a lead-lined coffin filled with 100-proof whiskey and placed in a black-draped wagon/hearse, led the way. When stopped by Indians, dad opened the coffin and after a quick look, a potentially hostile encounter was avoided. Willie's marked grave is along Highway 6 about 6 miles east of Raymond.

hill past some of the town's stately old houses for great views of the Willapa River and the Willapa Hills and, on the corner of Memorial and Cowlitz Streets, visit one of Washington's finest county courthouses. Open during business hours, this elegant 1910 building sports an impressive art-glass dome and historical scenes painted in the 1940s.

sundaythieves

An economically collapsing Oysterville was the Pacific County seat. An illegal election gave the honor to South Bend; in case an appeal was upheld (it was), eighty-five men crossed the Willapa Bay on a Sunday in 1893 and stole the records from Oysterville. They later sent a bill for services to the commissioners. It wasn't paid. The county seat remained South Bend.

The highway follows Willapa Bay's southeastern shore past South Bend, by rich wetland scenery, feasting grounds for migrating black brant geese. The estuary environment supports a mind-boggling array of life-forms, from mud-dwelling clams, shrimps, and oysters to the millions of marine birds that consume them. After crossing the Naselle River, see Long Island to the west, part of Willapa National Wildlife Refuge (360-484-3482). The island supports a coastal rain forest that includes a stand of old-growth cedars as well as mammal and songbird populations. But you'll need a kayak or boat to reach the island and its trail and campsites.

Long Beach Peninsula

The Long Beach Peninsula is an inviting place to explore for day or weekend rambles. The roar of the surf is never far off, the air is washed clean by ocean winds, and there are activities galore. The larger beachside communities are popular tourist destinations but you don't have to go far to find lesser-known treasures and quiet walking trails.

Enjoy a public art treasure hunt by searching for the numerous historical murals that grace the exteriors of many buildings in Ilwaco, Seaview, Long Beach, and **Ocean Park.** A free Muralogue guide is available from the Long Beach Peninsula Visitor Center (800-451-2542; www.funbeach.com).

Ilwaco is a fishing community at the peninsula's south end. The town's harbor is a great place to browse and see charter boats heading out to fish for salmon, sturgeon, bottom fish, or tuna. In the harbor area are canneries for fish and crab processing, fresh-fish markets, gift shops, and eateries. For gourmet food served up with Northwest wines and microbrews, the locals suggest The Port Bistro near the Ilwaco marina at 235 Howerton Way (360-642-8447), open daily for lunch and Thursday through Monday for dinner; and Pelicano's, a more recent addition to the marina by local chef Jeff McMahon at 177 Howerton Way (360-642-4034), open at 5 p.m. for dinner Wednesday through Saturday.

Between 1889 and 1930 the Ilwaco Railroad and Navigation Company transported goods and people up and down the peninsula, first by coach along the beach, then by narrow-gauge railway. We recommend stopping at the Columbia Pacific Heritage Museum (formerly the Ilwaco Heritage Museum). It's housed in the old telephone utilities building at 115 Southeast Lake Street (360-642-3446). There's a scale model of the 1890s narrow-gauge railway that ran along the beach between Ilwaco and tiny Nahcotta about 12 miles to the north. Often referred to as the Clamshell Railway, it ran on a schedule governed by tides. The old railway depot is on display in the museum's courtyard. Have a seat on an original Clamshell Railroad car. The museum is open year-round from 10:00 a.m. to 4:00 p.m. Monday through Saturday and noon to 4:00 p.m. Sunday. The first outdoor mural produced on the peninsula, a 1920s railway scene, is on the north side of the Doupe Brothers Hardware Store at Ilwaco's only traffic light.

Two and a half miles southwest of Ilwaco, off US 101, Cape Disappointment State Park (360-642-3078) offers beaches, forest trails, campsites, and two historic lighthouses. Although it's easy to snare a site in the winter without a reservation, all sites must be reserved in the summer. Call Washington State Parks for reservations, (888) 226-7688, or visit www.parks.wa.gov.

Waikiki Beach, a sheltered cove well-supplied with driftwood and smooth sand near the park entrance, is a great place to watch the Columbia River's busy shipping activities as well as a powerful storm's waves break high off the lighthouse cliff. For more dramatic views, hike along the trail to the North Head Lighthouse. The *Lewis and Clark Interpretive Center* (360-642-3029) offers views of the Columbia River. A stroll through the center takes

Storm Watching 101

When powerful winter storms batter Washington's ocean coast, it's time to pick a spot and enjoy the show. The trick is to be smart by wearing layers of warm clothing topped by raincoats, boots, gloves, and head gear. Then you can laugh in the face of 10-foot-high waves pounding cliffs and sand, 60 mph winds, and high-velocity spray. What you can't be casual about are huge driftwood logs being tossed about like toothpicks or rolling at the water's edge. People have been killed when swept out to sea by an extra-large sneaker wave or struck by a log. Five good storm-watching spots are Waikiki Beach at *Cape Disappointment State Park* (Ilwaco), Kalaloch, Ocean Shores, Ruby Beach, and Westport. For more information on the safest locations, call the Long Beach Peninsula Visitors Bureau, (800) 451-2542; and Westport/Grayland Visitor Information Center, (800) 345-6223.

Lewis and Clark Corps of Discovery

On November 7, 1805, William Clark wrote in his journal: "Great joy in camp we are in view of the Ocian. . . ." For the record, the party was still some 20 miles from the Pacific Ocean, but they finally arrived at the mouth of the Columbia River on November 15 and set up Station Camp. Although Clark scouted up the Long Beach Peninsula some 9 miles for a possible winter headquarters site, the party backtracked upriver and, on the advice of Clatsop Indians about food sources, started crossing to the Oregon side of the river on November 26. By December 7 the whole party was hunkered down at the Fort Clatsop site and began building their winter quarters. The *Fort Clatsop National Memorial* is near Astoria, which was established as a trading site at the mouth of the Columbia River in 1811. For more information, check *Discovering Lewis & Clark,* a multimedia site incorporating the entire route (www.lewis-clark.org) or *Lewis and Clark Trail Heritage Foundation* (www.lewisandclark.org).

you on Lewis and Clark's heroic journey from Camp Du Bois in Wood River, Illinois, to the Pacific Ocean.

Now head north on US 101 to *Seaview* for meandering back roads that offer pleasant views of quaint cottages, many established during the late nineteenth century as summer retreats. The *Shelburne Country Inn B&B* at 4415 Pacific Highway (800-466-1896; www.theshelburneinn.com) was built in 1896 and restored in the 1970s. Along with antiques, homemade quilts, and a bountiful herb garden, the inn features hearty country breakfasts, lunches, and dinners in the restaurant. The Shelburne also provides breakfast for the China Beach Retreat at 222 Robert Gray Drive, Ilwaco (360-642-5660; www.chinabeachretreat.com), an early 1900s waterfront cabin; the Audubon Cottage is also on the China Beach grounds. Nearby, the Depot Restaurant (1208 38th Place; 360-642-7880) operates in Seaview's original Clamshell Railroad Depot.

Long Beach, the largest town on up the Long Beach Peninsula, has a wooden boardwalk stretching a half-mile along the beach from Bolstad Avenue. The boardwalk provides easy access to the roaring surf, rustling dune grass, and the wide, sandy beach. Subtle lighting along the way makes the boardwalk ideal for a romantic evening stroll. From here you can see the array of multicolored kites that folks of all ages fly on the beach in late August during the *Washington State International Kite Festival* (and any time the wind's right). Discovery Trail, an eight-mile walk through the dunes, parallels the boardwalk for part of its journey from Long Beach to Ilwaco.

Be sure to stop at the *World Kite Museum and Hall of Fame* at 303 Sid Snyder Drive (360-642-4020; www.worldkitemuseum.com) in Long Beach, which features displays from delicate butterfly and dragon kites to huge fighting kites and videos. The museum's impressive collection numbers more than

1,400 kites representing cultures around the world. You can visit daily from 11:00 a.m. to 5:00 p.m. May through September and daily except Wednesday and Thursday October through April. Look in a small alley between Second Street and Third Street South and between Pacific Highway 103 and Boulevard Street to see if the kids can find *Fish Alley Theater,* great fun for the whole family with storytellers, clowns, jugglers, face painters, and musicians during the summer.

Good places to grab a bite to eat on the Long Beach Peninsula include the *Berry Patch* (1513 Bay Avenue in Ocean Park; 360-665-5551); *Sand Dollar Deli & Pizza* (401 South Pacific in Long Beach; 360-642-3432); the *Crab Pot* (1917 Pacific Highway; 360-642-8870); and *Cottage Bakery & Deli* at 118 Pacific Highway in Long Beach (360-642-4441).

Continuing north, travelers can find access to the beach at both Loomis Lake and Pacific Pines State Parks; walk on sandy paths lined with wild strawberry plants. The beaches are great spots for quiet seaside picnics. If you like being closer to the action, check out *Boardwalk Cottages* at 800 Ocean Beach Boulevard South in Long Beach (800-569-3804; www.boardwalk cottages.com) or the *Seaview Motel & Cottages* at 3728 Pacific Way, Seaview (360-642-2450). To bed down in the former digs of the lighthouse keepers, located just inland from North Head Lighthouse and Cape Disappointment State Park, inquire at (360) 642-3078. For information on other cottages, motels, and beachside RV parks, contact the Long Beach Peninsula Visitor Information Bureau (800-451-2542; www.funbeach.com).

Romantics can contact innkeepers Susie Goldsmith and Bill Verner at *Boreas Bed & Breakfast Inn,* also close to the ocean at 607 North Ocean Beach Boulevard in Long Beach (888-642-8069; www.boreasinn.com). There's a whirlpool spa in an enclosed cedar-and-glass gazebo. Breakfast is a lively event, with guests gathering on the main level for such tasty treats as roasted Washington pears stuffed with pecans, peach kuchen baked in custard, and a three-mushroom frittata sautéed with sherry. Another pleasant place to stay is the 1929 *Moby Dick Hotel, Restaurant and Oyster Farm* at 25814 Sandridge Road in Nahcotta (360-665-4543; www.mobydickhotel.com).

The tiny town of *Nahcotta* has been the center of the peninsula's oyster industry. Native oysters, a tribal staple for centuries, were wiped out by the

marinetrails

Four marine trails offer paddlers not only routes but camping sites accessible to non-motorized craft: the 140-mile Cascadia Marine Trail in Puget Sound, Willapa Bay Water Trail, Lakes-to-Lock Water Trail in Seattle, and the 146-mile Lower Columbia River Water Trail between Washington and Oregon.

1920s through overharvesting, disease, and freezing weather. The introduction of Japanese oysters and new cultivation techniques has made this Willapa Bay area one of the top oyster-growing places in the world. Pop over to **Oysterville Sea Farms** at First and Clark Streets in Oysterville (360-665-6585) to see the oyster-shucking process and to shop for fresh oysters and cranberry goodies.

Visit the **Willapa Bay Interpretive Center** at 273rd Place on Nahcotta's breakwater in a replica of an oyster station house. The center (360-665-4547) exhibits 150 years of oyster-growing and is open from 10:00 a.m. to 3:00 p.m. on weekends Memorial Day through Labor Day. The walls are covered with old photographs, memorabilia, oyster-harvesting tools, maps, and a 20-foot mural of Willapa Bay. From here continue north on Sandridge Road to **Oysterville,** established in 1854 to house oyster workers and families. You can see the local church, a one-room schoolhouse, the general store, and early 1900s houses as you stroll through this extremely quiet bayside village.

Three miles north of Oysterville, take the tree-lined Stackpole Road to **Leadbetter Point State Park,** adjacent to the **Willapa National Wildlife Refuge** at the far end of the 28-mile-long peninsula. A favorite place for bird-watchers, Leadbetter Point's tidal flats overflow with migrating shorebirds and geese in April and May. Four trails lead walkers and birders through park or refuge with Willapa Bay on the east and the Pacific Ocean on the west.

Along the Columbia River

From Ilwaco head east to little **Chinook** on US 12 along the Columbia River. It was one of the most prosperous communities in Washington during the 1880s when fishing traps lined the river and tons of fish were processed in waterfront canneries. The traps were banned in 1935, but the port of Chinook is still a major fishing center in the area. You can still see many old homes built in the late 1800s. Next door to the old Methodist church on the corner of US 101 and Hazel Street in Chinook is **Little Ocean Annie's** (360-777-8387), which offers tasty fish-and-chips and seafood to go.

Traveling north on Highway 401 and east on Highway 4, the landscape is mostly forestlands along the Columbia River, past the communities of Naselle, Rosburg, Grays River, **Skamokawa,** and **Cathlamet.** Stop for a photo opportunity in Grays River at the state's oldest remaining covered bridge used by the public. The 1905 wooden bridge stretches across the Grays River and is a 15-minute drive west of Cathlamet; call the Wahkiakum County Chamber of Commerce (360-795-9996) for directions.

Plan to stop at the *Julia Butler Hansen National Wildlife Refuge* (360-795-3915; 46 Steamboat Slough Road) near Cathlamet and drive through its 4,757 acres of diked floodplain covered with thick grass and woodland habitat for birds and land animals. There are also trails for walking or bicycling. The refuge was created to protect the endangered Columbia white-tailed deer

Travelers can find lodgings at Skamokawa Center and Cafe, 1391 West Highway 4, Skamokawa (888-920-2777; www.skamokawakayak.com). Their light and airy guest rooms are situated in the historic Skamokawa General Store building, constructed on a wide deck that extends about 40 feet over the north bank of the Columbia River. From your lofty perch on the second floor, enjoy views of one of the main sections of the *Lewis and Clark Columbia River Water Trail* (www.coasttrails.org) and to the adjacent Julia Butler Hanson and *Lewis and Clark National Wildlife Refuges*. Ask the innkeepers about kayak rentals, instruction, and guide services.

The Inn at Crippen Creek in Skamokawa offers two rooms on a secluded 14-acre valley setting with a meandering creek at 15 Oatfield Road (360-795-0585; www.crippencreek.com). A little more inland in the Willapa Hills is the Inn at Lucky Mud, 44 Old Chestnut Drive (800-806-7131; www.luckymud.com). Ask your musician hosts to tell you the story behind the B&B's name; if you're lucky, they'll sing and play for you at breakfast. For eateries in the Skamokawa area, try the *Duck Inn Restaurant* (360-795-3655), Grays River Café (360-465-2999), or *Duffy's Irish Pub* (360-465-2898), located a few miles west in Grays River.

The town of Cathlamet sits above the Columbia River, well situated for watching the parade of river traffic and enjoying views of the rural farmland of *Puget Island.* The 4-mile-long island is perfect for an easy bicycle ride, and from the south end you can board the last remaining passenger ferry on the Lower Columbia River to the Oregon side, connecting you to Highway 30 east to Portland or west to Astoria.

Puget Island innkeeper Winnie Lowsma welcomes bird and butterfly watchers to *Redfern Farm Bed & Breakfast* at 277 Cross Dike Road (360-849-4108; www.redfernfarmbnb). You'll find two second-floor guest rooms

femaleforce

Julia Butler Hansen, who had a national wildlife refuge named after her, won all 21 elections in her 43-year political career at three levels. As a Congressional representative, she was the first woman to chair a subcommittee of the House Appropriations Committee, and was an expert on the U.S. highway system. Her Cathlamet home, built in 1860, is the county's oldest building and the town's main attraction.

gogogogo

Wahkiakum County is the only county in the state without a stop light.

(each with a private bath), an outdoor spa, and a back deck overlooking the family garden and orchard. You could also call the innkeepers at the **Bradley House Inn,** 61 Main Street in Cathlamet (360-795-3030; www.bradleyhousebb .com). Bed down in comfort in this gracious 1907 Eastlake home built by an early lumber baron. Enjoy a stay at the Italian-style Villa at Little Cape Horn at 48 Little Cape Horn Road (360-578-9100; www.villalittlecapehorn.com) a few miles east of Cathlamet. The recently built four-bedroom lodging sits above the Columbia River with magnificent views and a private beach.

Cathlamet offers Riverview Restaurant (88 Main Street; 360-795-8033); the riverside River Rat Tap (90 Broadway; 360-795-0099) in an 1891 building that once housed a roller-skating floor; Sharon's Pizza & More (40 River Street; 360-795-3311), and the Eagle Mexican & Italian Restaurant (380 Una Avenue; 360-795-0559). The **Wahkiakum County Historical Museum** at 65 River Street (360-795-3964), which turned 50 years old in 2009, offers artifacts of work and daily life from when the town was young.

Places to Stay on the Washington Coast

AMANDA PARK

Lake Quinault Lodge
345 South Shore Road
(800) 562-6672

Lake Quinault Resort
314 North Shore Road
(800) 650-2362

Lochaerie Resort Cabins
638 North Shore Road
(360) 288-2215

CATHLAMET

Bradley House Inn
61 Main Street
(360) 795-3030

DUNGENESS

Groveland Cottage Bed and Breakfast Inn
14861 Sequim–Dungeness Way
(800) 879-8859

FORKS

Kalaloch Lodge
157151 Highway 101
(866) 525-2562

Miller Tree Inn Bed & Breakfast
654 East Division Street
(800) 943-6563

Shady Nook Cottages
81 Ash Avenue
(360) 374-5497

HOOD CANAL

Glen Ayr Hood Canal Waterfront Resort
25381 North Highway 101
Hoodsport
(866) 877-9522

Rest-a-While RV Park
Highway 101
(360) 877-9474

LA PUSH

Quileute Oceanside Resort
320 Ocean Drive
(800) 487-1267

LONG BEACH

Boardwalk Cottages
800 Ocean Beach
Boulevard South
(800) 569-3804

Boreas Bed & Breakfast
607 North Boulevard
(888) 642-8069

PORT ANGELES

Lake Crescent Lodge
416 Lake Crescent Road
(360) 928-3211

Sol Duc Hot Springs Resort
Sol Duc Road
(360) 327-3583

SEAVIEW

Seaview Motel & Cottages
3728 Pacific Way
(360) 642-2450

SEQUIM

Dungeness Bay Cottages
140 Marine Drive
(888) 683-3013

Juan de Fuca Cottages
182 Marine Drive
(866) 683-4433

Red Caboose Getaway
24 Old Coyote Way
(360) 683-7350

SKAMOKAWA

Inn at Lucky Mud
44 Old Chestnut Drive
(800) 806-7131

Skamokawa Center & Café
1391 West Highway 4
(360) 795-8300

TOKELAND

Tokeland Hotel & Restaurant
100 Hotel Road
(360) 267-7006

WESTPORT

Chateau Hotel Westport
710 Hancock
(360) 268-9101

SELECTED INFORMATION CENTERS AND OTHER HELPFUL WEB SITES

Forks
(800) 443-6757
www.forkswa.com

Grays Harbor County
www.co.grays-harbor.wa.us/info/
tourismGH

Hood Canal
(800) 576-2021
www.discoverhoodcanal.com

Lewis and Clark
www.lewisandclarkwa.com

Long Beach Peninsula
(800) 451-2542
www.funbeach.com

Olympic National Forest
www.fs.fed.us/r6/olympia

Olympic National Park
www.nps.gov/olym

Olympic Peninsula
(800) 942-4042
www.olympicpeninsula.org

Port Angeles
(360) 452-2363
www.portangeles.net

Sequim
(800) 737-8462
www.visitsun.com

Westport/Grayland
(800) 345-6223
www.2chambers.com/Westport

Places to Eat on the Washington Coast

ABERDEEN

Billy's Bar and Grill
322 East Heron Street
(360) 533-7144

Bridges Restaurant
112 North G Street
(360) 532-6563

CHINOOK

Little Ocean Annie's
US 101 and Hazel Street
(360) 777-8387

DUNGENESS

Three Crabs Restaurant
11 Three Crabs Road
(360) 683-4264

FORKS

Forks Coffee Shop Cafe
241 South Forks Avenue
(360) 374-6769

Kalaloch Lodge Restaurant
157151 US 101
(360) 962-2271

Smokehouse Restaurant
193161 US 101
(360) 374-6258

HOODSPORT/ELDON

Hoodsport Coffee Company
24240 North US 101
Eldon
(360) 877-0400

ILWACO

Pelicano Restaurant
177 Howerton Way
Ilwaco Marina
(360) 642-4034

The Port Bistro
235 Howerton Way
Ilwaco Marina
(360) 642-8447

LONG BEACH

Café Akari
203 Bolstad Avenue
(360) 642-3828

Cottage Bakery & Deli
118 Pacific Highway
(360) 642-4441

Peninsula Wine Merchants
509 Pacific Avenue South
(360) 777-8444

OCEAN PARK

Full Circle Cafe
1024 Bay Avenue
(360) 665-5385

PORT ANGELES

Elizabeth & Company Coffeehouse and Bakery
106 East First Street
(360) 452-5222

First Street Haven Cafe
107 East First Street
(360) 457-0352

Olympic Bagel Company
802 East First Street
(360) 452-9100

SEQUIM

The Buzz Coffee Shop
128 North Sequim Avenue
(360) 683-2503

Cedar Creek Restaurant
665 North Fifth Avenue
(360) 683-3983

Oak Table Cafe
292 West Bell Street
(360) 683-2179

ALSO WORTH SEEING

The Cranberry Museum & Farm
Long Beach

Lewis and Clark Discovery Dunes Trail
Port of Ilwaco to Long Beach

Moclips
Highway 109, north of Ocean Shores

Puget Sound Region

You could spend a lifetime exploring the Puget Sound region and still need more time. Its inland waterways, cut out by glaciers, offer travelers thousands of miles of shoreline, waterfront communities, and dozens of islands. The region's moist maritime climate supports lush forests and farms. A dynamic economy based on high-tech, natural resources, agriculture, and industry has attracted a diverse culture.

Although population explosions have made communities off Interstate 405 east of Seattle no longer off the beaten path, *Bellevue,* Redmond, Kirkland, and Woodinville also have their share of offerings. Plan an hour or more to enjoy the splendid *Bellevue Botanical Gardens* at 12001 Main Street, Bellevue (425-452-2750; www.bellevuebotanical.org). Stroll along a lush perennial border garden, a summer dahlia display, a traditional knot garden, a meditative Japanese garden, an alpine rock garden, and a loop trail through the reserve.

To the east, six miles north of Fall City on Highway 203, *Remlinger Farms* has 270 acres of fruits, vegetables, and berries, as well as a farm-animal petting zoo for children, picnic tables, a farm-fresh produce store, restaurant, and bakery. Remlinger Farms offers a Ripe 'n Ready Report of in-season produce

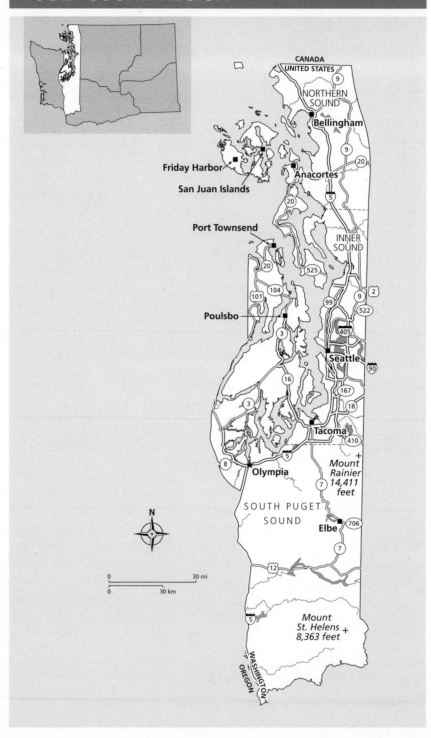

PUGET SOUND REGION

CANADA
UNITED STATES

NORTHERN SOUND

Bellingham

Friday Harbor

San Juan Islands

Anacortes

Port Townsend

INNER SOUND

Poulsbo

Seattle

Tacoma

Mount Rainier 14,411 feet

Olympia

SOUTH PUGET SOUND

Elbe

Mount St. Helens 8,363 feet

WASHINGTON
OREGON

N

0   30 mi
0   30 km

by calling (425) 451-8740 or browsing the farm's Web site, www.remlingerfarms
.com. The farm is located half a mile off Highway 203 on Northeast Thirty-
second Street, just south of Carnation.

Farther east is the picturesque **Snoqualmie Valley,** surrounded by the foothills of the Cascade Mountain range. The Snoqualmie River, flowing through the
valley, creates the spectacular 270-foot Snoqualmie Falls between Snoqualmie
and Fall City. Above the falls are a public overlook and the posh **Salish Lodge
& Spa** at 6501 Railroad Avenue (800-826-6124; www.salishlodge.com).

The **Northwest Railway Museum** (425-888-3030; www.trainmuseum
.org) at 38625 Southeast King Street in Snoqualmie is open daily. Scenic rides
on a diesel-electric train are on Saturday and Sunday April through October
plus Memorial Day and Labor Day, leaving from the restored Victorian train
station to the nearby community of North Bend and then to the top of Snoqualmie Falls and back.

For toothsome treats, be sure to stop by **Snoqualmie Falls Candy Factory** at 8102 Railroad Avenue Southeast (425-888-0439) for delicious fudge,
taffy, peanut brittle, and caramel corn as well as a great selection of ice cream.
You could also stop at **Gilman Village** in nearby Issaquah to sample chocolate
confections at **Boehm's Candies** at 255 Northeast Gilman Boulevard (425-
392-6652). For a cozy place to spend the night, call the **Roaring River Bed**

For Wine and Microbrew Aficionados

The grand duchess of wineries in the Seattle area is the elegant **Chateau Ste.
Michelle** at 14111 Northeast 145th in Woodinville. Tall Douglas fir, colorful rhododendrons, and lush beds of annuals and perennials greet visitors entering the chateau gates. Folks can enjoy shady picnic areas, the gift shop, seasonal events, and
a tour of the wine-making process. The winery's extremely popular summer concert
series attracts top names and large crowds who sit on the lawn. For information, call
(425) 415-3300 or check out www.ste-michelle.com. Wine and microbrew aficiona-
dos also have other options:

Alexandria Nicole Cellars
19501 144th Avenue NE
Woodinville
(425) 518-3300

Columbia Winery
14030 Northeast 145th
Woodinville
(800) 488-2347

Redhook Ale Brewery
14300 Northeast 145th Street
Woodinville
(425) 483-3232

Rock Bottom Brewery and Restaurant
550 106th Avenue NE
Bellevue
(425) 462-9300

For additional information check the Web site: www.eastkingcounty.org.

Seattle Tours

Seattle's Space Needle, Seattle Center, Pike Place Market and other landmarks are definitely not off the beaten path, so if you've been there, done that, opt for tours that will take you off the beaten path and behind the scenes.

Although Seattle is not known for its crime, it does have a dark side. *Private Eye Tours* (206-365-3739; www.privateeyetours.com) explores the unusual, macabre and sometimes just strange side of the city—if you're brave enough. Choose between the Mystery and Murder Tour (a mass murder, an axe man, brothels, Jimi Hendrix, serial killer Ted Bundy) or the Ghost Tour (phantoms and poltergeists, a mortuary, a gambling den, a poor farm, a castle, a haunted theater, a notorious rooming house).

If films or music are your passion, pick up **Reel Life in Seattle** (www.cityofseattle.net/filmoffice) or **Seattle Music Map** (www.seattle.gov/music.com) brochures for do-it-yourself tours. The city has been featured in hundreds of films and TV shows since *Tugboat Annie* in 1933. Sylvester Stallone made a leaping escape from the monorail in *Assassins; Sleepless in Seattle* featured a local houseboat and the Pike Place Market; and *Frasier* celebrated its 100th broadcast here. Follow the maps' numbers to trace the spots that hosted films and TV shows (*Black Widow, Northern Exposure, The Parallax View, The Fabulous Baker Boys,* etc.). On the music/dance scene, find the sites connected to Kurt Cobain, Duke Ellington, Gypsy Rose Lee, Pearl Jam, Martha Graham and Mark Tobey, the jazz era on Jackson Street, and Sub Pop Records, as well as soak up the nightlife.

Even the famous *Pike Place Market* is home to a different type of visit. If visitors go on their own, the sights, sounds, smells and crowds may be a little overwhelming and confusing. But at least three companies offer 2- to 3-hour walking food tours that include the culinary landmark, tours best taken early in a multi-day stay to introduce you to bakeries or restaurants worth a return visit. It's a chance to experience Pike Place Market like a local, and learn a few tips, perhaps how to pick the best fish or where the best local hang-outs are located. Not to mention nibbling your way through the tour.

Seattle Food Tours (800-979-3370; www.seattlefoodtours.com) covers the market and adjacent Belltown with its lunch tours. Guides share stories about area history, chefs' backgrounds, ethnic eateries, nightlife, and restaurant specialties, including Pacific Rim-inspired cuisine and award-winning chowder. *Taste Pike Place Market* (206-725-4483; www.tastepikeplace.com) has three tours—breakfast, lunch, and food-and-wine tasting—that might include local boutique wines, alderwood smoked wild salmon or crumpets. *Savor Seattle Tours* (800-838-3006; www.savorseattletours.com) is a food-

& Breakfast, 46715 Southeast 129th Street, North Bend (877-627-4647; www .theroaringriver.com), which offers one cabin and four rooms with private entrances, sitting areas, and decks overlooking the bubbling Middle Fork of the Snoqualmie River. For dining in the North Bend area, try Gaston's (425-888-1803) at 101 West North Bend Way, a mix of pasta, steaks, and seafood entrees and recommended by locals.

and-cultural adventure with cherry-inspired treats, Russian piroshky pastries, artisan-made cheeses and clam chowder.

Bill Speidel's Underground Tour (206-682-4646; www.undergroundtour.com) is worth the admission just to hear the guide's wildly entertaining spiel at the start of the tour inside a 1980s saloon. The tour takes groups under the streets and sidewalks into former downtown Seattle with plenty of humorous commentary.

For an Asian cultural tour, take a trip with **Chinatown Discovery** (206-623-5124; www.seattlechinatowntour.com) through the fragrances, foods, languages and history of the International District. While you're there, take time for an extended stroll through the **Wing Luke Asian Museum** (206-623-5124; www.wingluke.org), transformed in 2008 to more than eight times its original size in a 1910 building financed by Chinese immigrants. Parts of the museum are accessible only through Historic Immersion Tours. Or follow the long journey told in the **Northwest African-American Museum** (206-518-6000; www.naamnw.org, also opened in 2008. Tragedy and triumph, creativity and context, history and tales of new immigrants are part of the mix.

Specialty tours are also abundant. **Fifth Avenue Theatre** (206-625-1418; www.5th avenue.org.) has a free guided 20-minute tour that covers the building's past and ornate architecture. **Qwest Field** (www.qwestfield.com), home of the Seahawks, and Safeco Field (www.seattle.mariners.mlb.com), home of the Mariners, offer tours. Or join an architecture tour of the **Seattle Architecture Foundation** (www.seattlearchitecture.org).

But if you want more traditional tours, take a look at these options: **Show Me Seattle Tours** (206-633-2489; www.showmeseattle.com) takes visitors to the first Starbuck's Coffee Shop and the fish markets at Pike Place Market, Pioneer Square and the stadiums, the International District, quirky neighborhoods, great city views, the locks, floating homes and a whimsical giant troll crushing a VW. **Seattle Tours** (888-293-1404; www.seattlecitytours.com) is a 50-mile ride by popular attractions, including the salmon ladder at the Ballard Locks and the sports stadiums.

Short on time? **Let's Tour Seattle** (206-632-1447; www.letstourseattle.com) is a one-hour whirlwind stuffed with sights, history and humor as you roll by floating homes, the Fremont troll, Washington arboretum and many other sites. **See Seattle Walking Tours** (425-885-3173; www.seattlewalkingtours.com) offers easy to moderate on-foot excursions that can cover Bill Boeing to Bill Gates and the Duwamps as well as Sodo mojo. Among several options, Gray Line of Seattle (800-426-7532; www.graylineseattle.com) offers a hop-on, hop-off double-decker bus.

South Puget Sound

Using a generous definition of South Puget Sound, let's go southeast from The Sound toward picturesque Mount Rainier, a dominant feature seen from the lower sound and a stunning up-close backdrop to many interesting places in the area around Mount Rainier National Park.

PUGET SOUND'S FAVORITE ATTRACTIONS

American Camp, English Camp
San Juan Island

American Museum of Radio and Electricity
Bellingham

Bloedel Reserve Gardens
Bainbridge Island

Center for Wooden Boats
Seattle

Fort Worden
Port Townsend

Hovander Homestead Park
Ferndale

Island County Historical Museum
Coupeville

La Conner Quilt Museum
La Conner

Lynden Pioneer Museum
Lynden

Mason County Historical Society Museum
Shelton

Meerkerk Rhododendron Gardens
Whidbey Island

Mount Rainier National Park
Ashford

Mount Rainier Scenic Railroad
Elbe

Museum of Glass
Tacoma

Peace Arch Park and Gardens
Blaine

Pioneer Farm Museum
Eatonville

Port Townsend Marine Science Center
Port Townsend

Sidney Art Gallery
Port Orchard

Skagit Valley Tulip Festival
Mount Vernon

Suquamish Museum
Suquamish

Wolf Haven Wildlife International
Tenino

The steam-powered *Mount Rainier Scenic Railroad* excursion train takes riders on a slow jaunt from Mineral Lake near the southwest entrance to the park. On this one-and-a-half-hour round-trip, you'll pass through thick evergreen forests, cross bubbling mountain streams, and enjoy spectacular views of the sleeping volcano's summit. Passengers can sit in an open carriage or relax in a closed, heated car. Trains leave at 10:30 a.m. and 2:30 p.m. Saturday and 2:00 p.m. Sunday from Memorial Day through the end of September and daily from June 15 through Labor Day. For further information call (888) 783-2611 or check www.mrsr.com.

In the nearby *Elbe* railroad yard, about 14 miles from the park entrance, two classic dining cars of the *Mount Rainier Dining Company* are permanently parked on the tracks—a 1922 Southern Pacific and a 1910 Great

Northern, offering a railroad dining car experience. A lounge named the Side Track Room is located in a late-1930s Chicago, Burlington, and Quincy coach. The dining cars are open Wednesday through Sunday for breakfast, lunch, and dinner. Call (888) 773-4637 for reservations.

Six miles farther east on Highway 706 is **Ashford,** a small community of artists, outdoor enthusiasts, and old-timers who appreciate living at the entrance to **Mount Rainier National Park.** On your way from Elbe, look for Dan Klennert's Ex-Nihilo outdoor sculpture park (www.danielklennert.com) on the right-hand side of the road. Travelers are welcome to walk among large metal sculptures, such as elk, a skeleton on a Harley-Davidson motorcycle, a larger-than-life bicycle, and a 17-foot-tall giraffe named Aspen Zoe. Klennert's work was featured in the Disney movie *America's Heart and Soul.*

Ashford is Rainier-Climbing Central, home to Rainier Mountaineering Inc. at 30027 Highway 706 East (888-892-5462; www.rmiguides.com). RMI has guided thousands of climbers to the summit since 1969. It's owned by mountaineers Lou and Peter Whittaker with Joseph Horiskey. International Mountain Guides at 3111 Highway 706 East (360-569-2609; www.mountainguides.com) also works out of Ashford. Peter and Erika Whittaker's Whittaker Mountaineering at 30027 Highway 706 East (800-238-5756; www.whittakermountaineering.com) sells and rents climbing gear. The adjacent Rainier Base Camp Bar & Grill is open in the summer. Grab a bite and let the kids work off some energy on the nearby not-too-high climbing wall.

Also here is Whittaker's Bunkhouse Motels & Cabin (Win and Sarah Whittaker) and their Wireless Internet Café (30205 Highway 706 East; 360-569-2439). Win and Sarah were the force behind creating the annual Rainier Independent Film Festival at three venues in the Ashford Valley. On the east edge of Ashford, stop at **Ashford Creek Pottery** at 30516 Highway 706, (360) 569-

ultimatesummit

Each year about 10,000 climbers try to reach the top of 14,410-foot Mount Rainier, which has the most glaciers (twenty-six) of any U.S. mainland mountain. Only about half reach the summit; some die trying.

1000. The charming studio offers functional stoneware enlivened with irises and also displays pottery by local artists.

The **Mountain Meadows Inn** (28912 Highway 706 East; 360-569-2788; www.mountainmeadowsinn.com) is a comfortable bed-and-breakfast. It was the home of the superintendent of National Mill in 1910, once the biggest lumber mill west of the Mississippi River. Guests wake to a hearty, gourmet country breakfast. Wildlife is often visible from the generous front porch or on a stroll on forest trails.

Another favorite lodging and eatery in these parts is *Alexander's Old Country Inn Bed & Breakfast Day Spa* (37515 Highway 706 East; 800-654-7615; www.alexanderscountryinn.com), just 3 miles east of Ashford. Luminaries such as Theodore Roosevelt and William Howard Taft have bunked down at this twelve-room 1912 homestead. The pan-fried trout comes from its own glacier-fed pond; and the baked salmon and beef tenderloin in a green pepper and mango chutney are highly recommended.

Before heading up to the mountain, consider being pampered at Stormking Spa and Cabins at 37311 Highway 706 (360-569-2964; www.stormkingspa .com) or *Wellspring Spa and Log Cabins* at 54922 Kernahan Road (360-569-2514) where licensed massage therapist Sunny Thompson has created a

Old and New Blend on Mount Rainer

Mount Rainier National Park has two historic inns as well as the Henry M. Jackson Visitor Center at Paradise that opened in 2008. The 121-room **Paradise Inn,** which took six months to build in 1916 and two years and $22.5 million to renovate in a manner that kept that warm cozy feeling inside, re-opened in 2008. A German carpenter designed and built much of the decorative woodwork on the interior and most of that, as well as furniture and other items, was stored during renovation (including the rocks, all numbered, of each fireplace). So if you've been to the inn before, don't worry: the woodwork is still there, the rustic piano has a new soundboard, and the 14-foot grandfather clock carved by carpenter Hans Fraehnke sits in the same corner. The inn, at 5,400-foot elevation, is closed from late fall to late spring, although the Paradise area is accessible, weather-willing and if plows are able to keep ahead of the snowfall.

The 25-room *National Park Inn* at Longmire (elevation 2,761 feet), near the Nisqually entrance to the park, was renovated in 1990 and is on the Register of Historic Places. The rustic inn has a stupendous backdrop on a clear day—stand on the north porch and let your jaw drop at the sight of Mount Rainier, right there. It can be particular beautiful at sunset. The inn is complemented by a good restaurant, the Longmire Museum, a general store in a 1911 cabin, and a gift shop. It's open year-round so take advantage of off-season rates and bring your cross-country skis and snowshoes.

The star of the park, of course, is Mount Rainier. To folks who live within sight, it's called The Mountain, as in, "The Mountain is out today!" It has the most glaciers (twenty-six) of any mountain in the mainland United States; the Carbon Glacier is the largest mainland glacier by volume; and the Emmons Glacier is the largest by area. Its last major eruption was about 2,500 years ago but there was a minor blowing off steam and ash in the 1800s. Geologists say that the eruption that created the Osceola Mudflow (about 1,600 vertical feet of the peak slid away) sent mud roaring across the landscape to where Tacoma and south Seattle now sit. Seattle is about 50 miles from Mount Rainier.

mountain paradise of saunas, waterfalls, hot tubs, comfortable rooms, cozy log cabins, and a tree house. The outdoor hot tubs overlook landscaped gardens with terraced waterfalls and cooing doves.

Jasmer's at Mount Rainier at 30005 Highway 706 East (360-569-2682; www.jasmers.com) offers cozy cabins along Big Creek. Other accommodations close to Ashford include *Nisqually Lodge* at 31609 Highway 706 East (888-674-3554; www.escapetothemountains.com) for comfy lodge-style rooms; and *Mounthaven Resort* at 38210 Highway 706 East (800-456-9380; www .mounthaven.com) for cabins and RV spaces.

On the far north side of Mount Rainier, *Alta Crystal Resort* at 68317 State Route 410 East near Greenwater (800-277-6475; www.altacrystalresort.com) offers cabins and chalets at the Crystal Mountain Ski Area, a short walk from summer hiking and mountain biking trails through old-growth trees within the Mount Baker–Snoqualmie National Forest. For a complete list of area lodging, go to www.visitrainier.com.

Mount Rainier National Park celebrated its centennial anniversary in 1999; its jewel, Mount Rainier, rises to an elevation of 14,410 feet above sea level. Because of its height, ice and snow, weather-related changes can happen here almost without warning, and scientists say that the mountain can—one day—erupt again. But from June to early September, you can enjoy two scenic drives that lead to panoramic locations. The first, *Paradise,* is reached from Ashford or Packwood; the second, *Sunrise,* is reached from the east side near the Chinook Pass highway. Sunrise is the more winding drive but the rewards are many, including wonderful wildflower meadows with environmentally sensitive paths and trails among the native flora. Both Paradise and Sunrise are more than 5,000 feet in elevation, so travelers should take warm sweaters and jackets on this trek.

There are six developed campgrounds in Mount Rainier National Park; check the Web sites www.nps.gov/mora and www.mount.rainier.national-park .com for information about camping, hiking, horse camping, and backpacking in the park. Additional information can be obtained from park headquarters in Ashford (360-569-2211). During winter cross-country skiers can contact the *Mount Tahoma Trails Association* about skiing hut-to-hut on some 100 miles of logging road trails; check www.skimtta.com or call (360) 569-2451, Mount Tahoma Ski Trail office, for a recorded message and current information.

Good places to grab a bite to eat include Copper Creek Inn Restaurant in Ashford (360-569-2326; www.coppercreekinn.com); *Rainier Overland Restaurant and Lodge* in Ashford (360-569-0851; www.rainieroverland.com); *National Park Inn Restaurant* in nearby Longmire; (360-569-2275; http://

rainier.guestservices.com); and **Scaleburgers** (54109 Mountain Highway, Elbe; 360-569-2247). Located in a weigh-station building renovated in 1939, Scaleburgers has been serving juicy hamburgers since 1987.

In the lowlands near Eatonville, you can enter a time warp at the **Pioneer Farm Museum** at 7716 Ohop Valley Road (360-832-6300; www.pioneer farmmuseum.org). One-and-a-half-hour tours are run from 11:15 a.m. to 4:00 p.m. daily in summer and on weekends during spring and fall. The museum gift shop, housed in an 1888 trading post cabin, brims with old-fashioned treats.

flying saucers

In 1947 a pilot saw nine unusual-looking aircraft flying very fast by Mount Rainier. Kenneth Arnold made what is considered the first modern UFO sighting. The term flying saucers came out of his description: "flying like a saucer."

North of Eatonville is **Northwest Trek** at 11610 Trek Drive East (360-832-6117; www.nwtrek.org), an unusual park where a variety of wildlife live in a woodland setting, wildlife that you can see up close—really close. By taking the 55-mimute tram tour through 435 acres of forest, wetland, and meadow, you'll be (sometimes extremely) close to free-roaming bison, elk, moose, caribou, and bighorn sheep. Seen from walking trails in another area of the park will be captive cougar, lynx, bobcat, bear, and other animals. There are more than 200 North American animals in the park. It is open at 9:30 a.m. daily but closes at various hours depending on the season. Admission is $7.00 to $15.00 and includes the tram tour. For more information, call (360) 832-6117 or go to www.nwtrek.org.

To the northwest of Trek is Olympia, the state capital and former home of the now-shuttered Olympia Brewery plant. Many visitors tour only the capitol building, then move on, but there are many lesser-known sights worth experiencing. Start with a sidewalk tour of downtown as described in "Olympia's Historic Downtown: A Walking Tour," which highlights outstanding historic buildings, homes, and parks. This brochure is available from the Olympia-Lacey-Tumwater Visitor & Convention Bureau at 809 Legion Street Southeast (877-704-7500; www.visitolympia.com), open 8:00 a.m. to 5:00 p.m. weekdays.

icecream youscream

The world's first soft-serve ice cream machine was used in an Olympia Dairy Queen.

Families with young children will want to stop at Olympia's **Hands On Children's Museum** at 106 Eleventh Street Southwest (360-956-0818; www .hocm.org). This creative place offers a diverse collection of interactive exhibits for kids ten years old and younger.

Kids also love Tumwater Falls Park at Deschutes Way & C Street, Tumwater (360-943-2550; www.olytumfoundation.org). It's free, open during daylight hours, and the perfect park for a family picnic with a scenic waterfall, walking trails, and a salmon ladder.

Plan to visit the **Washington State Capital Museum** in the historic Lord Mansion at 211 Southwest Twenty-first Avenue (360-753-2580; www.wshs.org). The museum offers a look at South Puget Sound's early pioneer and Indian history in interpretive exhibits on two floors of the mansion. The nearby Lacey Museum also showcases the area's history from Oregon Trails Days to the present. Housed in a 1926 building that served as a private residence, 1940s fire station, and Lacey's first city hall, the museum features exhibits, artifacts, and old photos. It's free and open 11:00 to 3:00 p.m. Thursday and Friday and 9:00 a.m. to 5:00 p.m. Saturday at 829½ Lacey Street Southeast (360-438-0209).

thevenerable capitol

Olympia's Legislative Building, completed in 1928, was the last domed capitol built in the United States. Forty-two steps lead to the entrance, symbolizing that Washington was the forty-second state to join the Union. The granite for the steps and foundation was quarried in the Washington town of Index, and the sandstone of its face is from the foothills of Mount Rainier. The dome weighs more than thirty million pounds and sits 287 feet above the ground. The dome's five-ton Angels of Mercy chandelier was designed by Louis Comfort Tiffany. A Visitor Information Center at Fourteenth and Capitol Way offers more information; call (360) 586-3460 or visit www.ga.wa.gov/visitor. Hours are 8:00 a.m. to 5:00 p.m. daily and 9:00 a.m. to 4:00 p.m. weekends. For tour information, call (360) 902-8880.

After museum-hopping, stop downtown and grab a bite to eat at the **Urban Onion** at 116 Legion Way Southeast (360-943-9242), which reportedly has the best kids' menu in town. If you're there for breakfast, don't pass up the famous U.O. Smoothie, a concoction of orange juice, bananas, and yogurt.

Stroll along the **Percival Landing** boardwalk on Olympia's waterfront to see boats and ships and occasionally view the playful antics of a seal. The boardwalk begins on Fourth Avenue behind Bayview Market. A three-story tower at the landing's north end offers great views of the port, the city and, on a clear day, the Olympic Mountains. Also at Percival Landing is the Sand Man, Olympia's grand old tugboat launched there in 1910, a tireless workhorse until 1987, and now open to the public from 10:00 a.m. to 3:00 p.m. Saturdays and Sundays. Step aboard to relive Puget Sound maritime history as volunteer docents tell the tales.

You'll find several places to eat, including the **Olympia Farmers' Market,** located at the north end of Capitol Way. The spacious, covered market is open from 10:00 a.m. to 3:00 p.m. Thursdays through Sundays from April through October, and weekends only in November and December.

To absorb the atmosphere of Olympia's past, enjoy a meal at the historic McMenamins **Spar Cafe, Bar and Tobacco Merchant** at 114 East Fourth Avenue (360-357-6444). The Spar retains many details from its early days; chairs have a clip on the back to hold the patron's hat, sports scores are announced on a chalkboard, and the walls are decorated with old logging photos. With the McMenamins' ownership, handcrafted ales are now brewed onsite using the Spar's legendary artesian water.

Enjoy other eateries and coffee shops in the Olympia area, including **Tugboat Annie's Restaurant** located at 2100 West Bay Drive (360-943-1850); **Budd Bay Cafe** at 525 Columbia Street Northwest (360-357-6963); **Oyster House** at 320 Fourth Avenue West (360-753-7000); **Cafe Vita** at 124 Fourth Avenue East (360-754-8187); and **Wagner's European Bakery & Cafe** at 1013 Capitol Way (360-357-7268).

For lodgings near downtown, call the innkeepers at **Swantown Inn Bed & Breakfast,** a four-bedroom 1893 Queen Anne/Eastlake Victorian mansion located at 1431 Eleventh Avenue Southeast (360-753-9123; www.swantowninn .com). A sumptuous three-course gourmet breakfast is served in the grand dining room, or you can have a boxed continental breakfast to take on the road. In 2008, Swantown added a day spa.

moundmystery

Many theories try to explain the Mima Mounds, fairly evenly spaced 5- to 8-foot-tall mounds of rock and dirt about 30 feet in diameter on the Mima Prairie south of Olympia. Theories include: Ice Age pocket gophers; earthquakes; mounds used like raised beds for growing vegetables by American Indians; fish nests when the area was underwater; after the prairie thawed post-Ice Age, the ground fractured and melted and the mounds were what was left; and Paul Bunyan and his workers worked off a job leaving dirt-filled wheelbarrows that rotted, leaving the mounds behind.

From the **Puget View Cottage** at 7924 Sixty-first Avenue Northeast (360-413-9474), located a few miles northeast of Olympia on Puget Sound, guests enjoy wide water views of Nisqually Beach, Anderson Island, and Longbranch Peninsula. By prior arrangement, you can be dropped off by float plane. Walk the nearby beaches and trails of **Tolmie State Park** and watch for marine wildlife. The Nisqually River, which flows from glaciers on Mount Rainier, empties into Puget Sound at the nearby **Nisqually National Wildlife Refuge,** where visitors may see more than 200 bird species, including migratory waterfowl, and many small mammals. Enjoy walking on seven miles of trails with observation blinds, including the one-mile Twin Barn Loop to the Education Center, open 10:00 a.m. to 2:00 p.m. weekdays. For information, contact the refuge office at 100 Brown Farm Road Northeast, Lacey (360-753-9467) from 7:30 a.m. to 4:00 p.m. weekdays.

Splendid nature trails are found a few miles south of Olympia at *Mima Mounds Natural Area Preserve,* an unanswered "whodunit" of uniformly spaced giant mounds. An interpretive center is built into one of these geological wonders. An observation deck, a barrier-free interpretive path, and hiking trails are set among the riot of colorful wildflowers and native grasses that bloom in spring and summer. For directions, go to www.southsoundprairies .org/visit.htm or call (360) 596-5144.

A few miles east of Mima Mounds is *Wolf Haven International* at 3111 Offut Lake Road Southeast, Tenino (800-448-9653; www.wolfhaven.org). Forty-five-minute tours are offered on the hour and the tours are the only way to see the wolves. Wolf Haven is a privately owned refuge for abandoned wolves and other feral animals that can't be returned to the wild. Volunteers describe wolf biology and lore as well as the personalities of individual wolves living at the sanctuary. Camera lenses more than 80mm are not allowed although there are separate photography tours for a fee. Campfire sing fests and howl-ins happen Friday and Saturday nights in summer starting at 7:00 p.m.

adoptawolf

Folks can "adopt" a resident Wolf Haven International wolf either singly, as pairs, or in packs. This is a personal way to connect with and make a difference in the lives of these extraordinary animals, which for various reasons are no longer able to live in the wild. Lone wolves are paired whenever possible for companionship. See www .wolfhaven.org for current information or call (800) 448-9653.

Nearby, visit *Lattin's Country Cider Mill & Farm* at 9402 Rich Road Southeast (360-491-7328; www.lattins cider.com) and purchase freshly made cider, homemade pies, jams, and syrups as well as seasonal fruits and vegetables. Stop by on weekends to sample homemade doughnuts. For lodging, call *Blueberry Hill Farm Guest House Bed & Breakfast,* 12125 Blueberry Hill Lane in nearby Yelm (360-458-4726; www.blueberryhillfarmguesthouse.com). The innkeeper makes Grandma's Gourmet Berry Jam and also serves guests delicious farm-style breakfasts (at a nominal charge per person).

South of Wolf Haven on Highway 99 is the town of *Tenino,* a community famous around the turn of the twentieth century for its sandstone quarries. The scenic *Tenino City Park* was built around one of the abandoned quarries.

TOP ANNUAL EVENTS
IN THE PUGET SOUND REGION

Bumbershoot
Seattle, Labor Day weekend
(877) 885-9452

Scottish Highland Games
Hovander Park, Ferndale, early June
(360) 384-3444

Northwest Folklife Festival
Seattle, Memorial Day weekend
(206) 684-7300

Skagit Valley Tulip Festival
Mount Vernon area, all of April
(360) 428-5959

Oysterfest & Seafood Festival
Shelton, early October
(800) 576-2021

Water cascades down moss- and vine-covered sandstone walls into a pond, now used each summer as the community's public swimming pool.

Tenino was a railroad town named, some say, after the Number 10-9-0 engine that pulled local trains. The 1914 *Tenino Depot Museum* (399 Park Avenue West), adjacent to the city park, is one of many local sandstone buildings. Museum exhibits illustrate techniques used in the old quarries to transform raw stone into everything from bricks to flower pots, as well as railroad lore and local history. The museum is open noon to 4:00 p.m. weekends. For information, call the Tenino Chamber at (360) 264-5075; or go to www.tenino chamberofcommerce.com.

Steilacoom, just northeast of Olympia via I-5, is a small town perched on a bluff overlooking the southernmost part of Puget Sound and nearby Anderson Island. It's history is rich with stories of fast ships, quick business deals, and slow trains. Washington Territories' first incorporated town was established in 1854 by Maine sea captain Lafayette Balch. During the late-nineteenth century, it was an important seaport, county seat, and commercial center.

To learn more about the town, visit the Steilacoom Historical Museum (253-584-413; www.steilacoomhistorical.org) at the corner of Rainier and Main Streets, the Wagon Shop on Main below the museum, and the Nathaniel Orr Home, adjacent to the museum on Rainier Street. The museum buildings offer glimpses of the town's history, and docents are often available to explain and demonstrate old-time skills. Call for current times.

Stroll through the downtown National Historic District, with more than thirty buildings on the historic register. Ask for a walking tour map at the museum; guides are also available.

For a historic site that takes visitors back to the days of early American settlement, take in the nearby **Fort Steilacoom Museum** on the grounds of Western State Hospital, 9601 Steilacoom Boulevard (253-582-5838). Four officers' quarters are all that is left of the original twenty-six wood-frame structures. They interpret the early military history of that area. It's open 1:00 to 4:00 p.m. Sundays from June through August and the first Sunday of September through May.

Then, for a comfortable overnight stay in this historic village, call **Above the Sound Bed & Breakfast** at 806 Birch Street (253-589-1441; www .abovethesound.com), just a short walk for a twenty-minute ferry ride to Anderson Island. Or try the Inn at Saltar's Point, 68 Jackson Street (253-588-4522; innatsaltarspoint.com), a modern (2007) B&B a few blocks from downtown. For a treat, have dinner at a French restaurant, Le Crème Brulle (1606 Lafayette Street; 253-589-3001).

The island is only 4 miles from end to end but there are plenty of little nooks to explore. At the center of the island, you'll find the **Johnson Farm,** which was operated by the Johnson family from 1912 to 1975 and is now maintained by the Anderson Island Historical Society to display the labors and comforts of traditional rural life. Tools and artifacts are on display, including the wheelhouse of the ferry **Tahoma,** which plied the Anderson Island route for decades. The farm, always open, has summer weekend tours.

Anderson Marine Park, on the southwest shore, is a delightful and secluded place. Take the nature trail through the woods and down to Carlson's Cove. Well-marked signs point out the diverse plant life and bird activity in the evergreen forest. Short stretches of the trail are marked "skid road," "corduroy," and "puncheon." These terms, which describe the shape of the logs under your feet in the muddier parts of the walk, demonstrate historic road surfacing techniques to show how logging roads were once built. The last stretch includes a steep descent to a small dock floating in the sheltered cove rich with intertidal life. Beware of the poison oak beyond the marked path along the shore and be sure to wear good walking shoes.

Ken and Annie Burg offer families the fun and comfort of their large log home, **Inn at Burg's Landing Bed & Breakfast** at 8808 Villa Beach Road (253-884-9185; www.burgslandingbb.com), located near the Anderson Island ferry dock. From the inn's large decks, you can watch the boat traffic on Puget Sound with a backdrop of Mount Rainier and the Cascades on blue-sky days, or collect seashells on the private beach. Ken Burg, who grew up on Anderson Island and attended its one-room school, can tell stories of island life "back in the good old days." Annie guarantees that no guest goes hungry for breakfast.

Back on the mainland, take time to stop at the DuPont History Museum at 207 Barksdale Avenue (253-964-2399), near I–5 exit 119. In 1906, the DuPont Company bought nearly 5 square miles of land to manufacture black powder and explosives. Tar-paper shacks housed the construction crew, but those shacks soon morphed into the construction of a company town, with about 100 permanent homes built for the employees.

It had its own school, newspaper, post office, church, butcher shop, hotel, and clubhouse. Eventually DuPont moved on, sold the houses to the former employees, and donated park land and the infrastructure to the town. In 1976, Weyerhaeuser Company bought all 3,200 acres of the property from the company for the planned community of Northwest Landing. In 1987, the company town area, known as The Village, was placed on the National Register of Historic Places. The museum preserves pieces of the town's history, legacy, and artifacts.

For an overnight, the easily accessible Liberty Inn at 1400 Wilmington Drive (877-912-8777, www.libertyinn.com) is between I–5 and the museum. Weather willing, Mount Rainier dominates the view behind the inn. All rooms are smoke free and the complimentary breakfast options are many.

Inner Sound

Historically the home of the Puyallup and Nisqually Indian tribes, the **Tacoma** area did not see white people until 1833 when the British Hudson's Bay Company established a fur-trading post, Fort Nisqually. In the early 1850s the first permanent settlers, mainly lumbermen, arrived. They built sawmills along the Commencement Bay waterfront, which soon bustled with cargo ships and workers of many nationalities, including American, English, Scottish, Irish, Hawaiian, Native American, and Chinese. Back then the old Whiskey Row area sported saloons, brothels, and gambling houses. By the early 1870s the fledgling town successfully courted the Northern Pacific Railroad to designate Tacoma its western terminus. The railroad was completed in 1883, thus linking Tacoma to the rest of the country, and the city's population soared from some 5,000 in 1884 to 50,000 by 1892.

Today a twenty-first-century renaissance continues to transform Tacoma. Several historic neighborhoods, downtown hotels and museums, shops, and places to eat are varied. A Museum District has emerged along the Thea Foss Waterway, where visitors can find its stunning centerpiece, the **Museum of Glass** at 1801 Dock Street (866-468-7386; www.museumofglass.com). Its impressive tilted 90-foot-tall cone wrapped in shimmering stainless steel is reminiscent of the sawmill wood burners of the mid-1800s and symbolizes the city's transformation from an industrial to a cultural enclave. Indoors you can see artisans create with molten glass in the Hot Shop Amphitheater and enjoy rotating exhibits in the gallery spaces, as well as browse the museum store, which sells some of the Hot Shop creations. For good eats with views of the waterway, try Woody's on the Water at 1715 Dock Street East (253-272-1433).

The **Washington State History Museum** at 1911 Pacific Avenue (888-238-4373; www.washingtonhistory.org) is connected to the Museum of Glass by the spectacular Chihuly Bridge of Glass, a 500-foot pedestrian walkway over Interstate 705 that showcases the work of internationally respected glass artist and Tacoma native Dale Chihuly. Next door is historic Union Station, also displaying Chihuly glass in its rotunda. The **Tacoma Art Museum** (253-272-4258; www.tacomaartmuseum.org) is just one block away at 1701 Pacific Avenue. Another unusual museum is **Karpeles Manuscript Library Museum** at 407 South G Street (253-383-2575).

gallopinggertie

Washington has bragging rights to the most dramatic failure in U.S. bridge history. The third-longest suspension bridge in the world lasted less than five months in 1940. It behaved like a roller coaster when poor design met moderate winds. The 5,939-foot-long Tacoma Narrows Bridge's center span bucked, twisted, and tumbled into the water below, taking with it vehicles and one spaniel.

Downtown Tacoma's historic **Broadway Theater District** and, adjacent to it, Antiques Row on Broadway and St. Helens Avenues between Seventh and Ninth Streets, offer the restored 1918 Pantages and Rialto Theaters and the contemporary Theatre on the Square.

From here head north to the Stadium District, named for the imposing 1906 chateaulike fortress that began as an elegant hotel but now houses Stadium High School. Continue to **Old Town** to see the **Job Carr Cabin Museum** at 2315 North Thirtieth Street (253-627-5405), a replica of the 1864 home of Tacoma's first mayor, public notary, and postmaster. At the far northern tip of the city, **Point Defiance Park** at 5400 North Pearl Street (253-591-5337) offers a zoo, aquarium, gardens, saltwater beaches, and trails. The **Fort Nisqually Living History Museum** (253-591-5339; www.fortnisqually.org) has docents in period garb reenacting life at this Hudson Bay Company fur trading post ca. 1855. You can also find a flock of antiques shops along North Pearl Street.

For entertaining eating, try the **Antique Sandwich Company's** (5102 Pearl Street; 253-752-4069) specialty sandwiches; the **Spar Tavern** at 2121 North Thirtieth Street (253-627-8215) for tasty pub fare and local microbrews and ales; or the **Swiss,** a blues pub located near Union Station at 1904

Jefferson Avenue (253-572-2821). In the Theater District, Over the Moon features casual Northwest cuisine and cozy décor at 709 Opera Alley (253-284-3722). In southeast Tacoma at 516 Garfield Street, *Marzano's* (253-537-5191) offers tasty Italian fare.

Pearl Street ends to the north at Point Defiance, where a ferry leaves every hour until late evening for *Vashon Island,* one of the largest of Puget Sound's islands. When you ferry over to visit, stop at the *Blue Heron Art Center* at 19704 Vashon Highway (206-463-5131) to get a feel for the thriving island arts community.

Next, call the *Brian Brenno Blown Glass Studio & Gallery* at 17630 Vashon Highway (206-567-5423) to ask when their artists are blowing glass. Among the creations at the gallery are life-size glass hats in fabulous colors. If you're ready for a snack, pop into *Homegrown Cafe & Deli* at 17614 Vashon Highway (206-463-6302). Don't miss visiting the *Country Store and Gardens* at 20211 Vashon Highway Southwest (888-245-6136; www.tcsag .com) and its Ceiling Museum of antique kitchen appliances and kitchenware as well, and browse the natural foods, preserves, and garden goodies plus the 10-acre nursery. Head down to *Point Robinson* at the southeast tip of the island, called Maury Island, connected to Vashon Island by an isthmus created by the Army Corps of Engineers, to see the working lighthouse. Call the president of the Keepers of Point Robinson (206-463-6672) well ahead if you'd like to arrange a tour. Linger overnight on Vashon Island by arranging for cozy suites at the *Betty MacDonald Farm Bed & Breakfast* at 1200 Ninety-ninth Avenue Southwest (888-328-6753; www.bettymacdonaldfarm.com) where you can look across Puget Sound to see Mount Rainier. For additional lodging information browse the Visitor Information Center site, www.vashonchamber.com.

Gig Harbor is a delightful fishing village nestled in a protected bay on the northwest side of the Tacoma Narrows. The harbor is crowded with both pleasure and fishing boats. Harborview Drive, which hugs the shore, is lined with shops, sidewalk cafes, and galleries, making it a great place to stroll. On a clear day, Mount Rainier looms in the distance.

---

vintage automobiles galore

The city of Tacoma will add another major museum in 2010. LeMay: America's Car Museum (www.lemaymuseum.org) will showcase the huge vintage automobile collection of Tacoma collector Harold LeMay. Currently, part of LeMay's incredible collection can be toured 9:00 a.m. to 5:00 p.m. Tuesday through Saturday at 325 152nd Street East (253-536-2885).

Estates, Mansions, Villas, and Castles

A number of Pacific Northwest timber, ship, and industrial barons of the late 1800s and early 1900s exhibited a tendency to the immense, ornate, and showy when it came to building their houses. Many of these palatial homes eventually fell into disrepair; some were razed, but a number of these fine structures have recently been renovated. Here are six among the top-drawer variety, five of them open as bed-and-breakfast inns and one as a splendid estate garden, also open to the public. Each offers a fascinating history.

Branch Colonial House Bed & Breakfast Inn

6,000 square feet
Ca. 1904 home restored by Robin Korobkin
2420 North Twenty-first Street
Tacoma
(877) 752-3565
www.branchcolonialhouse.com

Chinaberry Hill Grand Victorian Inn and Cottage

6,000 square feet
Ca. 1889 home restored by Cecil and Yarrow Wayman
302 Tacoma Avenue North
Tacoma
(253) 272-1282
www.chinaberryhill.com

DeVoe Mansion Bed & Breakfast Inn

6,000 square feet
Ca. 1911 home restored by Dave and Cheryl Teifke
208 East 133rd Street
Tacoma
(888) 539–3991
www.devoemansion.com

Lakewold Gardens Estate

Ten-acre estate gardens developed in 1938 by owners Corydon and Eulalie Wagner. Gardens and a 1907 Georgian-style manor house now kept up by Friends of Lakewold; splendid gardens and gift shop open to the public.
12317 Gravelly Lake Drive SW
Tacoma
(888) 858-4106
www.lakewoldgardens.org

Thornewood Castle Inn and Gardens

36,000 square feet
Ca. 1911, renovation ongoing by Wayne and Deanna Robinson
8601 North Thorne Lane SW
Lakewood
Also shown by appointment
(253) 584-4393
www.thornewoodcastle.com

The Villa Bed & Breakfast Inn

10,000 square feet
Ca. 1925 home
705 North Fifth Street
Tacoma
(888) 572-1157
www.villabb.com

Gig Harbor's ***Rent-A-Boat and Charters*** at 8829 North Harborview Drive (253-858-7341; www.gigharboatrentals.com) offers several ways to explore Puget Sound year-round (daily spring and summer, by reservation fall and winter), from pedal boats and seagoing kayaks to larger sailboats and powerboats. Galleries featuring local artisans include The ***Ebb Tide Co-operative Gallery*** at 7809 Pioneer Way (253-851-5293), which started in 1984 and is open daily with colorful woven clothing, jewelry, watercolors, wood carvings, pottery, and other arts. You'll find great gifts also at the **Beach Basket** at 4102 Harborview Drive (253-858-3008) and the year-round Beach Basket Christmas Shop next door; **Seasons on the Bay** at 7804 Pioneer Way (253-858-8892); and **Strictly Scandinavian** at 7803 Pioneer Way (253-851-5959), which features authentic gift items from Denmark, Norway, Finland, and Sweden, both traditional and trendy. For a good selection of regional wines as well as gifts, stop by the **Keeping Room** at 7811 Pioneer Way (253-858-9170).

For comfortable lodgings, most of them with views of Henderson Bay, Carr Inlet, or Colvos Passage, check with the volunteers at the Gig Harbor Visitor Information Center, 3125 Judson Street (888-843-9444; www.gigharborguide.com).

Recommended eating spots in the Gig Harbor area include **Narrows Landing Restaurant,** located right beside the tower at the Tacoma Narrows Airport, 1208 Twenty-sixth Avenue Northwest (253-853-4114); **Anthony's Restaurant** at 8827 North Harborview Drive (253-853-6353); **Tides Tavern** at 2925 Harborview Drive (253-858-3982); and **Java & Clay Coffeehouse** at 3210 Harborview Drive (253-851-3277). For a million-dollar view of Mount Rainier and a casual menu, try Harbor Kitchen at 8809 North Harborview Drive (253-853-6040) with its cozy seating and colorful boat activity.

Other Friendly B&Bs, Tacoma–Gig Harbor–Vashon Island Area

Aloha Beachside Bed & Breakfast
8318 Highway 302
Gig Harbor
(888) 256-4222
www.alohabeachsidebb.com

Bear's Lair Bed & Breakfast
13706 Ninety-second Avenue NW
Gig Harbor
(877) 855-9768
www.bearslairbb.com

The Betty MacDonald Farm Bed & Breakfast
12000 Ninety-ninth Avenue SW
Vashon Island
(888) 328-6753
www.bettymacdonaldfarm.com

Green Cape Cod Bed & Breakfast
(ca. 1929)
2711 North Warner Street
Tacoma
(253) 752-1977
www.greencapecod.com

Waterfront Inn Bed & Breakfast
9017 North Harborview Drive
Gig Harbor
(253) 857-0770
www.waterfront-inn.com

Bloedel Reserve Bainbridge Island

Brimming with rich scenery and history and just a thirty-minute ferry ride from Seattle, Bainbridge Island is the perfect day-trip destination. It's also the gateway for the get-away-from-it-all activities on the Kitsap and Olympic Peninsulas. One of the most lovely and historic places on the island is the *Bloedel Reserve* at 7571 Northeast Dolphin Drive (206-842-7631; www.bloedelreserve.org). Once a private estate, the 150-acre reserve offers a feast for the senses with its beautifully maintained grounds, including a bird marsh, an English landscape garden, a moss garden, a reflection pool, a Japanese garden, and woodlands. The reserve is open to the public 10:00 a.m. to 4:00 p.m. Wednesday through Sunday; reservations are required.

From Gig Harbor you can backtrack a few miles to Tacoma via the Tacoma Narrows Bridge and rejoin I-5 heading north. For a pleasant day trip, head to the Seattle waterfront and board the ferry for a thirty-minute ride to nearby *Bainbridge Island.* Browse the shops and boutiques along Winslow Way in *Winslow,* the island's main town. The must-stop goal is Bainbridge Arts & Crafts (151 Winslow Way East; 206-842-3132). More than 250 artists participate in the co-op, which is open daily.

Enjoy the food at one of the several spots in downtown Winslow: try the breakfast waffles at the *Streamliner Diner* at 397 Winslow Way East (206-842-8595) near the ferry landing; *Blackbird Bakery* at 210 Winslow Way East (206-780-1322); and *Winslow Way Cafe* at 122 Winslow Way East (206-842-0517). Make it ice-cream time at Mora Iced Creamery at 139 Madrone Lane (206-855-8822), which serves delicious homemade sorbets and ice creams from stainless-steel, temperature-controlled ice cream cabinets. If tea is your thing, head to the Asian-style August Moon Teahouse at 123 Bjune Drive (206-842-1883), a 10-minute walk from the ferry, for loose teas and light fare.

To stay overnight on the island, check with the *Captain's House Bed & Breakfast* five blocks from the ferry at 234 Parfitt Way Southeast (206-842-3557). There you are just a block from a Winslow favorite for almost three decades, Pegasus Coffee House at 131 Parfitt (206-842-6725), located in one of the town's oldest buildings on the waterfront. It also has live music Friday, Saturday, and Sunday nights. For other lodging options, check www.bainbridge lodging.com. From Bainbridge Island you can access other Kitsap Peninsula destinations such as Poulsbo, Port Orchard, and Gig Harbor.

A ferry from Seattle takes visitors to Bremerton to explore the *Kitsap Peninsula* and the western sections of Puget Sound. Kitsap County has 236 miles of shoreline with every community on the water. When you reach Gorst, a tiny town on the edge of Sinclair Inlet, you'll find an ex-landfill and log

Family Excursions on the Kitsap Peninsula

Anna Smith Children's Park
Creative demonstration garden
7601 Tracyton Boulevard NW
Bremerton
(360) 337-5350

Northwest Electric Boat Rentals
18779 Front Street
Poulsbo
(360) 265-8300
www.northwestboatrentals.com

Point Defiance Zoo & Aquarium
Picnic and play areas, gardens
5400 North Pearl Street
Tacoma
(253) 591-5337
www.pdza.org

More information:

Kitsap County Parks & Recreation
(360) 337-5350
www.kitsapgov.com/parks

Kitsap Peninsula Visitor Information
(800) 416-5615
www.visitkitsap.com

dump transformed into the remarkable *Elandan Gardens and Gallery* at 3050 West Highway 16, Bremerton (360-373-8260; www.elandangardens.com). The garden's extensive bonsai collection and its gallery, which offers elegant antiques and art treasures, are open from 10:00 a.m. to 5:00 p.m. Tuesday through Sunday.

Port Orchard, a few miles east of Gorst on Highway 116, has a hospitable downtown ideal for window shopping. Bay Street, the main commercial street, has old-fashioned sidewalks with a wooden canopy for comfortable strolling, rain or shine. Murals on downtown walls illustrate life during the late nineteenth century, when Port Orchard was a major stop for the *Mosquito* Fleet, the small steamboats that were once a common form of transportation on the Sound. At the north end of Sidney Avenue, you can catch the *Carlisle II,* one of the original fleet, which carries pedestrians and bicycles across the bay to Bremerton every half hour. A waterfront observation deck offers views of marine activities in the bay and across the water to Bremerton's naval shipyards.

To get a taste of Port Orchard's early days as well as the richness of local artistic talent, stroll a few blocks south on Sidney Avenue to the *Sidney Art Gallery* at 202 Sidney Avenue, open in the summer from 11:00 a.m. to 4:00 p.m. Tuesday through Saturday and 1:00 to 4:00 p.m. Sunday (otherwise by appointment). The first floor of this former Masonic Temple, built in 1908, features monthly exhibits highlighting the works of Northwest artists. The second floor houses the *Sidney Museum,* featuring exhibits of turn-of-the-twentieth-century stores and coastal scenes. More Port Orchard history is at the *Log Cabin Museum,* located just up the hill at 416 Sidney Street. All three are owned by the Sidney Museum and Arts Association, which can be reached at (360) 876-3693; www.sidneymuseumandarts.com. The 1914 Log Cabin Museum includes six resident mannequins dressed in period costumes in historical scenes. Occasionally mannequin relations join the scenes.

For anyone into collectable dolls and bears or who loves Victorian teas, the place to stop is Springhouse Dolls & Gifts and Victorian Rose Tea Room at 1130 Bethel Avenue (360-876-0529; www.springhousegifts.com). It's a restaurant and gift shop in a pink Victorian home.

Reflections Bed and Breakfast at 3878 Reflection Lane East (360-871-5582), a spacious home filled with New England antiques, offers wide views of Bainbridge Island and Port Orchard Passage from each guest room and deck. One option is the Honeymoon Suite, complete with a private sitting room.

Poulsbo is a friendly community on the shores of *Liberty Bay.* It was settled in the 1880s by Norwegians. The Poulsbo business community has revived this heritage to create a Scandinavian-theme town. Scandinavian delights await at every turn in the town's historic district, from potato *lefse* (pancakes) to the painted folk art designs (rosemaling) adorning shutters and doorways. Be sure to visit *Sluy's Poulsbo Bakery* (360-779-2798) at 8924 Front Street, the town's main street, which is close to the water and the marina. They serve delicious Poulsbo bread and Scandinavian pastries. It's one of three wonderful bakeries on Front Street.

There's plenty of food to tempt the palate and quench the thirst: *Checkers Espresso and Gallery* at 18881 Front Street (360-697-2559); the funky and fun *Poulsbohemian Coffeehouse* at 19003 Front Street (360-779-9199); *JJ's Fish House* at 1881 Front Street (360-779-6609); or MorMor Bistro & Bar at 18820 Front Street (360-697-3449).

After browsing in the shops or learning about marine biology at the

berry nice

Western Washington's climate is conducive to growing a wide array of berries, beginning in early summer with strawberries and raspberries and ending in the fall with wild blackberries and huckleberries. You'll find U-pick farms and stands throughout your journeys in the Puget Sound area. Berries are especially abundant in the Pierce, Skagit, Snohomish, Snoqualmie, and Whatcom County areas. When you're at a restaurant and the server says there's fresh berry pie, don't pass it up. You could also try the loganberry, a cross between a blackberry and a raspberry.

Marine Science Center at 18743 Front Street Northeast (360-598-4460; www
.poulsbomsc.org), head for **Anderson Parkway** and its large wooden gazebo
(Kvelstad Pavilion), where you can relax and see the marina, the boats, Liberty
Bay, and the Olympic Mountains. A 612-foot boardwalk leads from the Viking
statue, along the shore, and up the forest-covered bluff. As you stroll you may
see loons or cormorants dive for fish offshore.

After all this waterside exploration, you may want to take to the waves
yourself. One way to explore Liberty Bay is through **Northwest Electric
Boat Rentals** at 18779 Front Street (360-265-8300; www.northwestboat
rentals.com). These almost silent boats, which seat up to 12, offer a chance
to get close to nature while staying warm and dry. The **Olympic Outdoor
Center** at 18971 Front Street (360-
697-6095; www.olympicoutdoorcenter
.com), across from Poulsbo's Marina
and **Waterfront Park,** can outfit and
prepare you for a kayaking adventure
on Liberty Bay. Experienced naturalists
are also available for scheduled or self-
designed day (or full-moon) trips.

paddlethetrail

If you were thinking about longer
paddling distances, the **Cascadia
Marine Trail** links more than
fifty accessible sites for human-
powered craft, from comfy
bed-and-breakfasts to camp
sites, throughout Puget Sound.
Kayaking visionaries foresee the
day when this network of trails and
campsites will take paddlers from
Olympia north as far as Skagway,
Alaska. Trail updates are available
through the Washington Water
Trails Association at (206) 545-
9161 or www.wwta.org.

To find out more about the early
people who first used these waters for
food and travel, take a right (south) turn
off Highway 305, south of Poulsbo, to the
Suquamish Museum at 15838 Sandy
Hook Road, Suquamish (360-598-3311;
www.suquamish.nsn.us/museum). The
museum's premier exhibit, *The Eyes of
Chief Seattle,* introduces the history and
traditional lifestyle of the Suquamish Nation. The museum is open daily from
10:00 a.m. to 5:00 p.m., May 1 to September 30. The new Suquamish Museum
should open late in 2009 or early 2010 in the downtown **Suquamish** area.

Just three miles northeast of the museum off Highway 305 is **Old Man
House State Park,** given to the tribe by the state. This is where Chief Sealth
(better known as **Chief Seattle**) lived and died. The Old Man House was a
huge plank building that once stretched along the beach. A display explains
how local tribes built and used the large house. The small park is ideal for
picnics and quiet reflection alongside Agate Passage. Up the hill, behind St.
Peter's Church, is Chief Sealth's gravesite. Construction is under way on the
new Suquamish Longhouse, the first welcoming house since the destruction of
Old Man House. It is expected to open in the summer of 2009.

For a relaxing rural interlude, contact the **Manor Farm Inn** (26069 Big Valley Road NE, Poulsbo; 360-779-4628; www.manorfarminn.com), a comfortable country-style bed-and-breakfast with six spacious guest rooms. For other overnight stays in the area, contact **Murphy House Bed & Breakfast** near the bustling waterfront at 425 Northeast Hostmark Street (800-779-1606; www.murphyhousebnb.com); **Foxbridge Bed & Breakfast,** an elegant Colonial-style manor close to town at 30680 Highway 3 Northeast (360-598-5599; www.foxbridge.com); Green Cat Bed & Breakfast at 25819 Tytler Road Northeast (360-779-7569; www.greencatbb.com); and Morgan Hill Retreat at 1921 Northeast Sawdust Hill Road (800-598-3926; www.morganhillretreat.com).

Shine Road becomes Paradise Bay Road north of Highway 104, which winds through the forests above Hood Canal, offering occasional glimpses of the water along the way. Past Port Ludlow and Oak Bay, you can turn off to **Indian Island** and **Fort Flagler,** or continue straight toward **Port Townsend.** The bridge to Indian Island offers great views of the narrow strait separating this island from the mainland. The road beyond the bridge has several places to pull off to admire the scenery. Turn right at the Jefferson County day-use sign and follow the gravel road to the beach to explore the pebbly tidelands, scattered with driftwood and salt marsh plants. Waterbirds are especially abundant here during their fall migration. Just above the shore you'll find the trailhead to the ½-mile South Indian Island Trail, an ideal hike through madronas and firs to a sandy beach, a narrow spit, a lagoon, and views of Mount Rainier.

The causeway from Indian Island to **Marrowstone Island** crosses lush wetlands and a lagoon between the two islands. Nearby is **Beach Cottages on Marrowstone,** 10 Beach Drive, Nordland (360-385-3077; www.beachcottage getaway.com), a rustic retreat surrounded by tall grass and wild beaches. Seven cedar guest cabins encircling the meadow come with kitchens and views of Oak Bay. The caretakers recommend that guests bring boots, warm clothing, blankets, and, if possible, a canoe or kayak. Linens, towels, basic kitchen utensils, and firewood are provided.

Fort Flagler covers the entire north end of Marrowstone Island, a mix of forests, former gun batteries, and coastline. The fort was used periodically for military training until it became a park in 1954. Although the campground is busy during the summer (888-226-7688 for campsite reservations; www.parks.wa.gov), the park is big and diverse enough to offer seclusion for those who seek it. Numerous hiking trails go through the forest to cliffs overlooking Admiralty Inlet. The **Roots of a Forest Interpretive Trail,** a short distance past the campground entrance, provides an inside look into forest ecology. There's an indoor interpretive display, open 1:00 to 4:00 p.m. weekends, and a long beach to explore at **Marrowstone Point.**

If you don't turn off to Marrowstone Island, Oak Bay Road will lead you to the turn-off for the *Ajax Cafe* in Port Hadlock (21 Water Street; 360-385-3450), an unexpected delight. With its funky decor the much-loved cafe offers superb dinners highlighting local coastal cuisine, including scallops, salmon, duck, and beef, and the most incredible Pot du Crème and other delicious freshly made desserts. The public wharves, ships, and boatyards across the street add to the ambience. A sign at the dock tells of the history of a once-booming industrial site from 1878 to 1916. The cafe is open for dinner Tuesday through Sunday, but daily during the summer.

Continue north on Highway 20 to Port Townsend for Northwest history, arts events, shopping, Victorian homes, and festivals. Contact the Port Townsend Visitor Center at 2437 East Sims Way (360-385-2722; www.enjoypt .com) for information. Residents enjoy meeting one another for coffee and sweets at *Tyler Street Coffee House* at 215 Tyler Street (360-379-4185) or for a fresh, healthful breakfast at the *Salal Cafe* at 634 Water Street (360-385-6532). Both establishments open onto *Franklin Court* with its flowers, wooden walkways, and fruit trees. On the bluff above the downtown area, *Sweet Laurette* at 1029 Lawrence Street (360-385-4886) offers French-inspired goodies such as tarts, galettes, truffles, and cheesecake, and lunch indoors and alfresco.

Port Townsend has a lively community of artists, so visitors find many fine galleries located downtown in the waterfront area as well as uptown, on the bluff. Try *Ancestral Spirits Gallery* at 701 Water Street (360-385-0078) for Inuit and Native American art, and *Northwinds Art Center,* which showcases artists throughout the year near the visitor center at 2409 Jefferson Street (360-379-1086).

The *Jefferson County Historical Museum* is located at 540 Water Street (360-385-1003; www.jchsmuseum.org) in the 1891 city hall building. The two-story brick structure houses exhibits that describe the area's nautical, native, and Victorian history. Call for hours. Be sure to explore the historic neighborhoods on the hill; follow the stairs up Taylor Street or take either Quincy or Monroe Street up the hill to see many Victorian homes that once housed the cultural and financial elite of Washington Territory.

Stop to see the *Old Bell Tower* on Tyler Street on the bluff, which once summoned the volunteer fire department. At the corner of Jefferson and Taylor Streets is the 1868 *Rothschild House,* which has been preserved as it was a century ago by the historical society. Tour the house 11:00 a.m. to 4:00 p.m. daily May through September. Be sure to stroll through the rose garden with its fragrant varieties, some dating to the early 1800s. Call the visitor information center (360-385-2722) for the current dates of Port Townsend's favorite annual events, including the *Annual Victorian Festival* in early May, the *Secret Garden Tour* in late June, the *Historic Homes Tour* in mid-September, and the *Cabin Fever Quilt Show* in early September.

If you can't spend a night at the opulent *Ann Starrett Mansion,* a boutique hotel at 744 Clay Street (800-321-0644; www.starrettmansion.com), call to see if tours are scheduled. It is a splendid example of Victorian architecture, complete with an octagonal tower, a sweeping circular staircase, and formal sitting rooms. Ask about the comfortable carriage house guest rooms on the garden level. Within walking distance on Jackson Street, find lovely

The Nautical Life: Wooden Boats, Tall Ships, Schooners, Wooden Boatbuilding, and Wooden Boat Festivals

Center for Wooden Boats
Located on Lake Union, offering exhibits, programs, and classic wooden boats to rent for informal paddling excursions on the lake
1010 Valley Street
Seattle
(206) 382-2628
www.cwb.org

The *Lady Washington*
Tall ship makes scheduled ports of call along the West Coast from its home port of Aberdeen
www.ladywashington.org

Northwest Maritime Education Alliance
Offers collaborative programs: lecture series, summer workshops, restoration projects, and historic vessel tours
www.nwmaritime.org

The Northwest School of Wooden Boatbuilding
Offers classes and workshops
42 North Water Street
Port Hadlock
(360) 385-4948
www.nwboatschool.org

Sound Experience
Offers environmental sailing programs in the waters of Puget Sound aboard the historic schooner *Adventuress*
2310 Washington Street
Port Townsend
(360) 379-0438
www.soundexp.org

Wooden Boat Festival
Held the first weekend after Labor Day in Port Townsend; includes the Symposium on Wooden Boatbuilding
www.woodenboat.org

The Wooden Boat Foundation
Center for maritime education located in the Cupola House at Point Hudson
380 Jefferson Street
Port Townsend
(360) 385-3628
www.woodenboat.org

Chetzemoka Park and its rose gardens, including a splendid rose arbor walkway, plantings from around the world, large glider swings, a gazebo, and views of Admiralty Inlet and the Cascade Mountains to the east. Other comfortable places to stay include *James House Bed & Breakfast,* a renovated 1889 home located on the bluff at 1238 Washington Street (360-385-1238; www .jameshouse.com); and *Ravenscroft Inn Bed & Breakfast,* also located on the bluff at 533 Quincy Street (360-385-2784; www.ravenscroftinn.com). From the bluff walk down a series of concrete stairs to the downtown waterfront area and beautiful Haller Fountain with a special drinking fountain for your four-legged friend.

Consider stopping at the *Fountain Cafe* at 920 Washington Street (360-385-1364) for seafood and pasta specialties; *Fins Restaurant* at 1019 Water Street (360-379-3474) for superb seafood; *Nifty Fifties* at 817 Water Street (360-385-1931) for juicy hamburgers and old-fashioned sundaes, shakes, malts, and sodas; and *Elevated Ice Cream,* 627 Water Street (360-385-1156), to enjoy homemade ice cream, Italian ices, and pastries, and to see local art.

While in Port Townsend, be sure to inquire about events at *Fort Worden State Park* (360-344-4400). Like Fort Flagler to the east, Fort Worden was once part of the fortifications that protected Puget Sound from invasion by sea. Located just a mile north of downtown, the fort is the site of *Port Townsend Marine Science Center* at 432 Battery Way (800-566-3932; www .ptmsc.org), which has marine and natural history exhibits as well as bird migration and Protection Island puffin cruises. The Coast Artillery Museum, Commanding Officer's Quarters Museum, and Centrum Foundation (360-385-3102; www.centrum.org) also are on park grounds. Events offered by Centrum include writing, music, and dance conferences, which usually offer activities open to the public. Their annual blues, jazz, and fiddle festivals sell out every year. There is also a rhododendron garden, nature walks, old military batteries to explore with a flashlight, and a long public beach. To stay in the park, choose from old barracks, comfortable officers' quarters, youth hostel, or campground.

Directly to the east of Port Townsend is *Whidbey Island,* accessible by the Port Townsend to Keystone ferry. It's the largest of the Puget Sound islands, populated for 10,000 years by Native peoples and one of the first areas on the Sound to be settled by Europeans. Its extensive coastline, lush forests, and location midway between the snowcapped Olympic and Cascade mountain ranges create outstanding views. Small working farms, artist studios, and innovative home businesses are scattered among meadows, shoreline, and evergreen forests. There are several historic communities and small-scale resorts.

Whidbey Island is also accessible from the Seattle area from the south via the Mukilteo ferry, which leaves about every half hour. For information call Washington State Ferries at (888) 808-7977; www.wsdot.wa.gov/ferries. The northern entry point is across the Deception Pass Bridge on Highway 20.

Highway 525, which becomes Highway 20 north of Keystone, runs down the center of the island and carries most of the through-traffic. It's also a designated Scenic Isle Way from Deception Pass to Clinton. Stop by one of the visitors centers for free guides and maps, call (888) 747-7777, or go to www .whidbeycamanoisland.com. You can also take the meandering local roads that follow the shoreline for better views and less traffic.

Langley, on Saratoga Passage, is one of our favorite communities. To get there, turn right on Langley Road off Highway 525 and follow signs into town. On the way, visit **Whidbey Island Vineyard and Winery** at 5237 South Langley Road (360-221-2040; www.whidbeyislandwinery.com) and taste samples of its rhubarb, pinot noir, and siegerrebe varieties. The tasting room is closed on Tuesday during July and August.

Langley has many antiques and art galleries. For a sampling, stop at the **Karlson/Gray Gallery** at 302 First Street (360-221-2978; www.karlsongray .com) or Museo at 215 First Street (360-221-7737; www.museo.cc). Although a busy tourist town during summer weekends, Langley is always pleasant, with plenty of spots to sit and view the nautical scenery on Saratoga Passage. On First Street, cozy up to the bronze statue of a sea-gazing boy (with dog) leaning over the railing above Saratoga Passage. From here a wooden staircase leads down to the beach; stroll along a grassy walkway or descend farther to the pebbly shore below a bulkhead sculpted with images of salmon and whales.

whidbeyisland trivia

Living on an island is not like living on the mainland. For example, when the locals leave the island they often say, "We're going shopping in America." Note from the islanders: Do not under any circumstances try to cut your automobile into the ferry line—you will incur the wrath of not only the islanders but also everyone else in line.

You'll find cafes, restaurants, espresso bars, and bistros to suit every taste on First and Second Streets, including Primo Bistra above the Star Store at 201½ First Street (360-221-4060); **Mike's Place** at 219 First Street (360-221-6575); **Cafe Langley** at 113 First Street (360-221-3090); or for true New York-style pizza, the Village Pizzeria at 106 First Street (360-221-3363). The **Braeburn Restaurant** at 197 Second Street (360-221-3211) is one of the locals' favorite breakfast hangouts. Also on Second Street is **Useless Bay Coffee Company.**

For fine dining locals suggest **Fish Bowl** at 317 Second Street (360-221-6511). For more casual fare try **Edge Cliff Restaurant** at 510 Cascade Avenue (360-221-8899). Stop at Chef's Pantry at 112½ Anthes Avenue (360-221-2060) for a custom picnic crafted by Donna Leahy, nationally acclaimed chef and author of several cookbooks. Chocolate lovers should not miss 1 Angel Place for European-style chocolate delicacies at 138 Second Street (360-221-2728).

For a spin on live theater, plan to attend the **Langley Mystery Weekend** sponsored by the Chamber of Commerce (360-221-6765; www.whidbey .com/langley/lc/mystery) and held during the last full weekend of February. Mystery buffs meet over coffee in local cafes and coffee shops to pore over clues in order to nab the character that did the nefarious deed. It's great fun, with locals dressed in vintage garb and helping with the special effects. For an authentic walk through the past, visit the South Whidbey Historical Society Museum at 312 Second Street (360-221-2101), curated by renowned artist Lee Wexler.

To stay overnight in the Langley area, contact accommodations referrals for South Whidbey (360-221-6765; www.visitlangley.com). Treat yourself for a night or two at one of our favorites, the Boatyard Inn at 200 Wharf Street, Langley (360-221-5120; www.boatyardinn.com), with Saratoga Passage's incoming tide lapping within feet of your living room. Ten 600-square-foot studio and 1,000-square-foot loft suites include mini-kitchen and views of the shipping lanes, Cascade Mountains, and maybe a gray whale or two. Or call the innkeepers at **Country Cottage of Langley Bed & Breakfast** at 215 Sixth Street (800-713-3860; www.acountrycottage.com) and one of the first vintage homes in the area to be remodeled for bed-and-breakfast travelers. Innkeepers Jerry and Joanne Lechner offer fine hospitality at **Eagles Nest Inn Bed & Breakfast,** a contemporary octagonal-shaped home situated with a fine view of Saratoga Passage at 4680 Saratoga Road (360-221-5331; www.eaglesnestinn.com).

The rhododendron, Washington's state flower, is especially prolific on Whidbey Island. If these pique your interest, you'll want to visit the very special **Meerkerk Rhododendron Gardens** at 3531 South Meerkerk Lane, Greenbank (360-678-1912; www.meerkerkgardens.org). The rhododendron

Ferry time

The largest ferry fleet in the United States serves 26 million passengers on 28 ferries stopping at 20 ports of call in Puget Sound, the San Juan Islands, and Victoria, B.C. The 11 classes of ferries range from 112 to 460 feet long and can carry from 250 to 2,500 passengers and up to 218 vehicles.

blooms are usually at their peak the last two weeks of April and the beginning of May, but the gardens also include a magical Japanese section and are lovely at any time. Featuring more than 800 mature rhododendron and companion plants, the landscape includes ponds, forest, and waterside nature trails.

Great dining in this area is available at the Beachfire Grill at Holmes Harbor Golf Course at 5023 Harbor Hill Drive (360-331-2363) or Gordon's on Blueberry Hill at 5438 Woodard Avenue (360-331-7515), both in Freeland. Check to see if the charming log cottages are available at ***Guest House Log Cottages*** at 24371 Highway 525, Greenbank (360-678-3115; www.guesthouselogcottages .com). If not available, try ***Farmhouse Bed & Breakfast*** at 2740 East Sunshine Lane, Clinton (800-997-3115; www.farmhousebb.com) or call innkeeper Peggy Moore to ask about the romantic ***Seacliff Cottage*** at 727 Windmill Drive, Freeland (360-331-1566; www.cliffhouse.net).

An integration of nature, art, and spirit and a 500-year plan has created Earth Sanctuary near Freeland. In 2002, Chuck Polson (author of *Secrets of Sacred Space*) and like-minded souls began restoring a 72-acre site to its old-growth glory with the maximum diversity of wildlife, birds, fungi, and plants. Earth Sanctuary is also a retreat center. A self-guided map leads you on numerous trails past ponds, a bog, medicine plant restoration area, streams, small artworks made of natural materials, and much larger structures.

A dolmen (table-shaped stone structure and surrounding 5-foot to 7-foot tall Montana sandstone stones) serves as a meditation room. A cottonwood stone circle may one day attract great blue herons to mature trees, and a fen stone circle is made of eight standing stones up to 7 feet high, each weighing 600 to 1,000 pounds. The stones are aligned

creationof
pugetsound

Puget Sound has about 500 square miles of water and 1,400 miles of shoreline. This was a glacier-carved valley about 13,000 years ago until an ice dam broke and the valley was flooded by the Pacific Ocean.

with true north and south, the summer solstice sunrise and sunset, and the winter solstice sunset. The fee is $7 per person. Consider it your contribution to a remarkable vision. For information, call (360) 637-8777 or go to www .earthsanctuary.com.

Hillsides covered with vines at the historic ***Whidbey's Greenbank Berry Farm & Winery*** (360-678-7700; www.greenbankfarm.com) create a pleasant setting for a picnic. Visitors are welcome to tour the farm with its new cheese and antiques shops. The farm features Loganberry Dessert Wine by Greenbank Cellars. A wine-tasting barn offers a wide selection of Northwest wines. Pick up a homemade pie for your picnic at Whidbey Pies Café. The farm is just north of **Greenbank** and is open daily from 10:00 a.m. to 4:30 p.m. For tasty takeout entrees, try the deli at **Coupe's Greenbank Store** (360-678-4326) up the hill from the winery.

Historic **Coupeville** is another favorite. It's located several miles to the north, about midway up the island on scenic **Penn Cove.** Saratoga Passage lies to the east and Admiralty Inlet to the west. Look for a gaggle of mussel rafts floating out on Penn Cove where the famous Penn Cove mussels are grown and harvested. The annual **Penn Cove Mussel Festival** takes place the first weekend in March.

To learn about Coupeville's Native American, pioneer, and maritime history and to pick up a walking-tour guide, visit the **Island County Historical Museum** at 908 Northwest Alexander Street (360-678-3310) at the end of Front Street near the wharf. The museum is open every day but call for the hours. After browsing the museum go across the street to the wharf, which overlooks Penn Cove and the mussel-growing rafts. Poke around the **Gallery at the Wharf** and check out the underwater sea camera to view marine life.

Walk along Front Street and up Main Street to see more historic buildings. Stop at **Mariti Chocolate Company** at 17 Northwest Front Street (360-678-5811) for locally made chocolates. Shopping could not be more fun than in Back to the Island (360-678-6860), Beyond the Sea (360-678-6317), or One More Thing (360-678-1894), all on historic Front Street. If you are in the area on Saturday, take in the **Coupeville Farmers' Market** (April through October; 360-678-4288) on the corner of Main and Eighth Streets to mingle with friendly locals and load up on fresh berries, flowers, and vegetables. For fabulous freshly baked cinnamon rolls, soups, and salads, stop at **Knead & Feed Restaurant** on Front and Main Streets (360-678-5431), a former storehouse and laundry built in 1871 and nestled one level down the bluff facing Penn Cove. Its original post-and-beam structure adds to the ambience of this pleasant waterside spot. Local folks swear by the steamed mussels and garlic bread at **Toby's Tavern** on Front Street (360-678-4222).

To stay overnight in the Coupeville area, contact **Anchorage Inn Bed & Breakfast** at 807 North Main Street (877-230-1313; www.anchorage-inn .com), where children over ten are welcome; the Blue Goose Inn B&B, which offers three historic Victorian homes at 702 North Main (877-230-1313; www .bluegoosecoupeville.com); and **Garden Isle Guest Cottages** at 207 Northwest Coveland Street (877-881-1203; www.gardenislecottages.com) near the downtown area.

For evening dining in Coupeville, check out local restaurants that do great things with mussels, seafood, and steaks: **Oystercatcher** at 901 Northwest

Grace Street (360-678-0683) and *Christopher's* at 103 Northwest Coveland Street (360-678-5480). A dining-and-lodging alternative is the 1907 *Captain Whidbey Inn* at 2072 West Whidbey Island Inn Road (360-678-4097; www .captainwhidbeyinn.com) on the west shore of Penn Cove. The lodge, built of madrona logs, has comfortable rooms, a cozy beachstone fireplace, and a restaurant. Newer cabins are also available.

The impressive *Admiralty Head Lighthouse* interpretive center is located near the Keystone landing at *Fort Casey State Park.* Call (360) 678-4519 for information on seasonal tours. The park is open year-round for camping on a first-come, first-served arrangement. There are old fort structures to explore and long stretches of undeveloped public beaches to walk.

Before continuing north to scenic Deception Pass at Whidbey Island's north end, a spectacular sight in practically any kind of weather, you can find pleasant eateries in the Navy town of *Oak Harbor.* Or replenish your cooler, put together an impromptu picnic, and continue north to *Deception Pass State Park.* Pull into any large grocery outlet for supplies or *Seabolt's Smokehouse* at 31640 Highway 20 (360-675-6485) for fresh seafood deli fare. *Zorba's* at 841 Southeast Pioneer Way (360-279-8322) offers Italian and Greek fare. For a special occasion, book a reservation at Fraser's Gourmet Hideaway at 1191 Southeast Dock Street (360-279-1231). Promoting the bounty of the Northwest, Fraser's specializes in local seafood, meats, game, and wines. Look for the large Dutch windmill to help find lodging at the *Auld Holland Motor Inn* at 33575 Highway 20 (800-228-0148).

Drop in at A Knot in Thyme at 4233 De Graff Road (360-240-1216), about three miles before Deception Pass. The 14 acres includes a five-acre holly farm for seasonal use, a lavender garden, and a quilted garden that's planted in designs. The nature-inspired gift shop has a few surprises, including bean pod candles. If you have children, stop between 10:00 a.m. and 6:00 p.m. on summer Saturdays for wagon rides.

ferryalert

Who knows what the ferry-catching status of the Keystone–Port Townsend ferry will be in 2009–2010. Long in denial over the state of its ferries, Washington State Ferry officials shuffled boats in shell-game fashion for years. Once there were two large, fast boats but that deteriorated to one small, slow boat; once trips were every 45 minutes, now 90 minutes. A bid to build two new ferries came in $28 million over expectations. It's extremely smart to make a vehicle reservation (888-808-7977) anytime during summer and shoulder-season weekends. Standby is not a good choice. As one official put it, "This is not a perfect system." Ya think?

Deception Pass

Joseph Whidbey, master of the *HMS Discovery,* sailed through the narrow pass in 1792. He thought the crew would sail into a small bay, but was "deceived," finding instead another large channel between islands; thus, the name *Deception.* Before the bridge, an unscheduled ferry took passengers between islands. To bring the ferry to your side, you had to strike the mallet against a very large metal lumberjack saw and the sound would tell the ferry pilot that it was time to cross the challenging channel. For years, Berte Olson, the first female ferry captain in the state, and her husband ran the ferry at Deception Pass and Hood Canal. She later owned her own company and was in charge of four ferry routes in the 1920s into the 1950s. She had enough swing that she convinced the governor to veto a legislative bill to build a bridge across Deception Pass.

One of the best ways to see spectacular Deception Pass, the deep, turbulent waters rushing between Whidbey's cliff-bound north end and Fidalgo Island, is aboard the Island Whaler (888-909-8687; www.deceptionpasstours .com). Take the one-hour tour with an interpreter out of Oak Harbor, keep an eye out for bald eagles and seals, and go under the Deception Pass Bridge, built with more than 1,500 tons of steel in 1935 over Deception and Canoe passes and named a National Historic Landmark in 1982. It now costs more to paint the bridge than it did to build it. There are parking areas and view points as well as trails on either side of the bridge, and 3-foot-wide sidewalks on both sides allows safe viewing.

Northern Sound

Just across the Deception Pass Bridge from Whidbey Island is Fidalgo Island. For a bird's-eye view of this island, turn west from Highway 20 just south of Pass Lake and follow Rosario Road as it forks right, away from Burrows Bay. At the Lake Erie Grocery take an acute left onto Heart Lake Road, then turn right to enter **Mount Erie Park.** The steep road (not recommended for trailers or RVs) has several trails and observation points along the way, and the wide-angle views of northern Puget Sound and its islands from the 1,300-foot summit are spectacular. Continue right on Heart Lake Road toward **Anacortes,** which makes a great base camp for exploration. Leave your bags, drive to the ferry landing, leave your car, and walk on the ferry for a day trip to **Friday Harbor** on San Juan Island. But before you head for the ferry terminal, take time to explore.

Named one of the top small art towns in America, Anacortes has a rich history and a wonderful ambience in part reflected in more than 100 murals.

Bill Mitchell initiated the idea for the life-size cutouts accenting a century of the community's history. Pick up a map from the Anacortes Visitors Information Center at 819 Commercial Avenue (360-293-3832; www.anacortes.org) and go wandering. Murals include Ann Bessner and the Guemes Island Girls, a self-portrait of Bill Mitchell with a 1954 Autoette electric cart and wheelchair, the Black Ball Line and Washington State ferries from 1928 to 1972, Edna Whitney with a tandem bicycle, and Wild Bill Bessner and his Indian motorcycle (1920).

Meander past the **Burlington Northern Railway Station** at 611 R Avenue. The revitalized station houses the **Depot Arts Center** (360-293-3663), open 12:30 to 5:00 p.m. Tuesday through Friday and 12:30 to 3:30 p.m. Saturday.

Located nearby and a local favorite, **Gere-a-Deli** at 502 Commercial Avenue (360-293-7383) offers clam chowder, salads, and sandwiches. For arguably the best take-out food in Anacortes (unless you're lucky and you snag the one inside table or one sidewalk table), run, don't walk, to Geppetto's at 3320 Commercial Avenue (360-293-5033). The shop may be small but the variety is not; classic Italian specialties with homemade sauces, freshly made pizza and pasta, daily specials, and garlic parmesan rolls are in high demand. **Calico Cupboard Cafe and Bakery** at 901 Commercial Avenue (360-293-7315) offers tasty luncheon fare; and **Anacortes Chocolate Factory & Cafe** at 2302 Commercial Avenue (360-293-8042) is well-known for its sinful chocolates, scones, and espresso, as well as salads, sandwiches, and homemade soups. **Randy's Pier** 61 at 209 T Avenue (360-293-5108) has waterfront dining with great views of Guemes Channel; it's open daily for lunch and dinner and Sunday for brunch. **Rock Fish Grill & Anacortes Brewery** at 320 Commercial Avenue (360-588-1720) is a long-time local favorite for microbrews and ales, seafood, and pizza done in a wood-fired oven. One of the best-kept secrets in Anacortes is **SeaBear Specialty Seafoods** off the main drag at 605 Thirtieth Street (360-293-4661). Here you'll discover alderwood-smoked salmon, soups, chowders, and barbecued salmon.

The older neighborhoods are just west of Commercial Avenue on Sixth through Twelfth Streets. **Causland World War I Memorial Park,** on Eighth Street between M and N Avenues, is a pleasant green hideaway surrounded by mosaic walls made of white quartz and red argillite swirling in brown and gray sandstone. Across the street you can review the history of Fidalgo Island at the **Anacortes History Museum** at 305 Eighth Street (360-293-1915), once the town's Carnegie Library.

For an overnight stay, try the historic Majestic Inn & Spa at 419 Commercial Avenue (877-370-0100; www.majesticinnandspa.com), a 21-room inn restored in 2005. Other choices include **Autumn Leaves Bed & Breakfast** at 2301 Twenty-first Street (866-293-4929; autumn-leaves.com); **Heron House Guest House** at 11110 Marine Drive (360-293-4477; www.heronhouseguestsuites .com); and **Ship Harbor Motor Inn,** 5316 Ferry Terminal Road (800-852-8568; www.shipharbor.com). For splendid evening dining try il Posto Ristorante at 2120 Commercial Avenue (360-293-7600) and **Flounder Bay Café** at 2201 Skyline Way (360-293-3680).

Way too early for the ferry to the San Juans? Take Twelfth Avenue westward past the ferry exit and follow Sunset Avenue onto Loop Road around **Washington Park** and check out the beaches. At Fidalgo Head, stop at the viewpoint on a high promontory overlooking Burrows Island and Bay. When you can tear yourself away from the great views, circle back to Sunset Drive.

All four San Juan County islands with regular Washington State Ferries service from Anacortes—Lopez, Shaw, Orcas, and San Juan—offer exploration and relaxation. Lopez and **Shaw** Islands are the most off the beaten path, especially during the off-season. Shaw, the smallest San Juan island accessible by state ferry and the most residential, offers a step back in time. Franciscan Sisters once ran the ferry dock and the **Shaw Store** (360-468-2288) but it's now run by a local family, which maintains the tradition of running a tab for the locals. Old baskets, fruit boxes, and nautical paraphernalia decorate the walls, and a wide assortment of foods and beverages are part of the mix.

This is strictly a quick day trip because there are no motels or B&Bs on Shaw. The main road runs down the center of the island, past the **Shaw Island Library** at the intersection with Blind Bay Road. It's run by islanders and is open from 2:00 p.m. to 4:00 p.m. Tuesday, 11:00 a.m. to 1:00 p.m. Thursday, and 10:00 a.m. to 2:00 p.m. Saturday. Ask the volunteer librarian for a key to the adjacent log-cabin museum. Opposite the library is the still-in-operation red schoolhouse, part of it more than one hundred years old.

Head south by the school on Hoffman Cove Road, then left on Squaw Bay Road. Drive past scenic and secluded Squaw Bay to the turnoff to **South Beach County Park,** with several campsites overlooking the bay. Then follow Squaw Bay Road back to Blind Bay and right to the ferry dock.

Lopez Island is larger and more developed than Shaw but still offers many opportunities for quiet. Its rolling hills and agricultural views are attractive to bicyclists. Located 4 miles from the ferry landing, Lopez Village, with a museum, a store, and restaurants, is the island's commercial center. The **Lopez Island Historical Museum** at 28 Washburn Place (360-468-2049) is full of island history and lore and worth a stop. The museum is open from noon to 4:00 p.m. Wednesday through Sunday May through September. For good food in the village, try *Love Dog Cafe* (360-468-2150), *Holly B's Bakery* (360-468-2133), *Isabel's Espresso* (360-468-4114), and *Lopez Old Fashioned Soda Fountain* (360-468-4511), the last located in the pharmacy. *Bay Cafe* at 9 Old Post Road (360-468-3700) is an island favorite for fine dining and reservations are recommended. At scenic *Fisherman Bay* try the *Galley* (360-468-2713) for the best water views along with tasty fish-and-chips, juicy hamburgers, and good Mexican dishes. Remember that island restaurants are rarely open seven days a week so call before counting on a meal.

For a comfortable overnight stay in *Lopez Village,* call *Edenwild Inn Bed & Breakfast* at 13 Lopez Road (800-606-0662; www.edenwildinn.com). It has eight guest rooms, cozy fireplaces, and delicious European-style breakfasts. At *MacKaye Harbor Inn Bed & Breakfast* (ca. 1904) at 949 MacKaye Harbor Road (888-314-6140; www.mackayeharborinn.com), travelers find five guest rooms and great water views along with kayak rentals and the use of the inn's mountain bikes. Lopez Island Lodge (800-736-3434; www.lopezislander .com) is the largest accommodation on Lopez and also operates the marina and store at the dock in Fisherman Bay. Or choose to be tucked in the woods with eagles and ravens as neighbors at *Ravens Rook Cabin,* a secluded family-friendly cabin (877-321-2493; www.rockisland.com/~ravensrook/) at 58 Wildrose Lane, done in rustic post-and-beam style.

Orcas 101

It's no wonder that *Free Willy* was filmed in the San Juans, as three pods of orcas make their home in these waters. You can watch by sea or land in the San Juans, and you might see one without even trying. Here are some facts you can use to embellish your own whale tales:

- Males average 29 feet in length; females average 24 feet. Females outnumber males four to one and can live to age eighty. The average male lives to about thirty.

- Males weigh up to 16,000 pounds, females up to 12,000 pounds.

- Whales give birth to one calf at two- to six-year intervals.

- Typical diet for the Southern Resident Community (the local orcas) is fish, and most of that is salmon. Transient orcas sometimes eat other marine mammals. Orcas eat from 100 to 300 pounds of food a day.

- The whales "talk" to each other with a dialect unique to each pod.

- Orcas navigate the waters at about 2 to 6 mph.

- Orcas are members of the dolphin and porpoise family.

From here a short walk through adjacent Shark Reef Sanctuary takes you to the scenic shoreline and perhaps sunning harbor seals on a nearby rock. Public beaches on Lopez Island include the west side of Fisherman Bay off Bay Shore Road, *Shark Reef Park* (good tide pools here) at the end of Shark Reef Road on the island's southwest tip, and *Agate Beach* off MacKaye Harbor Road at the island's south end. *Spencer Spit State Park and Campground* (360-468-2251; www.parks.wa.gov) on the island's east shore is a very popular destination, very scenic, and with ample hiking trails and beaches. *Odlin County Park* (360-378-1842) is closest to the ferry landing and offers camping and RV spaces (no hookups).

An extremely popular destination is horseshoe-shaped *Orcas Island.* It's easy to spend two or three or more days on Orcas, the largest island of the four ferry-served islands. Drive over to popular *Moran State Park and Campground* (360-376-2326; www.parks.wa.gov), hike its many trails, and then drive up to *Mount Constitution.* One of the grandest views of the islands is from the top of its tower, especially fine at sunset. Poke into the small communities of *Deer Harbor, Eastsound,* Westsound, Olga, and Doe Bay. Have a picnic by the water. Visit art galleries and artists' studios.

Especially during the summer and shoulder-season weekends, call well in advance to make overnight reservations at one of the bed-and-breakfast inns or campgrounds. Not far from the ferry landing, Turtleback Farm Inn at 1981 Crow Valley Road (800-376-4914; www.turtlebackinn.com) offers guests pastoral views and excellent cuisine along with resident sheep and chickens. At Kingfish Inn Bed & Breakfast and West Sound Cafe at 4362 Crow Valley Road (360-376-4440; www.kingfishinn.com), located 3 miles from the ferry landing, Lori and Bob Breslauer offer four light and airy guest rooms with water views on the second floor of a historic building that they restored in 1997. Your stay includes tasty morning fare served in the couple's pleasant cafe on the first floor, along with views of the marina, water, and islands beyond. The café is open for dinners 4:00 to 8:00 p.m. Wednesday through Saturday. For those who like getting farther away from it all, contact the innkeepers at Otters Pond Bed & Breakfast (888-893-9680; www.otterspond.com), located at 100 Tomah Drive beyond Eastsound on the way to Moran State Park.

If you're interested in private cottages available by the day or week on Orcas, call *Buckhorn Farm Bungalow* at 17 Jensen Road (360-376-2298; www.buckhornfarm.com). The bungalow is close to the beach, sleeps four, and comes with a woodstove as well as electric heat, cozy sitting areas, and a cheerful kitchen. At the *Old Trout Bed & Breakfast* at 4272 Orcas Road (360-376-7474; www.oldtroutinn.com), ask about the *Water's Edge Cottage,* where a couple can snuggle up with a view of the pond.

For food and drink in and near Eastsound, the largest community on Orcas, try Teaser's Cookies & Coffee House (360-376-2913) at the corner of North Beach and A Streets; *Bilbo's Festive* at 310 A Street (360-376-4728) for regional Mexican dishes, an island tradition for more than three decades; and *Christina's Food & Wine Restaurant* at 310 Main Street (360-376-4904) for Northwest seafood. It's always smart to make reservations. For morning, midday, or takeout, locals suggest *Roses Bakery & Café* at 382 Prune Alley (360-376-5805). Enjoy a scenic drive past Rosario Resort and beyond Moran State Park and Campground to try *Cafe Olga* (360-376-5098) in the historic Orcas Island Artworks building (360-376-4408), 1½ miles east of Moran State Park. The Olga Store, across from the post office and a stone's throw from the Olga dock, reopened in 2008. A store-deli mix, it's closed on Mondays.

For a comfortable overnight stay right in the village of Eastsound, contact the friendly innkeepers at *Kangaroo House Bed & Breakfast* (888-371-2175; www.kangaroohouse.com).

Bustling Friday Harbor is the only town on San Juan Island, the second largest of the ferry-served islands. Folks find a busy marina, the ferry landing, and a plethora of shops and eateries. From mornings to early evening try *San Juan Coffee Roasting Co.* at the Can-nery Landing (360-378-4443) and Gar-den Path Café at 135 Second Street North (360-378-6255). Check out the *Place Bar & Grill* (360-378-8707) on Spring Street next to the ferry landing, *Haley's Bait Shop & Grill* (360-378-4434) at 175 Spring Street near the local movie theater (360-378-4434), *Vinny's Ristorante* at 165 West Street (360-378-1934), and *Friday Harbor House* at 130 West Street (360-378-8455) overlooking the harbor and marina. For fine dining away from town, try the much-loved *Duck Soup Inn* at 50 Duck Soup Lane (360-378-4878), a fixture for more than 30 years; and, at *Roche Harbor Village* (www.rocheharbor.com) at the north-west tip of the island, *Madrona Grill* (360-378-2155, ext. 405) or *McMillin's Dining Room* (360-378-5757). Also at Roche Harbor, enjoy *Lime Kiln Cafe*

thepigwar

In 1859 on San Juan Island, a longstanding border dispute between British and American residents nearly resulted in an all-out war. The catalyst and only casualty, however, was an Englishman's pig. An American shot the pig when he found the errant animal rummaging in his potato patch. The resulting "Pig War" lasted until 1872, when the island's ownership was awarded to the United States. Today you can visit American Camp at the south end of the island, where the American troops were stationed, and English Camp, on Garrison Bay near the north end, where the Royal Marines of Britain were posted. Both offer interpretive displays, hiking trails, and scenic beaches.

elwhaillahee

Some of the ferries that sail from Anacortes to Shaw, Lopez, Orcas, and San Juan Islands have Native American names in their languages, and are rotated through depending on the time of year and those pulled for maintenance or sent to another route. They include the *Elwha* ("elk"), *Kaleetan* ("arrow"), *Sealth* (named after the chief of the Suquamish and Duwamish tribes), the *Yakima* ("people of the narrow river"), the Evergreen, and Chelan. Remember that ferries operate on island time, roughly translated as they'll get there when they get there, and leave when they leave. For information call Washington State Ferry at (888) 808-7977 or check www.wsdot.wa.gov/ferries.

(360-378-6809) at the end of the wharf and a good spot for breakfast or lunch. Note: Some island eateries close during the winter months and reopen in the spring, or are open a few days each week; call ahead.

For bedding down in Friday Harbor, call well ahead for information and reservations. Check with the Shayo family at Kirk House Bed & Breakfast, 595 Park Street (800-639-2762; www.kirkhouse.net); **Harrison House Suites** at 235 C Street (800-407-7933; www.harrisonhousesuites.com); or Tucker House Bed & Breakfast at 260 B Street (800-965-0123; www.tuckerhouse.com), an 1898 B&B with cottages.

Outside of Friday Harbor try **Highland Inn Bed & Breakfast** (888-400-9850; www.highlandinn.com) near Lime Kiln Point State Park, also known as Whale Watch Park; Trumpeter Inn at 318 Trumpeter Way (800-826-7926; www.trumpeterinn.com); and **Lakedale Resort at Three Lakes,** 4313 Roche Harbor Road (800-617-2267; www.lakedale.com). Several miles from Friday Harbor is **Olympic Lights Bed & Breakfast** at 4531 Cattle Point Road (360-378-3186; www.olympiclights.com), a renovated 1895 farmhouse that sits in a wide meadow near the bluff that overlooks the Strait of Juan de Fuca. From here you can walk to the site of **American Camp** and enjoy scenic walks at 4th of July Beach. Find scenic camping and RV sites on the island as well as other lodging options by checking with the San Juan Island Chamber of Commerce Visitor Information Center in Friday Harbor (360-378-5240; www.sanjuanisland.org) and with the San Juan Islands Visitors Bureau (888-468-3710; www.visitsanjuans.com).

Be sure to check out American Camp and English Camp and their historic displays about the infamous Pig War, both part of the San Juan Island National Historic Park, the largest chunk of public land on the island. Don't miss a visit to The **Whale Museum** in Friday Harbor at 62 First Street (360-378-4710; www.whalemuseum.org). The public is encouraged to report any signs of stranded marine mammals to the San Juan County Marine Mammal Stranding Network, operated by the Whale Museum (800-562-8832).

Leaving the islands for Anacortes takes a bit of planning. Double-check the ferry departure times and plan to arrive at the ferry landing at least a couple of hours early (seriously) on summer weekends. Vehicles line up in a first-come, first-served arrangement. Remember to bring a book and entertainment for the kids.

After returning to the Anacortes ferry terminal from the *San Juan Islands,* head southeast for a few miles to La Conner or *Mount Vernon.* In March and April, about 1,100 acres are carpeted with blooming daffodils, tulips, and irises that thrive in the rich loamy soil of the lower Skagit Valley. On clear days, enjoy views of distant snowcapped *Mount Baker.* Check (360) 428-5959 and www.tulipfestival.org for information on the annual Skagit Valley Tulip Festival in April. If possible, visit midweek to avoid weekends when the narrow farm roads are often clogged with traffic.

From Highway 20 heading east from Anacortes, turn right on La Conner-Whitney Road and drive to La Conner at the edge of the Swinomish Channel. The scenic waterway carries a parade of small boats between *Padilla Bay* to the north and Skagit Bay to the south. Once a quiet village serving local farmers and fishermen, *La Conner* is now a popular tourist destination with restaurants, antiques shops, and boutiques clustered along First and Morris Streets.

Be sure to stop and visit one of the town's three museums. The *Skagit County Historical Museum* at 501 Fourth Street (360-466-3365; www.skagit county.net/museum) includes exhibits on the area's history, industries, and lost towns. The museum is open from 1:00 p.m. to 5:00 p.m. Tuesday through Sunday. Don't miss visiting the *La Conner Quilt & Textile Museum* in the 1891 Gaches Mansion at 703 South Second Street (360-466-4288; www.laconner quilts.com). It houses a wonderful collection of quilts from the Northwest and ongoing exhibits of quilts and fiber art throughout the year. It is open daily in April and Wednesday through Sunday the rest of the year.

The Museum of Northwest Art features world-class art exhibits and educational programs at 121 South First Street (360-466-4446; www.museumof nwart.org). Its inspiration began with four Northwest artists, Guy Anderson,

amoveable winterfeast

During February on the tidal flats and fields of Fir Island, visitors can marvel at some 30,000 Arctic snow geese, 1,500 trumpeter swans, and hundreds of tundra swans in addition to more than twenty species of ducks that pause to munch and rest while winging it along the Pacific Flyway. For maps and directions to the best viewing spots, contact the La Conner Chamber of Commerce Visitor Center at 606 Morris Street (888-642-9284; www.laconner chamber.com).

Kenneth Callahan, Mark Tobey, and Morris Graves. They drew their inspiration from nature and Asian influences. All spent time in the Skagit Valley and two lived here.

Afterward, have a bite to eat at one of several fine cafes and restaurants along First and Morris Streets. Consider the wood-fired Greek pizza at La Conner Brewing Co. at 117 South First Street (360-466-1415), the upstairs restaurant of Nell Thorn of La Conner at 205 East Washington Street (360-466-4261), or Calico Cupboard Café & Bakery for breakfast and lunch at 720 South First Street (360-466-4451).

Head north from La Conner on La Conner-Whitney Road and cross Highway 20 onto Bayview-Edison Road, which offers views of the islands and Padilla Bay. Walk or bicycle along the 2¼ mile Padilla Bay Shore Trail. Then pass Bay View State Park and Padilla Bay National Estuarine Research Reserve and stop at the recently remodeled *Breazeale–Padilla Bay Interpretive Center* at 10441 Bayview-Edison Road (360-428-1558; www.padillabay.gov). In addition to fish tanks and displays of local birds and mammals, children can enjoy environmental games and hands-on activities. Because of its fertile waters, Padilla Bay is a major stop for migrating birds. The center offers many programs for all ages, and is open year-round from 10:00 a.m. to 5:00 p.m. Wednesday through Sunday.

Small, comfortable inns entice travelers to rest in the Skagit Valley area, including the romantic Queen of the Valley Inn at 12757 Chilberg Road, Mount Vernon (360-466-4578; www.queenofthevalleyinn.com), one of the last remaining country inns in the valley. Every room has a farmland view, and a four-course regional and organic breakfast is served. *Benson Farmstead Bed & Breakfast* at 10113 Avon–Allen Road, Bow (800-441-9814; www.bbhost .com/bensonbnb), is run by descendants of the original Norwegian pioneers, with gardens, a family cottage, and the Garden Tower Suite by the waterfall garden. *Alice Bay Bed & Breakfast* offers intimate waterside views at 11794 Scott Road on Samish Island, Bow (800-652-0223; www.alicebay.com), as does La Conner Channel Lodge at 205 North First Street, La Conner (360-466-1500; www.laconnerlodging.com), with all but seven of its rooms at the edge of the Swinomish Channel.

Everyone should experience scenic *Chuckanut Drive* (Highway 11). Continuing north from Padilla and Samish Bays for about 20 miles, the winding road skirts high bluffs and offers breath-taking glimpses of the San Juan Islands before entering the Fairhaven Historic District of *Bellingham* soon after passing *Larrabee State Park.* Many of Bellingham's old commercial and residential buildings have been renovated to their nineteenth-century grandeur, especially in Fairhaven and downtown Bellingham.

Or to reach Fairhaven from I-5 take exit 250 and follow Highway 11 west to Twelfth Street. From Tenth Street walk the South Bay Trail, which has a section called Taylor Dock that takes you over the water. Or from mid-May to Sept. 1, take a Victoria-San Juan Cruises' foot-passenger scenic cruise (800-443-4552; www.islandcommuter.com) from the Bellingham Cruise Terminal for a day trip over to Friday Harbor on San Juan Island. Or, twenty minutes west of downtown, follow signs to the Lummi Island ferry landing for a six- to eight-minute ferry ride to enjoy a leisurely drive on this scenic little island.

While exploring the eclectic Fairhaven District near the waterfront, check out *Colophon Cafe,* 1208 Eleventh Street (360-647-0092), with its funky cow memorabilia and bovine decor; or *Skylark's Hidden Café* at 1308-B Eleventh Street (360-715-3010), a first-rate restaurant along a cobblestone path. Skylark's recently expanded and now offers a saloon.

The *Whatcom Museum of History and Art* (360-676-6981), in the Old City Hall at 121 Prospect Street, is a good place to pick up a walking map of downtown Bellingham. The museum is open noon to 5:00 p.m. Tuesday through Sunday; donations are appreciated. *Allied Arts of Whatcom County* operates a bright, friendly gallery at 1418 Cornwall Street. Try to take to take in the *Downtown Gallery Walk* offered five times each year (www.alliedarts .com).

Also check out the *American Museum of Radio and Electricity* located at 1312 Bay Street (360-738-3886; www.amre.us). From 11:00 a.m. to 4:00 p.m. Wednesday through Saturday, history buffs can browse the museum's collection of more than 1,000 radios and broadcasting memorabilia dating from the early 1940s. This special museum also houses an FM station that broadcasts locally radio shows from the World War II era. Visit *Sehome Hill Arboretum* (360-676-6985) on 180 acres with several miles of trails adjacent to Western Washington University. And don't miss the terrific Bellingham Farmers Market at 1200 Railroad Avenue (360-647-2060), 10:00 a.m. to 3:00 p.m. Saturday April through Christmas. Be sure to go early.

Historic Fairhaven's Dirty Dan Harris

He sported the customary beard, mustache, and longish hair worn in the 1880s. It's said that he was a sailor, trader, and rumrunner. He wore a shabby frock coat over a red undershirt. A dusty black plug hat was jammed on his head. On his feet he wore a pair of unlaced dirty boots. He also didn't bathe very often. But Dirty Dan, or Daniel Harris, in 1883 filed the original plan to create the community of Fairhaven. Dirty Dan is memorialized at 1211 Eleventh Street at the popular Dirty Dan Harris' Restaurant (360-676-1011), open daily at 5:00 p.m.

For dining in Bellingham, locals suggest finding pasta, seafood, and great desserts at **Pastazza** at 2945 Newmarket Street (360-714-1168; www.pastazza .com), the city's first fresh-pasta eatery; fresh Southwestern fare at **Pepper Sisters** (1055 North State Street; 360-671-3414); and drinks and food at Boundary Bay Brewery at 1107 Railroad Avenue (360-647-5593). **Chocolate Necessities** at 4600 Guide Meridian Street (800-804-0589) offers decadent chocolate truffles. For a great view while dining, head to **Harborside Bistro** at 1 Bellwether Way (360-392-3200) in the Bellwether Hotel. Lodging options include the Fairhaven Village Inn at 1200 Ten Street South in Fairhaven (360-733-1311; www.fairhavenvillageinn.com); the upscale-with-Northwest-flair Chrysalis Inn on the waterfront at 804 Tenth Street (888-808-0005; www.chrysalisinn.com); or the 65-room Hotel Bellwether on Bellingham Bay at One Bellwether Way (877-411-1200; www.hotelbellwether.com). If you're splurging, go all the way with Bellwether's three-story freestanding 900-square-foot Lighthouse Suite with a 360-degree observation deck.

The small community of **Ferndale** just north of Bellingham is a great place to explore both history and nature. Two blocks south of Main Street on First Avenue, **Historic Pioneer Park** is home to the largest collection of nineteenth-century log structures in the state. Tour these sturdy buildings, hewn from giant cedars, in the afternoon May 1 through September 30. Housed in the restored turn-of-the-twentieth-century Nielsen Farmhouse, 1 mile south of Ferndale via Hovander Road, the **Tennant Lake Natural History Interpretive Center** (360-384-3064; www.co.whatcom.wa.us/parks/tennantlake) provides information about the wetland environment. Next to the 1906 farmhouse and its beds brimming with summer perennials, stroll the paths of the

Lummi Island

Lummi Island, near Bellingham and a quick ferry ride from Gooseberry Point across Hale Passage, is one of the smaller populated San Juan isles. Only 9 miles long and 2 miles wide, it offers a few surprises. For one, during the month of August, you can watch the ancient fishing technique of reef-netting from boats at Legoe Bay on the west side of the island. Riley Starks and Judy Olsen, owners of **Nettles Organic Farm** and of **Willows Inn,** a historic B&B retreat at 2579 West Shore Drive (888-294-2620; www.willows-inn.com), buy reef-net-caught wild salmon for their gourmet entrees at the inn's cafe Thursday through Sunday. Rooms at the octagonal **West Shore Farm Bed & Breakfast** (360-758-2600; www.lanierbb.com) at 2781 West Shore Drive offer comfort and overlook Rosario Strait. For a special treat, ask Carl Hanson to play his Scottish bagpipes. On Memorial Day or Labor Day weekend, attend the annual artist tours to see splendid watercolors, oils, sculpture, jewelry, glass, pottery, and fiber arts for sale at artists' studios around the island.

Fragrance Garden, then follow the path past the viewing tower and toward the lake. Walk along the half-mile system of elevated boardwalks to see a variety of wetlands vegetation along with raptors and waterfowl, including large flocks of trumpeter swans in winter. Climb the 50-foot-tall observation tower and look for birds.

Find another historic site by following the signed ½-mile road from Tennant Lake to **Hovander Homestead Park** at 5299 Nielsen Road (360-384-3444), open daily 8:30 a.m. to 4:00 p.m. The restored family farmhouse was built in 1896 by Hakan Hovander, a Swedish architect who helped rebuild Chicago after the Great Fire of 1871. Volunteers in period-style clothing show visitors through the elegant rooms (call for dates). There are farm animals on the grounds in summer and antique farm equipment at the big red barn, as well as a demonstration garden. Experience traditional Scottish fun when the park hosts the **Bellingham Highland Games** in June.

You could now detour from I-5 and head east into the Cascade Mountain foothills on Highway 542 (Mount Baker Highway) and follow the road for glorious views of 10,778-foot Mount Baker. At Glacier, near milepost 38, stop at the Glacier Public Service Center (360-599-2714) in late spring, summer, and early fall for information on scenic hiking trails and campgrounds in the North Cascades. From here it's an easy summer drive up to the Shuksan Picnic Area, Heather Meadows, and on to **Artist Point Viewpoint** at road's end, 58 miles from Bellingham, at an elevation of 5,140 feet.

If you're not going east to Mount Baker, try sea level adventures by heading to **Birch Bay** just northwest of Ferndale (exit 270 from I-5) and close to the U.S.–Canadian border. Plan your visit for Thursday through Monday from Mother's Day to Labor Day so that you can stop at the **C Shop** at 4825 Alderson Road (360-371-2070), a Birch Bay institution and a combination bakery, candy shop, and hometown cafe. After munching the goodies, take a brisk walk along the beach at **Birch Bay State Park** (360-371-2800; www.parks.wa.gov) for seabirds and shorebirds, beachcombing, and wonderful water views of Birch Bay, Georgia Strait, and the San Juan Islands. Go to www.birchbaychamber.com (360-371-5004) for current tide tables and events.

Pause for good eats and wide-angle water views of Birch Bay at **Shores Restaurant** at 7848 Birch Bay Drive (360-371-3464). CJ's Beach House at 7878 Birch Bay Drive (360-371-3400) is another good option. For overnight stays inquire at Birch Bay Getaway at 824 Birch Bay Drive (877-627-2229; www.birchbaygetaway.com) for luxury cottages and suites; or Cottages by the Beach (425-339-8081; www.ilovecottages.com).

Lynden, a friendly community with a proud Dutch heritage, is located in the fertile Nooksack Valley farmlands east of Birch Bay. Stroll down Front

Quick Guide to Victoria and Vancouver, British Columbia

Victoria, located at the southern tip of Vancouver Island, and the city of Vancouver, situated on the mainland and not far from the U.S.–Canadian border, are destinations worth exploring if your travel arrangements include this part of Puget Sound. Both cities offer splendid public gardens, wide water vistas, impressive scenic drives, great coffeehouses and eateries, and comfortable overnight lodging options. You can travel to Victoria by passenger ferry from Seattle; by passenger and vehicle ferries from Port Angeles, at the tip of the Olympic Peninsula; by vehicle ferries from Anacortes, in northern Puget Sound; and by ferry from Tsawwassen, located just a few miles across the Canadian border from Blaine. Check these helpful resources to implement your planning:

Victoria Clipper
(from Seattle)
(206) 448-5000
From outside Seattle call (800) 888-2535
www.clippervacations.com

Victoria Express
(from Port Angeles)
(800) 633-1589
www.victoriaexpress.com
www.bcferries.com
Distance and driving time from Seattle to Vancouver, B.C., via border crossing at Blaine: 117 miles/3 hours

Vancouver Highlights
Downtown, Yaletown, Gastown, Chinatown, Queen Elizabeth Gardens, Granville Island on False Creek, English Bay, Burrard Inlet, Stanley Park, Sooke, and Lions Gate Bridge to North Shore, Grouse Mountain, Whistler Ski Area
(604) 683-2000
www.tourismvancouver.com

Victoria and Vancouver Island Highlights
Inner Harbour, Empress Hotel, British Parliament Buildings, Royal Provincial Museum, Butchart Gardens, Sidney/ Swartz Bay and up-island to Nanaimo, Tofino, Campbell River, and Port Hardy
(250) 953-2033
www.tourismvictoria.com

Tourism British Columbia
(800) 435-5622
www.HelloBC.com

Street, bedecked with flowers and quaint Dutch décor, and stop in for fresh pastries at a destination bakery—***Lynden Dutch Bakery*** (360-354-3911) at 421 Front Street or authentic European cuisine at Dutch Mothers Restaurant, 405 Front Street (360-354-2174).

Lynden Pioneer Museum, 217 West Front Street (360-354-3675) is open 10:00 a.m. to 4:00 p.m. Monday through Saturday and 1:00 to 4:00 p.m.

Sunday. Stroll through a re-created turn-of-the-twentieth-century main street with stores, a café, doctor and dentist offices, a school, a church, and a train station. Admire the collection of early automobiles, more than forty restored horse buggies and wagons, and antique farm machinery. In midsummer, the steam tractors and threshing machines are fired up at the Puget Sound Antique Tractor and Machinery Association's Threshing Bee. The land around Lynden features well-kept working farms, many open seasonally for U-pick adventures.

One area really off the beaten path is a tiny peninsula situated just below the 49th parallel, south of British Columbia. *Point Roberts* (population 860) became U.S. territory in the late 1840s. But before crossing the border, walk the gorgeous gardens of *Peace Arch State Park* by taking exit 276 in Blaine.

Pass through Canadian Customs at the border at Blaine, about 20 miles north of Bellingham on I-5. For border crossing requirements go to the U.S.–Canadian Border Crossing Web site at www.cbp.gov or call (206-553-0770).

Once in Canada, continue north into British Columbia and follow the signs to Tsawwassen, about 23 miles, then follow signs to Point Roberts and a small U.S. Customs station used to re-enter the United States. For a spectacular water view, stop at Point Roberts' *Lighthouse Marine Park* (360-945-4911) at the peninsula's southwest corner. Check out the Orca Center and two-story whale-watching tower with its great views of Georgia Strait and the Canadian Gulf Islands.

At *Point Roberts Marina* (360-945-2255) at the south end of Tyee Drive, inspect a flotilla of sailboats and motor craft, then stop for a snack at the *Dockside Cafe* (360-945-1206). A fine place to have dinner while taking in the splendid views is *South Beach House* (360-945-0717), east of the marina at 725 South Beach Road.

Places to Stay on Puget Sound

ANACORTES

Fidalgo Bay Resort RV Park
1107 Fidalgo Bay Road
(800) 727-5478

Ship Harbor Motor Inn
5316 Ferry Terminal Road
(800) 852-8568

ANDERSON ISLAND

Above the Sound Bed & Breakfast
806 Birch Street
Steilacoom
(253) 589-1441

Inn at Burg's Landing Bed and Breakfast
8808 Villa Beach Road
(253) 884-9185

ASHFORD

Mountain Meadows Inn
28912 Highway 706 East
(360) 569-2788

Nisqually Lodge
31609 Highway 706
(888) 674-3554

HELPFUL WEB SITES
IN THE PUGET SOUND REGION

Anacortes
www.anacortes.org

Bellingham-Whatcom County
www.bellingham.org

Ferry Information
www.wsdot.wa.gov/ferries

Gig Harbor
www.gigharborguide.com

Kitsap Peninsula
www.visitkitsap.com

La Conner
www.laconnerchamber.com

Langley
www.visitlangley.com

Mount Rainier National Park
www.visitrainier.com
www.nps.gov/mora

Oak Harbor
www.oakhborcomeashore.com

Olympia-Lacey-Tumwater
www.visitolympia.com

Port Townsend Area
www.enjoypt.com

San Juan Islands
www.guidetosanjuans.com

Seattle
www.visitseattle.org

Tacoma-Pierce County
www.traveltacoma.com

Washington State Parks
www.parks.wa.gov

Whidbey Island
www.whidbeycamanoislands.com

BELLINGHAM

Days Inn
215 Samish Way
(360) 734-8830

BIRCH BAY

Birch Bay Beachside RV
Park
7630 Birch Bay Drive
(800) 596-9586

Driftwood Inn Motel
Birch Bay Drive
(360) 371-2620

GIG HARBOR

Best Western Wesley Inn
6575 Kimball Drive
(253) 858-9690

**LA CONNER/MOUNT
VERNON/BOW**

Benson Farmstead Bed &
Breakfast
10113 Avon-Allen Road
Bow
(800) 441-9814

Katy's Inn
503 South Third Street
La Conner
(866) 528-9746

LOPEZ ISLAND

Raven's Rook Cabin
58 Wildrose Lane
(877) 321-2493

LUMMI ISLAND

West Shore Farm Bed &
Breakfast
2781 West Shore Drive
(360) 758-2600

ORCAS ISLAND

Bay Side Cottages
65 Willis Lane
Olga
(360) 376-4330

Buckhorn Farm
Bungalow
17 Jensen Road
Eastsound
(360) 376-2298

Cayou Cove Cottages
Deer Harbor
(360) 376-3199

Turtleback Farm Inn Bed & Breakfast
1981 Crow Valley Road
(800) 376-4914

POINT ROBERTS

Maple Meadows Inn and Madrona Yoga Bed & Breakfast
101 Goodman Road
(360) 945-5536

PORT ORCHARD

Reflections Bed and Breakfast
3878 Reflection Lane East
(360) 871-5582

PORT TOWNSEND

Ravenscroft Bed & Breakfast
533 Quincy Street
(360) 385-2784

POULSBO

Foxbridge Bed & Breakfast
30680 Highway 3 NE
(360) 598-5599

SAN JUAN ISLAND

Harrison House Suites
235 C Street
Friday Harbor
(800) 407-7933

Lakedale Resort At Three Lakes
4313 Roche Harbor Road
Friday Harbor
(800) 617-2267

Tucker House Bed & Breakfast
206 B Street
Friday Harbor
(360) 378-2783

TACOMA

Chinaberry Hill Grand Victorian Inn & Cottage
302 Tacoma Avenue North
(253) 272-1282

DeVoe Mansion Bed & Breakfast Inn
208 East 133rd Street
(888) 539-3991

VASHON ISLAND

Betty MacDonald Farm Bed & Breakfast
12000 Ninety-ninth Avenue Southwest
(888) 328-6753

WHIDBEY ISLAND

Anchorage Inn Bed & Breakfast
807 North Main Street
Coupeville
(877) 230-1313

Auld Holland Motor Inn
33575 Highway 20
Oak Harbor
(800) 228-0148

Guest House Log Cottages
24371 State Route 525
Greenbank
(360) 678-3115

Places to Eat on Puget Sound

ANACORTES

Anacortes Chocolate Factory & Cafe
2302 Commercial Street
(360) 293-8042

Gere-a-Deli
502 Commercial Avenue
(360) 293-7383

Penguin Coffee House
2119 Commercial Avenue
(360) 588-8321

BAINBRIDGE ISLAND

Blackbird Bakery
210 Winslow Way East
(206) 780-1322

ALSO WORTH SEEING

Microsoft Visitor Center
Redmond
(425) 703-6214
www.microsoft.com

Pacific Rim Bonsai Collection
Weyerhaeuser Campus
Federal Way
(253) 924-5206

SELECTED INFORMATION CENTERS

Anacortes
(360) 293-3832

Bellingham-Whatcom County
(360) 671-3990

Blaine
(800) 624-3555

Gig Harbor
(888) 843–9444

Kitsap County
(800) 416-5615

La Conner
(888) 642-9284

Langley
(360) 221-6765

Oak Harbor
(360) 675-3535

Olympia-Lacey-Tumwater
(877) 704-7500

Port Townsend
(888) 365-6978

San Juan Islands
(888) 468-3701

Seattle
(206) 461-5840

Tacoma-Pierce County
(800) 272-2662

Pegasus Coffee House & Gallery
131 Parfitt Way
(206) 842-6725

BELLEVUE/REDMOND

Rock Bottom Brewery & Restaurant
550 106th Avenue
Northeast
Bellevue
(425) 462-9300

BELLINGHAM

Colophon Cafe & Deli
1208 Eleventh Street
(360) 647-0092

Harborside Bistro at Bellwether Hotel
1 Bellwether Way
(360) 392-3200

Skylark's Fairhaven Cafe
1308-B Eleventh Street
(360) 715-3010

BIRCH BAY

The C Shop Bakery & Cafe
4825 Alderson Road
(360) 371-2070

ISSAQUAH

Boehm's Candies at Gilman Village
255 Northeast Gilman
Boulevard
(425) 392-6652

LA CONNER

La Conner Brewing Company
117 South First Street
(360) 466-1415

LOPEZ ISLAND

The Galley Cafe
Fisherman Bay
(360) 468-2713

Holly B's Bakery
Lopez Plaza
(360) 468-2133

LYNDEN

Lynden Dutch Bakery
421 Front Street
(360) 354-3911

OLYMPIA

Budd Bay Cafe
525 Columbia Street
Northwest
(360) 357-6963

Tugboat Annie's
2100 West Bay Drive
(360) 943-1850

ORCAS ISLAND

Bilbo's Festivo
310 A Street
Eastsound
(360) 376-4728

Café Olga at Orcas Island Artsworks
11 Point Lawrence Road
Olga
(360) 376-5098

Teezer's Coffee Shop
North Beach and A Streets
(360) 376-2913

POINT ROBERTS

The Breakers Bar & Grill
531 Marine Drive
(360) 945-2300

PORT HADLOCK

Ajax Cafe
271 Water Street
(360) 385-3450

PORT TOWNSEND

Elevated Ice Cream & Candy Shop
627 Water Street
(360) 385-1156

Manresa Castle
Edwardian Lounge
651 Cleveland Street
(800) 732-1281

Nifty Fifties Cafe
817 Water Street
(360) 385-1931

POULSBO

JJ's Fish House
1881 Front Street
(360) 779-6609

SAN JUAN ISLAND

Garden Path Cafe
135 Second Street
Friday Harbor
(360) 378-6255

Haley's Bait Shop & Grill
Spring Street
Friday Harbor
(360) 378-4434

San Juan Coffee Roasting Co.
Cannery Landing
Friday Harbor
(360) 378-4443

SEATTLE

Pike Place Public Market
1501 Pike Place
(206) 682-7453

SNOQUALMIE

Snoqualmie Falls Candy Factory & Cafe
8102 Railroad Avenue
Southeast
(425) 888-0439

TACOMA

Engine House #9
611 North Pine Street
(253) 272-3435

Over the Moon Cafe
709 Opera Alley Court C
(253) 284-3722

WHIDBEY ISLAND

Deception Cafe & Grill
5596 Highway 20, north of
Deception Pass bridge
(360) 293-9250

Knead & Feed Cafe
4 Front Street
(360) 678-5431

North Cascades and North Central Washington

Tremendous geological forces shoved huge chunks of granite thousands of feet into the air to form the far north section of the Cascade mountain range. We're talking mountains that reach 8,000 or more feet topped off with craggy snow-covered peaks, a picket fence that divides the wet western third from the drier two-thirds of the state.

Abundant water, rich volcanic soil, and hot summers make the Okanogan, *Chelan,* and Wenatchee river valleys on the east side of the Cascades ideal for fruit growing. Depending on the season, you'll find juicy cherries, apples, pears, and peaches, as well as field-ripened vegetables.

Farther east, the landscape mellows into dry, tan hills covered with sagebrush or bitterbrush. Explore back roads, ghost towns, and a scattering of small lakeside fishing resorts. National forests and state parks offer thousands of miles of trails, making it easy to hike, cross-country ski, trail ride, or mountain bike your way off the beaten path.

North Cascades

The North Cascades puncture the skyline, covered with forests up to the higher elevations, cut by dozens of rivers, waterfalls,

and lakes. At the timberline between 4,500 and 5,500 feet elevation, alpine meadows carpeted with brightly colored wildflowers draw hikers. Crossing over the passes to the eastern side of the Cascades, you'll see how the mostly blocked clouds leave the hills and canyons to drought-tolerant species of lodgepole, Western white pine, and ponderosa pine.

Highway 20, Washington's only paved road across this northern wilderness, was completed in 1972. It connects northern Western Washington and the north-central section of the state. The highway closes with the first heavy snowfall, usually around Thanksgiving. It normally opens again in late April. For current highway conditions call the Washington State Department of Transportation at (800) 695-7623. Late spring (wildflowers) or early fall (fall color) are the best times to view nature's displays. The U.S. Forest Service and

NORTH CENTRAL WASHINGTON'S FAVORITE ATTRACTIONS

Baker Lake
Concrete

Cascadian Farm Organic Market
www.cascadianfarm.com

Chimposiums
Ellensburg
www.cwu.edu

Ginkgo-Wanapum State Park
Vantage
www.parks.wa.gov

John Wayne Pioneer Trail
Ellensburg
www.parks.wa.gov/trails

Lake Chelan and Stehekin
Chelan
www.nps.gov/lach
www.lakechelan.com

Lower Yakima River Canyon
Yakima
www.visityakima.com

Methow Valley
Highway 20
www.methownet.com

Molson School Museum
Molson
www.okanogancountry.com

North Cascades National Park
North Cascade Mountains
www.nps.gov/noca

Ohme and Rocky Reach Dam Gardens
Wenatchee
www.ohmegardens.com
www.rockyreachdam.com

Ross Lake Resort
Newhalem
www.rosslakeresort.com

Run of the River Inn and Refuge
Leavenworth
www.runoftheriver.com

Skagit River Bald Eagle Natural Area
Rockport

Nature Classes

An excellent adventure is to incorporate a nature or natural history class into your vacation plans. The premier organization to offer a wide range of weekend classes and field experiences, many designed with the family in mind, is the nonprofit North Cascades Institute (360-856-5700 ext. 209). NCI has a $10.5 million learning center in partnership with North Cascades National Park and Seattle City Light, giving it a base high in the mountains.

Topics range far and wide: outdoor photography, high desert ecology, spring birding, nature journaling, poetics of the wild, landscape watercolor, Ross Lake by boat and boot, volcanic geology of Mount Baker, and treetop forest ecology are just the surface of a long list of experiences. Check out NCI's Web site, www.ncascades.org, or call for a catalog.

the **North Cascades National Park** office complex at 810 Highway 20 in **Sedro-Woolley** (360-856-5700) is a good place to stop for information as you approach from the west. The office is open Saturday through Thursday from 8:00 a.m. to 4:30 p.m. from Memorial Day weekend through mid-October and Monday through Friday (same hours) during the rest of the year.

Many visitors to north-central Washington enjoy river-rafting adventures. More than a dozen rivers are popular for rafting, ranging from a relaxing Class I to suicidal Class VI. Several professional rafting companies supply the equipment, information, and confidence beginners need to tackle a river. Most guided rafting trips concentrate on Class III and IV rivers—that is, rivers that have enough riffles, rapids, and white water to guarantee a great adventure. Some easy float trips also are scheduled to observe eagles. For current information about trips on the Skagit, Twisp and Methow Rivers, contact the North Cascades National Park office complex in Sedro-Woolley (360-856-5700). Another good contact is the Washington Outfitters & Guides Association (509-997-1080; www.woga.org), the only industry organization in the state that represents outfitters, sport-fishing guides, horse and llama packers, white-water rafters, hunting guides, and other outdoors professionals.

Traveling east on Highway 20 from Sedro-Woolley, follow the winding Skagit, a National Wild and Scenic River that's colored blue-green with glacial meltwaters. Take the turnoff north on Baker Lake Road to visit **Baker Lake,** a lovely mountain reservoir with campsites, trails, and lake access. Enjoy spectacular views of Mount Baker, known to the local Nooksack Tribe as Koma Kulshan, "the steep white mountain." **Shadow of the Sentinels,** on your right just past the Koma Kulshan Guard Station at Baker Lake's south end, is a pleasant half-mile, wheelchair-accessible trail and interpretive hike through old-growth forest. For information about forest and lakeside campgrounds in the North Cascades, stop in or contact the North Cascades Visitor Center on Highway 20 in Newhalem (206-386-4495; www.nps.gov/noca).

Located about 23 miles east of Interstate 5, the town of **Concrete** is worth a stop before continuing east on Highway 20. The Superior Portland Cement plant here was once the largest in the state, producing nearly half the cement used in the Grand Coulee Dam and supplying plenty more for construction of the local dams on Diablo and Ross Lakes. The plant closed in 1968. Concrete now serves as a jumping-off point for recreation in the Upper Skagit Valley and North Cascades. The 1916 concrete bridge that spans the Baker River at the town's east end is listed in the National Register of Historic Places. A jaunt across the bridge leads to East Shannon Road and an overlook to Baker Dam.

didyouknow?

Glacial water that feeds the North Cascades' rivers and lakes comes from melting glaciers. The milky blue or green or gray color of the lakes is caused by rock flour, what's left after rocks are ground down underneath the glaciers' movements. The fine powder is suspended and refracts sunlight, producing the colors.

Staying here is an option before exploring the scenic North Cascades Highway and mountainous regions to the east. At **Ovenell's Heritage Inn & Log Cabins at Double O Ranch,** 46276 Concrete-Sauk Valley Road (866-464-3414; www.ovenells-inn.com), travelers are greeted by a noisy but cheerful welcoming committee of ducks, geese, and other farm animals. There are four comfortable guest rooms in the main house and five log cabins. Enjoy views of Mount Baker—when it's "out."

Food options along Highway 20 in the Concrete area include the **Cajun Bar & Grill** (360-853-8518) at the corner of Main and Baker Streets for tasty Cajun-style favorites; **Annie's Pizza Station** (360-853-7227) for good pizza and other Italian fare; and, a bit farther east, **Perks** (360-853-9006) for espresso drinks and sandwiches.

Rockport, 8 miles east of Concrete, has excellent off-the-beaten path credentials. **Rockport State Park,** opened in 1961, is a 670-acre park in an ancient forest, although the camping area has been closed because of hazardous conditions. The trees are worth the stop, a rare never-logged forest with a dense canopy at the foot of Sauk Mountain. Folks can thank the old Sound Timber Company owners who declined to log the old-growth trees, selling the almost 600 acres to the state for $1.

The Skagit River Interpretive Center (open weekends from mid-December to mid-February) is located in Rockport, 1 block south of Highway 20 on

Birding on the North Cascades Loop

The Great Washington State Birding Trail includes the Cascade Loop, featuring 225 of the state's 365 bird species from inland coastal waters through conifer forests and over high passes of the Cascade Mountains to sagebrush and grassland plateaus, desert canyons, and the Columbia River. The state is known for its large populations of shorebirds and waterfowl, bald eagles, snow geese, neotropical migrants, and trumpeter and tundra swans. Grab your binoculars, scope, and bird book and hit the road, or incorporate some of these stops into one of your outings. The best birding times are generally early mornings and late afternoons and in spring and fall.

Tennant Lake Wildlife Area (www.co.whatcom.wa.us/parks/tennantlake) is near Ferndale, northwest of Bellingham. Use the 1-mile-long elevated boardwalk Loop Trail around lush wetlands and a marshy lake, and climb the observation tower.

Bayview State Park (www.parks.wa.gov), part of the 10,000-acre Padilla Bay National Estuarine Research Reserve near Mount Vernon; offers gravel beaches, salt marsh, and mud flats.

Larrabee State Park (www.bellingham.org), north of Mount Vernon via scenic Chuckanut Drive, offers 2,683 acres of mountain lookouts, lakes, conifers, saltwater coves with fascinating rock formations, and tidepools. Watch for waterfowl and shorebirds. Explore 8 miles of trails that start at the day-use area.

Rockport State Park (www.parks.wa.gov), near Rockport, has 465 acres with 5 miles of trails through old-growth conifers. Spring visits are best except for December-February when it becomes bald eagle country with eagles converging to feed on salmon coming up the Skagit River to spawn.

Pearrygin Lake State Park (www.parks.wa.gov), north of Winthrop, is a 580-acre park with a large lake; bird viewing is best along its east side. Try spring and summer mornings.

Barn Beach Reserve (www.ncw.audubon.org/bbreserve.htm) in Leavenworth is home to an environmental learning center, arts facility, and museum. The reserve and an adjacent park create a 50-acre greenbelt along the river, including a mature streamside forest and Blackbird Island.

Get a copy of the *Great Washington State Birding Trail* map through www.wa.audubon .org; www.wos.org; www.birdweb.org; or the Washington Department of Fish and Wildlife in Mount Vernon, (360) 445-4441.

Alfred Street in the Rockport Fire Hall (360-853-7283). Contact the center for information about the Upper Skagit Bald Eagle Festival (www.skagiteagle.org) held the weekend before the Super Bowl. Guided float trips on the Skagit River allow folks to see the eagles during this yearly event. This is home to one of the largest wintering bald eagle populations in the continental United States. Hundred of eagles are counted here annually by expert birders, with mid-December to late-January being the best times to see the majestic birds in the Upper Skagit River. On any given day, visitors might see up to 100 eagles from pullouts off Highway 20.

Just east of Rockport is the **Skagit River Bald Eagle Natural Area** with its viewpoints and interpretive signs overlooking the river. Designated sites such as this are the best places to watch eagles without disturbing them. Volunteers from the Eagle Watchers program provide information and birding scopes at the best sites. The eagles start heading here in late autumn from as far away as Alaska to feast on chum salmon that are exhausted and dying after navigating many miles upstream from the Pacific Ocean.

At milepost 101 is the **Cascadian Farm Organic Market** (55749 Highway 20; 360-853-8173), a roadside stand that sells the company's outstanding organically grown products; the organic foods are shipped all over the country. At this busy little stand, taste delicious berry shortcakes, low-sodium pickles and sauerkraut, fresh salads, sweet corn, all-fruit sorbets, and espresso. There are shaded picnic tables and self-guided tours of the experimental gardens. The market is open May through mid-September from 10:00 a.m. to about 6:00 p.m. weekdays and to 9:00 p.m. on weekends.

Skagit River Resort & Clark's Eatery, at 58468 Clark Cabin Road (www .northcascades.com) near Rockport (360-873-2250), offers cabins, bed-and-breakfast guest rooms, a number of RV sites, tent sites, laundry facilities—and about 175 rabbits hopping about the grounds. The small restaurant features Tootsie Matilda Clark and her famous cinnamon rolls.

Near the confluence of the Skagit and Cascade Rivers, Marblemount has been the last-chance stop for food, fuel, and news for travelers heading into the high country ever since miners trekked through these rugged mountains in the 1880s. **Buffalo Run Restaurant,** open for breakfast, lunch, and dinner at 60084 Highway 20 (360-873-2461), features buffalo steaks and burgers as well as venison and elk. For a more-traditional menu, stop at **Marblemount Diner** (360-873-4503) at the east end of town. If you're not fond of tents, check out the Buffalo Run Inn at 60117 Highway 20 (360-873-2103), originally an 1889 roadhouse and a watering hole for gold miners and traders.

This area is a backpacker's nirvana. If you don't mind steep trails of 3 to 5 miles in length that end in superb views of alpine lakes, jagged peaks, and long-range vistas, contact the visitor center in Marblemount at 59831 Highway 20 (360-873-4150) or the Wilderness Information Center (7280 Ranger Station Road; 360-854-7245) for maps, advice, and backcountry permits for the Pasayten Wilderness and North Cascades National Park. Also ask about hiking trails to high vistas from nearby Cascade Pass and Thornton Lakes trailheads. Note:

Do not attempt backcountry hikes without being completely prepared. See "Ten Essentials for Backcountry Hikers" on page 93.

The Skagit River Valley widens at milepost 120 at **Newhalem,** a company town on Highway 20. Stop at the 1922 **Skagit General Store** (206-386-4489) to gather picnic goodies and try samples of Skagit fudge that's made on the premises. Find a shady picnic spot near Old Number Six, the restored Baldwin locomotive engine that ran between Newhalem and Rockport before the highway was built.

The North Cascades Visitor Information Center and Ranger Station (206-386-4495) is located at 59831 Highway 20, behind the Newhalem Campground. It's open daily from 9:00 a.m. to 5:00 p.m. with hiking and camping information, helpful maps, and wildlife information.

Just past Skagit General Store, cross the Skagit River on a small suspension bridge and walk the **Trail of Cedars,** a 1-mile self-guided and wheelchair-accessible nature trail that loops through old-growth forest. Cross the river on another pedestrian suspension bridge next to the gorge powerhouse and continue a short distance on a woodland trail with benches and native plantings for close-up views of **Ladder Creek Falls,** which plunges about 75 feet through a narrow chasm of basalt.

The open-grate bridge at the **Gorge Creek Scenic Lookout,** between mileposts 123 and 124 on Highway 20, provides breathtaking views of the 242-foot gorge below. The big parking lot makes this spot easily accessible to highway travelers.

unpassable

Highway 20 is closed from Ross Dam east over 5,477-foot Washington Pass and down to Mazama with the first large snow storms in late October or early November and doesn't open again until April after the highway has been plowed.

Call Skagit Tours (206-233-2709; www.skagittours.com) to inquire about scenic lake cruises on Diablo Lake. On the two-and-one-half-hour tour, you'll see Ross Dam, Diablo Dam, craggy mountain peaks, North Cascades wildlife, and learn the history of the Skagit hydroelectric project including the old Incline Railway, which took project workers 560 feet up and back down Sourdough Mountain in the early 1920s. The boat tours are offered on weekends in June and September and on Thursday through Monday during July and August.

To get farther from the crowds and thoroughly enjoy yourself in the process, stay at the floating **Ross Lake Resort** at 503 Diablo Street, Rockport (206-386-4437; www.rosslakeresort.com) as thousands have done since 1950. A dozen cabins and three bunkhouses built on cedar log floats are on the

Ross Lake Resort

west side of Ross Lake just north of Ross Dam. It's the only resort on the lake and has no direct road access. To reach the resort, meet the passenger ferry (for a nominal fee) and truck that delivers guests to the resort in less than an hour or hike a 2-mile mountain trail from Highway 20. It's open mid-June to October.

Piles of food (there is no store or restaurant at the resort), ice chests, baggage, and people all jumble together in the Seattle City Light boat as it chugs past rocky islands and into a narrow passageway between steep canyon walls up to Ross Dam. Then, with gear and everyone safely loaded onto open trucks, it's a short but bumpy ride up switchbacks through the forest to Ross Lake. Speedboats from the resort ferry guests across the lake to the cluster of lodgings.

The cabins, built in the 1930s for logging crews, have been modernized with kitchens, plumbing, and electricity. Hardy hikers can arrange water-taxi service to trailheads for backcountry adventures. Pets are not allowed, and boat rental is required for cabins on weekends; rentals include boats with outboard motors, aluminum canoes, and single and double kayaks.

Back on Highway 20 heading east, you can stop for sweeping views of Diablo Lake and the hanging glaciers of Colonial and Pyramid peaks beyond from the overlook just before milepost 132. A few miles farther, the very short *Happy Creek Forest Walk,* south of the highway, provides a barrier-free boardwalk past huge fallen and standing old-growth trees. Interpretive signs tell the forest's story amid the sounds of the bubbling creek. Ross Lake stretches before you from the *Ross Lake Overlook,* north of the highway.

A few miles farther east, at the *East Bank trailhead,* a quarter-mile hike will take you to Ruby Creek, an important spawning area for native trout (no

Creative Vacations

One way to wander the state is to attend a creative workshop, conference, or personal retreat that would take you to a part of the state that is not familiar. Set aside a few days after that experience and explore the area before heading home.

Centrum. Port Townsend, (360) 385-3102, www.centrum.org

Coupeville Arts Center. (866) 678-3396, www.coupevillearts.org

Earth Sanctuary. Freeland, (360) 637-8777, www.earthsanctuary.com

Field's End. Bainbridge Island, (206) 842-4162, www.fieldsend.org

Flick Creek Photography Workshops. Stehekin, www.barnhartphoto.com

Hedgebrook. Whidbey Island, (360) 321-5786, www.hedgebrook.org

Inland Northwest Literary Arts. Spokane, (509) 623-4286, www.ewu.edu/getlit

North Cascades Institute. (360) 856-5700, ext. 209, www.ncascades.org

Northwind Arts Center. (360) 379-1086, http://northwindarts.org

Pacific Northwest Writers Conference. (425) 673-2665, www.pnwa.org

Port Townsend Writers Conference. (360) 385-3102, www.centrum.org

Puget Sound Guitar Workshop. www.langston.com/psgw

San Juan Art Workshops. (866) 374-4272, www.sanjuanartworkshops.com

Song & Word Retreats & Workshops. Shaw Island, (360) 468-3964, www.song andword.com

Westcott Bay Institute for Art & Nature. San Juan Island, (360) 370-5050, www .wbay.org

Whidbey Institute. Clinton, (360) 341-1884, www.whidbeyinstitute.org

Whidbey Island Writers Conference. (360) 331-6714, www.whidbey.com/writers

Write on the Sound. Edmonds, (425) 771-0228, www.ci.edmonds.wa.us/arts commission/wots.stm

fishing allowed). After 3 miles on the trail, you reach the shore of Ross Lake, and in 28 miles hardy backpackers can reach the Canadian border. ***Canyon Creek trailhead,*** where Highway 20 veers southeast, marks the beginning of a short walk over a bridge to a turn-of-the-twentieth-century mining site. About 2 miles up the trail, you'll see Rowley's Chasm, a 200-foot cleft in the rocky hillside.

The roadside scenery gets even more spectacular as you approach the high mountain passes. Creeks cascade down steep gullies; alpine meadows are dotted with purple fireweed and red Indian paintbrush in the summer; and avalanches have left their mark on hillsides by sweeping away trees and bushes. There are several places to pull off the road to ogle at the awesome mountain views, such as the **Whistler Basin Overlook** at milepost 160, the barrier-free **Rainy Lake Trail,** or the point at which the 2,600-mile **Pacific Crest National Scenic Trail** from Mexico to Canada crosses the highway at 4,855-foot-high Rainy Pass.

Cast your gaze on 7,720-foot Liberty Bell Mountain, a jagged-edged precipice that looms above the don't-miss **Washington Pass Overlook** (milepost 162), a spot with some of the most spectacular views in the state from 700 feet above the highway. The wheelchair-accessible loop path to the overlook offers close-up views of alpine plants and geology, from spiral-grained trees to smooth, glacier-carved rocks. At 5,477 feet above sea level, Washington Pass is the North Cascades Highway's highest point. From here it winds down a steep U-shaped valley into the drier terrain of Central Washington, drier because the Cascade Mountains block most of the rain clouds coming from the west.

Driving into east-of-the-mountains landscape is a surprise to most newcomers. This land is dominated by tall cinnamon-barked ponderosa pine on the eastern slopes as you descend into the Methow Valley. There are pleasant, streamside campgrounds along the way at **Klipchuck** and **Early Winters.**

Tiny **Mazama** is located a quarter-mile north of Highway 20 at the upper end of the scenic Methow Valley. Its country store, gas station, and post office appear to be all that is left of this once-booming mining town. **Mazama Country Inn** (509-996-2681; www.mazamacountryinn.com), an all-season retreat nestled in the forest between mountains, has a restaurant that's open to travelers as well as overnight guests. Located at the edge of the **Pasayten Wilderness,** the inn's eighteen-room lodge and comfortable cabins open onto miles of hiking and mountain-bike trails. In the winter, you can cross-country ski out your door on one of the largest groomed trail systems in the United States or book a helicopter to fly you into to ski trackless snow higher in the Cascades.

For advice, information, and maps on hiking and camping in the North Cascades, call the Mount Baker Ranger

peakdriving

From Mazama, take Hart's Pass and Slate Peak Roads to the highest point one can drive to in Washington State. RVs—don't. Drive an altitude-gaining, switchbacking, sometimes edge-of-the-cliff, asphalt or gravel road with occasional blind curves. The reward is Slate Peak (7,440 feet), a fire lookout and 360 degrees of spectacular views of peaks and valleys. The best time is late July to September (call 509-997-2131 to check the snow level).

District, (360) 856-5700, ext. 515, at the complex that also houses the North Cascades Institute (ext. 209), or go to the Mount Baker-Snoqualmie National Forest Web site, www.fs.fed.us/r6/mbs. Another option is to contact the North Cascades National Park Service complex, (360) 854-7200, www.nps.gov/noca, which also provides information on Stehekin and the Ross Dam.

In Mazama eateries include the *Freestone Inn Dining Room* at 31 Early Winters Drive (800-639-3809; www.freestoneinn.com) for Northwest gourmet specialties and *Mazama Country Store* (50 Lost River Road; 509-996-2855), which offers homemade soups and baked goods along with deli sandwiches, pizza, and information about seasonal recreation. During the winter when Highway 20 is closed, Mazama is accessible only from Highways 97 and 153 from Wenatchee.

Activities abound in this area during all four seasons. *Rendezvous Outfitters* (www.methow.com/huts) offers backcountry hut-to-hut cross-country ski touring on the *Methow Valley Winter Trail System* in the Okanogan National Forest for a combination of daytime adventure and overnight comfort. If scenic horseback-riding adventures are more your style, consider a wilderness pack trip with *Early Winters Outfitting* in Mazama (509-996-2659; www .earlywintersoutfitting.com). Scenic horseback rides are also an option for guests staying at *Freestone Inn at Wilson Ranch,* 31 Early Winters Drive near

Ten Essentials for Backcountry Hikers

1. Flashlight or headlamp, spare batteries

2. Map of your hiking area

3. Compass or GPS (global positioning system) device

4. Extra food

5. Extra clothing

6. Sunglasses and sunscreen

7. First aid supplies and medications

8. Pocketknife

9. Matches in waterproof container

10. Fire starter

We suggest adding a few more items to the traditional ten: extra water or a water filter, a whistle, insect repellent, and sunscreen. But the most important "essential" is common sense, which includes making thoughtful decisions and erring on the side of safety, especially with children in tow.

Mazama (800-639-3809; www.freestoneinn.com) and at the excellent mountaintop *Sun Mountain Lodge* (800-572-0493; www.sunmountainlodge.com), about 10 miles from town via Twin Lakes and Patterson Lake Roads.

Hikers and mountain bikers can obtain current information for all types of trails from the Methow Valley Visitor Information Center and U.S. Forest Service Ranger District (509-996-4000) and from *Methow Valley Sports Trails Association* (509-996-3287; www.mvsta.com).

Even if you're not camping, the *Winthrop KOA Campground* (509-996-2258) is worth a detour from Highway 20 about a mile east of Winthrop for a look at its display of license plates from around the world, all collected by local resident Mike Meyers.

Highway 20 traffic slows as it winds through the small town of *Winthrop,* an early 1900s trading post now spruced up with a touristy Western theme. The *Schafer Museum,* in a historic log home on the hill 1 block above town,

bookworms

Winthrop was named after Theodore Winthrop, a 19th-century Yale graduate and author. Author Owen Wister, town founder Guy Waring's Harvard roommate, spent his honeymoon here and came up with ideas for his first Western novel, *The Virginian.*

is worth a visit to glimpse some of the early history. It's open from 10:00 a.m. to 5:00 p.m. daily from Memorial Day to Labor Day. Stop at *DJ's Winthrop Blacksmith Shop* at 236 Riverside Avenue (509-996-2703). You can often see the blacksmith working at his gas-fired forge, or browse their gallery of hand-forged gifts and home accessories.

Eateries along Winthrop's main street, Riverside Avenue (Highway 20), include *Rocking Horse Bakery & Coffee* (509-996-4241) for awesome baked goods and java; *Boulder Creek Deli* (509-996-3990) for great specialty sandwiches; *Grubstake & Co.* for local organic cuisine with seasonal gourmet pizza (509-996-2375); *Sheri's Sweet Shoppe* (509-996-3834) for freshly made fudge, chocolates, cinnamon rolls, and handmade ice cream; *Winthrop Brewing Company* (509-996-3183), located in a wedge-shaped building that was once a schoolhouse, for fine handcrafted ales and tasty pub fare; and *Heenan's Burnt Finger Bar-B-Q & Steakhouse* (509-996-8221) for Texas-style ribs, chili, and steaks along with views of the Methow River. For a gourmet feast at a crisp altitude of 2,850 feet with a great view of the *Methow Valley,* 1,000 feet below, try the elegant dining room at Sun Mountain Lodge (509-996-2211).

Comfortable places to bed down in the scenic Winthrop area include the inviting, family-oriented *WolfRidge Resort* (509-996-2828; www.wolfridge resort.com), the casually elegant *Chewuch Inn Bed & Breakfast* (800-747-

3107; www.chewuchinn.com), and *River Run Inn & Cabins* (800-757-2709; www.riverrun-inn.com), located close to the Methow River.

The Winthrop–Twisp Eastside Road is a pleasant, less-traveled route to the small community of Twisp. On the way, about 5 miles east of Winthrop, explore the world of firefighting at the *North Cascades Smokejumpers Base* operated by the U.S. Forest Service. Contact the base (509-997-2031) Monday through Friday, 7:45 a.m. to 4:30 p.m., for tour information. The USDA Forest Service Methow Valley Ranger Station (509-996-4003, www .fs.fed.us/r6/oka) offers maps and information for backcountry hikes in the region.

In the small community of Twisp, pause for espresso drinks and superb pastries at *Cinnamon Twisp Bakery,* at 116 North Glover Street (509-997-5030), and for waist-bulging entrees at *BJ's Branding Iron Restaurant & Saloon,* 123 North Glover Street (509-997-3576). For an overnight stay here in the scenic Twisp Valley, call *Methow Valley Inn Bed & Breakfast,* 234 Second Avenue (509-997-2253; www.methowvalleyinn.com).

The highway forks a couple of miles past Twisp and Highway 20 continues east to Okanogan. Highway 153 proceeds southeast along the Methow River as it winds and bubbles over its pebbly bed to Pateros. On this route you'll pass the pleasant community of Methow, then plunge into orchard country as the river gorge deepens before its confluence with the Columbia River.

Okanogan Valley

The Okanogan Valley stretches from the British Columbia border at *Oroville* south to the Columbia River. Much of the land along the river is planted with fruit orchards. The area above the river valley is drier, covered with rolling grass and sagebrush meadows dotted with occasional stands of ponderosa pine, glacially deposited boulders, and pristine lakes. *Okanogan* is the Kalispel Tribe's word for "rendezvous," or "gathering place."

Highway 20 merges with U.S. Highway 97 in the city of Okanogan. Visit the *Okanogan County Historical Museum* at 1410 Second Avenue North adjacent to Legion Park. Fine displays cover local geography and history of Indian and pioneer life. Outside, inspect a collection of log buildings, including a settler's cabin, a blacksmith's shop, and a saloon. Call the Okanogan Chamber of Commerce (888-782-1134) for more information.

If time allows, check out the *Rusty Shovel* at 123 Second Avenue South (509-422-0558), where the owners offer all kinds of western-style gifts and rustic handmade treasures for homes and gardens. The Rusty Shovel is also a garden store and gourmet food store. Another Okanogan option is the 1940s-style

On the Avenue Restaurant & Ice Cream Parlour at 134 Second Avenue South (509-422-2278), open Wednesday to Sunday.

A few miles north is *Omak* with its highly thought of *BreadlineCafé* at 102 South Ash Street (509-826-5836). The Breadline offers locally grown beef, Thursday night wine-tasting, and live blues and folk music. It's in the former Omak Beverages building that bottled soda pop from the 1920s through the 1950s. Locals suggest *Rancho Chico's* at 22 North Main Street (509-826-4757) for an excellent Mexican feast. Stop by *Novel Delights* at 19 North Main Street (509-826-1113) for tasty espressos, bagels and cream cheese, or delicious cookies made by the owner. Find home knick-knacks and a mini-soda fountain at Grandma's Attic at 12 North Main Street (509-826-4765). You can also browse the large selection of used books. *Magoo's Restaurant* at 24 North Main Street (509-826-2325) is a good choice for breakfast and lunch.

No words can be written about this town without mentioning the Big Show, the Omak Stampede (800-933-6625; www.omakstampede.org), which includes a rodeo and the World-Famous Omak Suicide Race, in which horses and their Native American riders plunge down impossibly steep 200-foot-long Suicide Hill into the Okanogan River. It's become infamous, too, because at least twenty horses have died since 1983.

Heading north again on US 97, stop at *Riverside* on any day except Saturday to browse *Historic Detro's Western Store* at 10 Main Street (509-826-2200). The all-purpose outfitter offers clothes and gear for tourists, residents, and professional cowboys and cowgirls. Although the building was rebuilt as a store after a fire in 1916, it became Detro's Western Wear in 1945, making it one of Washington's oldest and largest historic stores. Pick up some food at Riverside Grocery (102 North Main Street; 509-826-2049) and check out its Front Porch antiques.

cowboycaviar

Conconully has gone upscale with its Cowboy Caviar Fete in June. Local restaurants compete for the best dish made with bull testicles, otherwise known as cowboy caviar. Try the spicy Balls of Fire.

For a pleasant overnight campout, head about 15 miles northwest of Omak to *Shady Pines Resort Cabins and RV Park* at 125 West Fort Salmon Creek Road (800-552-2287) on the shores of 350-acre Conconully Reservoir. Four small cabins each sleep four, and a log cabin duplex sleeps six, all shaded from summer's heat by tall pines. Appreciate full kitchens, queen-size beds, and cozy sitting areas. Beachfront RV sites offer full hookups, and a few tent sites are also available. Rent a boat to go fishing for rainbow trout or just a relaxing row around the scenic lake. And yes, wireless Internet service has come to *Conconully.*

Conconully Jail, Sam's Story

Although it was built for impenetrability, the Conconully jail became the butt of many a local joke for the frequent prisoner escapes between 1891 and 1915. Perhaps the most amusing is the story of Sam Albright, who found out that two of his friends were guests of the hoosegow and went with another man to pay them a visit. Finding the jailer absent, he and his partner unlatched the window and climbed through. The four friends then engaged in a lively poker game, after which Sam and his friend left candy and books for the inmates, then exited back through the window, latching it behind them.

Head into the town of Conconcully and catch one of the small town's many festivals: Miners Day, Grubstake Open Golf Tournament, Outhouse Races (since 1983), Snow Dog Super Mush, and the ever-popular Cowboy Caviar Fete (see sidebar). For a quieter way to spend your time, check out the Conconully Museum; hours are 10:00 a.m. to 4:00 p.m. weekends and holidays. The town was nearly destroyed three times in its youth: an 1892 fire, an 1893 mining depression, and an 1894 flood.

Conconully's culinary options include the ***Tamarack Historic Saloon*** at 316 North Main Street (888-746-8137) for good hamburgers, ales, and pub grub; and ***Lucky D's Restaurant*** at 215 North Main Street (509-826-2573) for hearty breakfasts and lunches.

About 23 miles east of Tonasket on Highway 20, the tiny community of ***Wauconda*** offers a great introduction to the open beauty of the Okanogan high desert. You'll pass a scattered collection of homes, old homestead cabins, and barns on the 3,000-foot-high plateau. The ***Wauconda Store and Cafe*** (509-486-4010), a store/cafe/post office, is worth a stop. The wood-paneled cafe, decorated with local art and historical photos, offers great views of the rolling valley and high desert tree species including western larch, ponderosa pine, lodgepole pine, Engelmann spruce, and aspen.

Bonaparte Lake Resort, located near Tonasket at 695 Bonaparte Lake Road (509-486-2828), has cabins with kitchens, camping, gas, and a lodge with a small store and cafe famous for its great hamburgers. To get there, turn north about 3 miles west of Wauconda off Highway 20 onto a 6-mile-long country road that winds along Bonaparte Creek through meadows and forests. The Okanogan National Forest also has several campgrounds in the area. ***Lost Lake Campground,*** about 8 miles beyond the resort, offers several fine hiking trails, including the easy Big Tree Trail with 600-year-old Western larches, and the Strawberry Mountain Trail, offering panoramic views from hillsides covered with wild strawberries. For information, contact the Tonasket Ranger Station at 1 West Winesap; (509) 486-2186; www.fs.fed.us/r6/oka.

Located about 15 miles east of Oroville, Molson's two historical museums are worth seeing. The **Molson School Museum,** open daily from 10:00 a.m. to 5:00 p.m. Memorial Day weekend through Labor Day, offers three floors of well-organized displays. After browsing through the classrooms and library upstairs, the vintage clothing and furniture on the main floor, and the huge tool collection downstairs, enjoy homemade treats provided by museum volunteers. The **Old Molson Outdoor Museum** (509-485-3292), open during daylight hours for self-guided tours from April through December, exudes an Old West feeling with its nineteenth-century cabins, original bank building, mining and farm tools, and storefronts. Both museums are free, but donations are appreciated. **Sidley Lake** and **Molson Lake,** just north of town, are popular with travelers who like to fish. Bird-watchers also delight in the array of waterfowl, from blue-billed ruddy ducks to canvasbacks, feeding amid reeds and islands in the tiny lakes.

From Molson retrace your route back to Oroville and US 97. Oro, Spanish for gold, links us to the town's early history as a miner's mecca. But in 1925 it was nicknamed Queen Tomato for its large tomato-canning factory, and it was an honor to be elected Tomato Queen.

Oroville's original Great Northern Depot has been restored as a museum and community hall on the corner of Twelfth and Ironwood Streets. The **Oroville Old Depot Museum** (509-476-2570), open 10:00 a.m. to 3:00 p.m. Monday through Saturday from the first weekend in May to the second weekend in September, provides insight into the town's history as a railroad, mining, and agricultural center buffeted by changing times.

For meals, try Fat Boy's Family Diner at 1518 Main Street (509-476-4100) for hamburgers, malts, and shakes amid a nostalgic 1950s decor; Expressions

Old Molson Outdoor Museum

TOP ANNUAL EVENTS IN NORTH CENTRAL WASHINGTON

Ellensburg Rodeo
Ellensburg, late summer

'49er Days
Winthrop, May

Leavenworth Spring Bird Fest
May

Spirit of the West Cowboy Gathering
Ellensburg, mid-February

Upper Skagit Bald Eagle Festival
Rockport I
Weekend before Super Bowl

Espresso at 817 Apple Way (509-476-2970) for light sandwiches, baked goods, and soft ice cream; or **Home Town Pizza** at 1315 Main Street (509-476-2410) for made-from-scratch pizza, Italian pastas, and gourmet desserts to die for.

Continue southwest to **Loomis,** traversing dry hillsides above the green Sinlahekin Valley. Loomis is another quiet village that boomed during the gold rush of the 1890s and busted soon after. You'd never know from the orchards, old houses, and 1-block-long main street that this was once the largest city in the county. South from Loomis take the primitive but scenic Sinlahekin Road through the **Sinlahekin Wildlife Area** (509-223-3358), the oldest (1939) wildlife area in the state, back to Conconully.

East of Loomis on the Loomis–Oroville Road is narrow Spectacle Lake, rimmed with cattails, dry hills, and remnants of an old wooden irrigation flume. There are several rustic resorts along this roadside lake, but the best one is hidden away to the north on secluded Wannacut Lake. Watch for the sign past spring-fed Spectacle Lake for **Sun Cove Resort and Guest Ranch,** located at 93 East Wannacut Lane (509-476-2223). Or arrive directly from Oroville on a 10-mile, partially graveled road by following signs on Twelfth Avenue west of the Oroville Depot Museum. There are camp sites, log cabins, and larger cottages with splendid lake views, excellent fishing opportunities, wooded grounds that provide plenty of fun activities for both children and adults, including hiking trails, a heated swimming pool, a playground, and sports equipment. The resort is open from April through November.

If you don't take the turnoff to Sun Cove, you can continue straight on the Loomis–Oroville Road past Whitestone Lake and merge right onto the Tonasket–Oroville Westside Road. This less-traveled route traverses the hills west of the Okanogan River, parallel to US 97. During summer, keep an eye out for fresh-fruit stands along the way to refill your picnic hamper with locally grown apples, pears, peaches, cherries, and apricots.

Cross the river to US 97 at *Tonasket;* before heading south toward *Lake Chelan,* pause for refreshments at *Shannon's Ice Cream Parlor & Cafe* at 626 South Whitcomb Avenue (509-486-2259). You'll find many flavors plus tasty sandwiches, soups, salads, and desserts in this welcoming oasis. Or try the Mav Burger at Maverick Bar & Grill, 220 South Whitcomb Avenue (509-486-1411). An option for hearty meals is *Whistler's Restaurant* (509-486-2568) at 616 South Whitcomb Avenue, and also *Tonasket Saloon & Tavie Café,* 302 South Whitcomb Avenue (509-486-2459). Enjoy local artist J.B. Lucas' murals painted on the saloon's walls, some dated 1949.

fruitsandveggies

Washington grows 57 percent of all U.S. cherries, almost 60 percent of the country's apples (including two-thirds of the U.S. organic crop), almost 50 percent of our pears, 91 percent of red raspberries in the United States, and more Concord and Niagara grapes than any other state in the country. It's also the top producer of lentils, dry peas, and hops.

Two lodgings in the lightly populated area to the east and south of Tonasket deserve mentioning: to the east, Canaan Guest Ranch Bed & Barn, between Tonasket and *Republic;* to the south, Eden Valley Guest Ranch. Both are year-round operations with activities that fit snow and sun. The 500-acre Canaan Guest Ranch, 474 Cape LaBelle Road, Tonasket (866-295-4217, www .canaanguestranch.com), sits at 3,500-foot elevation. Bring your horses or ride the ranch's stock; enjoy the beautiful gardens and use the ranch as a base to explore the area. The 900-acre Eden Valley Ranch, 31 Eden Lane, Oroville (509-485-4002; www.edenvalleyranch .net), offers 10 deluxe cabins. It's adjacent to the Okanogan National Forest.

If you are in the area during the winter ski season, the Tonasket District ranger station at 1 West Winesap (509-486-2186; www.fs.fed.us/r6/oka) can provide information about the *Sitzmark Ski Area,* the Highland Cross Country Snow Park, and nearby snowmobile trails.

Mountain Passes, Valleys, and Canyons

If you like being surrounded on three sides by rugged, 8,000-foot-high mountain peaks, dense alpine forests, and miles of hiking trails; don't mind a long boat ride to the end of a 55-mile-long lake that reaches deep into the Lake Chelan Recreation Area and the Sawtooth Wilderness; love the allure of winter moonlight snowshoe treks and staying overnight in rustic tent-cabins or cozy lodge rooms without TVs, telephones, daily newspapers, or Internet access, do we have a destination for you.

Skiing Washington

Individual Web sites offer specific information about downhill runs; the extent of cross-country trail systems; snowboarding areas; snowshoeing; day lodge amenities; directions, weather, snow conditions, Sno-Park fees, and overnight accommodations in the area. For additional information, visit **www.skiwashington.com.**

49 Degrees North Ski Area
42 miles north of Spokane via U.S.
Highway 395
(509) 935-6649
www.ski49n.com

Hurricane Ridge
18 miles south of Port Angeles in Olympic National Park
www.hurricaneridge.net

Loup Loup Ski Area
Between Okanogan and Twisp off Highway 20
(509) 557-3401
www.skitheloup.com

Methow Valley Winter Trail System
North of Wenatchee and near Mazama, Winthrop, and Twisp via
Highways 97, 153, and 20
(509) 996-3287
www.mvsta.com

Mission Ridge
12 miles from Wenatchee
(509) 663-6543
www.missionridge.com

Mount Baker
56 miles east of Bellingham via Highway 542
(360) 734-6771
www.mtbakerskiarea.com

Mount Spokane
23 miles north of Spokane
(509) 238-2220
www.mtspokane.com

Sitzmark
20 miles east of Tonasket off US 97
(509) 485-3323
http://skisitzmark.org

Stevens Pass
between Seattle and Leavenworth via Highway 2
(206) 812-4510
www.stevenspass.com

Summit at Snoqualmie
45 miles east of Seattle via Interstate 90
(425) 434-7669
www.summitatsnoqualmie.com

White Pass
90 miles southeast of Olympia near Mount Rainier National Park via I-5 and Highway 12
(509) 672-3101
www.skiwhitepass.com

It's an extraordinary adventure to **Stehekin** and the scenic Stehekin Valley, one of the most isolated outposts in the state. The good news is that Stehekin also offers a small restaurant (in the lodge), a bakery, mountain-bike rentals, and shuttle van rides up-valley to trailheads. We're talking small, low key and down-home friendly. And it's possible to see the immediate area in a few hours, or stay for a vacation.

Two passenger ferries leave daily from the town of Chelan to the village of Stehekin. The **Lady of the Lake** takes four hours to travel each way with a 1½-hour stopover in Stehekin. The **Lady Express** does the same trip in 2½ hours with an hour stopover. Or go on the *Lady Express* and back on the *Lady of the Lake* and earn a three-hour layover. During the trip, a guide comments on natural history and the wilderness environment. For schedules, contact **Lake Chelan Boat Company** (509-682-4584; www.ladyofthelake .com). Chelan Airways (877-682-5556) offers fast floatplane trips from Chelan to Stehekin as well as a glacier tour and a fly/boat combination.

If you're interested in camping, hiking, and other recreational activities in the Stehekin Valley area, start with www.nps.gov/noca and www.stehekin valley.com. Then call the National Park Service/U.S. Forest Service Visitor Information Center in Stehekin (360-856-5700, extension 340, then extension 14). Rangers can help with trail maps, weather conditions, campgrounds and camping sites, other lodging in Stehekin, equipment lists, guide services, and permits for backcountry excursions. The center is open daily from 8:00 a.m. to 4:30 p.m. from mid-May through mid-October. There is also a National Park Service and **Lake Chelan Recreation Area** information center in Chelan at 428 West Woodin Avenue (509-682-2549). Note: Do not hike into wilderness areas without being fully equipped and fully informed about the areas you plan to explore. See "Ten Essentials for Backcountry Hikers" on page 93.

For a gentler outdoor adventure, try the **Stehekin Valley Ranch** (509-682-4677; www.courtneycountry.com or www.stehekin.biz), open from mid-

Recreation and Picnicking in the Lake Chelan Area

Chelan Falls Park
Picnic area, swimming beach, boat ramp, and docks 5 miles north of Chelan.

Chelan Riverwalk Park
Scenic 1-mile shoreline trail along the Chelan River near downtown.

Lake Chelan Mural Walk
Over a dozen murals in and around the downtown area, each containing an apple in some form. Pick up a mural map from the visitor information center.

Old Mill Park
Picnic sites, boat launch, short-term moorage, and marine wastewater station located in the Manson area, 10 miles up the north lakeshore.

Willow Point
Scenic and quiet lakeside spot near Manson.

June to the last week of September. At the ranch 9 miles up-valley from the boat landing, the Courtney family offers rustic one-room tent-cabins; a few come with electricity and baths. In the open-air dining lodge, guests hunker down at huge log slab tables to enjoy steaming cups of coffee and hearty meals cooked by ranch staff. There are no water views here, but you can arrange for scenic horseback rides and rafting trips.

thehousethat jackbuilt

The House That Jack Built, a small log cabin near the Golden West Visitor Center in Stehekin, is popular with long-distance hikers because of its gear-mending kits and other hiker items and a draw for visitors for its locally made gifts.

Another option is the **North Cascades Stehekin Lodge** (509-682-4494; www.stehekinlanding.com) near the boat landing. The lodge offers a restaurant and a small convenience store. **Silver Bay Inn** at 10 Silver Bay Road (800-555-7781; www.silverbayinn.com) has cozy and self-contained accommodations in the Lake Cabin (sleeps four), the Bay Cabin (sleeps six), the River View Room (sleeps two), and the Lakeview House (comes with two bedrooms, two baths, and a full kitchen). The property offers panoramic views of Lake Chelan and those 8,000-foot-high steep mountains. The inn is close to restaurants, a bakery, and the Stehekin Valley shuttle bus.

Bring sturdy walking shoes and water on the easy 3½-mile hike to **Rainbow Falls** (or take the shuttle bus). Just a short walk from the main road brings you to a good view of 312 feet of cascading water. For a taste of history, explore the old one-room Stehekin School, down the road from the falls, then walk a short distance to the Buckner orchard and their early 1900s homestead. On your return walk, stop at the **Stehekin Bakery** for delicious, fresh-baked treats (open May 15 through October 15). If you can hold off munching everything, carry your snack the 2 miles back to Stehekin and enjoy your pastries

Dammed River

The Columbia River is tamed in the center of the state by the Rocky Reach, Rock Island, Wanapum, and Priest Rapids dams, which create long, narrow reservoirs, generate electricity, and provide irrigation for the Wenatchee Valley region. Like the Okanogan Valley to the north, nearly all available plots of land along the east side of the Columbia River and several smaller valleys to the west toward Cashmere are planted in orchards, making this one of the nation's prime sources of apples, pears, peaches, and apricots. Boating, swimming, fishing, and bicycling are popular during the long, sunny summers; skiing and snowshoeing are popular in winter.

with grand views of the lake at one of the picnic tables on the large deck near the boat landing.

On the populated end of the lake is Chelan. The downtown area is a pleasant place for strolling, shopping, and leisurely eating. Chelan Riverwalk Park offers a shoreline walking trail and a pavilion where outdoor concerts are scheduled during the summer. There are many good eating options in the area, including the historic **Campbell House Cafe** in downtown Chelan at 104 West Woodin Avenue (509-682-2561), which has a full-service dining room on the main floor. But the best place to eat is in the pub on the second floor, which offers outdoor seating on its veranda along with superb views of the lake.

deliciousapples

The world's oldest strain of Delicious apples, a green-and-red-striped one called Common Delicious, grows in the abandoned Buckner Orchard, about 3 miles up the Stehekin Valley. Be prepared to share the orchard with black bears.

For a casual family-style eatery, stop at **Apple Cup Cafe** at 804 East Woodin Avenue (509-682-2933), which serves breakfast all day; for good takeout pizza try **Local Myth Pizza** at 122 South Emerson (509-682-2914); and for giant cinnamon rolls, bagel sandwiches, salads, and specialty espressos, find **Latte Da Coffee Stop Cafe** at 303 East Wapato Avenue (509-682-4196).

In the **Manson** area on Lake Chelan's north shore, a few miles from Chelan, sample Mexican specialties at **El Vaquero Restaurant** at 75 Wapato Way (509-687-3179). If you have a deli picnic planned, follow the signs to scenic **Willow Point Park** near Manson. While city parks can get lively and noisy with kids and families, this small shoreside park offers a quiet alternative and great views of the lake. While in Manson, don't miss Blueberry Hills, a popular U-pick blueberry farm and restaurant featuring from-scratch cooking surrounded by eight acres of blueberries; (509-687-2379; www.wildabout berries.com).

Another popular destination is **Banjo Creek Farms** (509-687-0532; www .banjocreekfarms.com). Activities include wagon rides, a petting zoo, corn maze, and "gold-panning." For a round of golf, check out Bear Mountain Ranch Golf Course (877-917-8200; www.bearmt.com), voted one of the six favorite new courses in the country by PGA Professionals, or call for tee times at the scenic **Lake Chelan Municipal Golf Course** (800-246-5361; www.lake chelangolf.com).

For a side trip, head south on US 97 east on U.S. Highway 2, about 28 miles south of Chelan to **Waterville.** The Douglas County seat since 1887, its cattle-based economy changed in the course of the terrible winter of 1889–90,

Eating the Slow Foods Way

Many Washington inns, B&Bs, and restaurants are embracing the Slow Foods movement that originated in 1989 in Italy by Carlo Petrini, who recognized that the industrialization of food was standardizing and limiting options and tastes while eliminating varieties. The supporters appreciate the concept of leisurely dining with family and friends, sustainable agriculture, experimenting with new foods and flavor, eating locally produced food, protecting the environment from chemicals by eating organic, and recognizing the cost of importing food hundreds or thousands of miles. A combination of positive steps can help create good, clean, and fair (field workers should be adequately compensated) food. The Slow Food movement also includes wines and meat. Yakima-area hosts speak of visitors coming from Portland and Seattle to enjoy the ambience and community-supported agriculture; there are about a dozen Slow Food USA chapters in Washington state.

when temperatures were subzero and snow drifts continued into April. The cattle industry was essentially wiped out, and farmers turned to wheat.

Waterville's **Douglas County Historical Museum** on US 2 has interesting displays, including an extensive rock collection. But its main claim to fame is the state's first recovered meteorite, found by a farmer and weighing 82 pounds. In front of the museum rests a large metal bucket, once part of an overhead conveyor system that in the early 1900s carried wheat 2,400 feet down to the river, where it was loaded onto grain barges. The museum also has a two-headed calf and a horse mannequin that was used to model saddles and bridles.

Waterville is a pleasant community with many old houses and a fine county courthouse. Directly across from the museum at 102 East Park Street, the 1903 **Waterville Historic Hotel** (888-509-8180; www.watervillehotel .com) has been restored by owner Dave Lundgren. One large suite and ten comfortable rooms (some with private baths and claw-footed tubs) are now available. Some of the original oak and leather Mission-style furnishings are on the main floor in the cozy lobby and tearoom area, where a light continental breakfast is served. Ask about the Nifty Vaudeville Theater, which occasionally screens old movies.

From Chelan, head south to **Wenatchee** on U.S. Highway 97A on the west side of the Columbia River. Tan-colored hills looming on your right (west) are now clothed in sagebrush, bitterbrush, and aromatic juniper. But across the river to the east, you see compact orchards that are lush and green from irrigation. Detour at **Rocky Reach Dam** (509-663-7522; www.chelanpud.org) and enjoy a rest stop and perhaps an impromptu picnic amid a splendid perennial garden, hanging baskets of summer flowers, and a children's playground. With camera in hand, climb the steps to the top of the children's slide and snap a picture of the large floral U.S. flag in the Old Glory Garden, planted in red, white, and blue annuals. More than 5,000 annuals bloom on Petunia Island surrounding the fish ladders. Take a tour of the dam, check out the visitor center, and watch migrating fish through a viewing glass.

Just prior to reaching Wenatchee, look for the sign to **Ohme Gardens** and detour to 3327 Ohme Road (509-662-5785; www.ohmegardens.com) to

sky high

The sunny oasis of Waterville, where grain fields have replaced sage brush and cattle, claims the distinction of being the town with the highest altitude in the state: 2,622 feet above sea level.

visit this lush and cool alpine wonderland. Herman and Ruth Ohme started to develop the family gardens on their barren hilltop 600 feet above the Columbia River in 1929. Ten years later, friends and community members urged the Ohmes to allow public visits to their splendid creation. Travelers still flock to this nine-acre alpine garden atop the bluff that allows wide views of the Columbia River, Cascade Mountains, and **Wenatchee Valley.** Irregular stepping stones and narrow flagstone pathways meander up, down, and around shaded fern-lined pools, next to large ponds, and around immense boulders. You'll see many varieties of sedum along with creeping thyme, creeping phlox, alyssum, and dianthus. Tall western red cedar, mountain hemlock, grand fir, Douglas fir, and alpine fir grow around the garden's perimeter. The garden is open from April 15 to October 15, 9:00 a.m. to 6:00 p.m. There's a nominal admission fee.

For other activities, stop by the Wenatchee Valley Visitor Center at 25 North Wenatchee Avenue (800-572-7753; www.wenatcheevalley.org). A pleasant overnight option is **Apple Country Bed & Breakfast** at 524 Okanogan Avenue (509-664-0400; www.applecountryinn.com). Innkeepers Jerry and Sandi Anderson welcome guests to their 1920 Craftsman-style home with its deep and inviting porch. Guest rooms in the main house are named for the apples that grow in the valley—Gala, Fuji, Red Delicious, Golden Delicious, and Cameo. A separate carriage house is a cozy and private haven. About 4 miles from downtown and toward Mission Ridge Ski Area is the **Rimrock Inn Bed & Breakfast** at 1354 Pitcher Canyon Road, where Judy Rector welcomes guests to three spacious guest rooms (888-664-5113; www.rimrockinn.com).

For good eats in the Wenatchee area, try **Jeepers It's Bagels Cafe** at 619 South Mission Street (509-663-4594) in the Victorian Village; the **Cellar Cafe** in a vintage house at 249 North Mission Street (509-662-1722); **Lemolo Cafe & Deli,** 114 North Wenatchee Avenue (509-664-6576); **McGlinn's Public House** at 111 Orondo Street (509-663-9073) for pastas, gourmet pizza, homemade desserts, and live jazz; **Mission Street Bistro,** 202 North Mission (509-665-2406); and the **Windmill** at 1501 North Wenatchee Avenue (509-665-9529) for legendary steaks and freshly baked pies to die for.

Walk off the calories on a scenic section of the 11-mile **Apple Capital Recreation Loop Trail** that skirts the Columbia River. Find parking and trail access at Riverfront Park at the end of Fifth Street in downtown Wenatchee or at Walla Walla Park off Walla Walla Avenue at the north end of town. The path is wheelchair accessible.

As you head west on US 2 from Wenatchee toward Leavenworth, detour first at the small town of **Cashmere** to tour the Liberty Orchards' **Aplest & Cotlets Candy Factory,** located at 117 Mission Avenue (509-782-4088, extension 1). The tour includes samples of the delicious fruit and nut confections. If time allows plan an hour or so to tour Cashmere's **Pioneer Village and Museum,** located at 600 Cotlets Avenue (509-782-3230; www.cashmere museum.org; there is a nominal admission fee). Volunteers in pioneer dress encourage you and the kids to snoop into some twenty pioneer structures dating from the 1800s that are outfitted with vintage furniture, linens, dishes, kitchenware, clothing, and accessories of those earlier times. Browse the well-stocked wine and gift shop, which offers a selection of wines from Wenatchee Valley wineries. For a bite to eat in Cashmere, try **Walnut Cafe,** 106 Cottage Avenue (509-782-2022), open Wednesday through Sunday.

In the 1960s **Leavenworth** was a worn-out 1920s-style railroad and lumber town. Now, with years of revitalization by enthusiastic townsfolk, Leavenworth is a vibrant Bavarian-style village with a bit of Austria and Switzerland thrown in for good measure. It sits at the edge of the central Washington Cascades in the Icicle River Valley, where the towering mountains look very much like the Alps. The compact village is a good place for walking. Carved window boxes and hanging baskets spill over with bright flowers and greenery; shop signs are hand-painted in old Germanic script; building exteriors show gingerbread detailing and rich carving; and tiers of second- and third-floor exterior decks and dormers are also done in the carved and richly appointed Bavarian style.

apletsandcotlets

The top-selling concoction of Liberty Orchards in Cashmere has been a hit since 1920. Think crisp Washington apples, ripe apricots, and crunchy English walnuts and a secret family recipe. Take a tour of the candy kitchens.

Enjoy strolling and poking into shops like **Die Musik Box** at 933 Front Street (509-548-6152), where you'll find more than 5,000 music boxes from around the world; and **Der Sportsmann** at 837 Front Street (509-548-5623) for clothing related to hiking, biking, fishing, climbing, and skiing as well as bike rental and ski rental/repair. For those with a sweet tooth, try the **Rocky Mountain Chocolate Factory** at 636 Front Street (509-548-6525); Schocolat, at 843 Front Street (509-548-7274), makes handmade European-style chocolates; the Fudge Hut at 933 Front Street (509-548-0466) offers thirty-five varieties of fudge; or **Sweet Dreams** at 220 Ninth Street (509-548-5144) for chocolates from Switzerland and Howard Miller grandfather clocks. Try **Cheesemonger's Shop** at 819 Front Street (509-548-9011) for international cheeses, beer, and sausages. Visit the Feathered Nest, 715 Front Street (509-548-2064) or Alpen Haus Gifts, 807 Front Street (509-548-7122). The **Cuckoo Clock** at 725 Front Street has a large selection of cuckoo and other kinds of clocks.

After all this ogling and shopping, you'll be ready to enjoy coffee and a great meal. Your alpine-influenced choices include **Andreas Keller,** downstairs at 829 Front Street (509-548-6000), for rotisserie-cooked chicken, German potato salad, sausages, sauerkraut, beer, and wine; Munchen Haus, 709 Front Street (509-548-1158), an authentic Bavarian grill and beer garden; King Ludwig's (509-548-6625), famous for pork hocks; Café Mozart, 829 Front Street (509-548-0600), offering fine European dining; and Café Christa, 801 Front Street (509-548-5074) for authentic Central European cuisine.

christmas
traditions

Don't miss **Leavenworth Nutcracker Museum,** 735 Front Street (509-548-4708; www.nutcrackermuseum.com), which has one of the largest collections of old nutcrackers in the world and is the only nutcracker museum in the United States.

There are more than 1,175 rooms available in and around Leavenworth, including motels, bed and breakfasts, condos, and cabins. They handle up to thousands of tourists at one time, some arriving by the busload. Visit www.leavenworth.org for a complete listing. Consider these hospitable inns: The only one with a 24-foot-tall knight in shining armor outside is Der Riotterhof (190 US 2; 800-255-5845); **Enzian Inn** (590 US 2, 800-223-8511) offers European-style Old World ambience; and **Bosch Garten Bed & Breakfast** at 9846 Dye Road (800-535-0069) offers three guest rooms, a well-stocked library, and a hot tub in an enclosed Japanese teahouse in the garden.

One of our favorites, **Run of the River Inn and Refuge,** is a log cabin–style inn located at 9308 East Leavenworth Road (800-288-6491). It has elegant amenities in six guest rooms with fireplaces, sitting areas, whirlpool tubs, decks overlooking the Icicle River, and heavenly breakfasts in the great

room. ***Pine River Ranch,*** located at 19668 Highway 207 (800-669-3877; www
.prranch.com) and close to ***Lake Wenatchee,*** has suites with river-rock fireplaces, whirlpool tubs, and gourmet breakfasts.

Into fine wines? If so, hit the tasting rooms downtown before traveling to
Eagle Creek Winery, 10037 Eagle Creek Road (509-548-7668); ***La Toscana
Winery*** located 6 miles east of Leavenworth and open by appointment (509-
548-5448); ***Icicle Ridge Winery,*** 8977 North Road in nearby Peshastin (509-
548-7851); Wedge Mountain Winery (509-548-7068), also in Peshastin; Berghof
Keller Winery, 11695 Duncan Road (509-548-5605); and Cascadia Winery,
10090 Main Street, Peshastin (509-548-7900).

The Wellington Disaster

A half-mile-wide avalanche roared down Windy Mountain near Stevens Pass, moving
everything in its path, including two Great Northern trains.

"It seemed as if the world were coming to an end," one railroad worker was quoted.

At 1:42 a.m. on March 1, 1910, it became the worst natural disaster in terms of the
greatest number of deaths—96—in Washington State history and one of the worst
train disasters in U.S. history.

The two trains were heading for Puget Sound, a combination of several steam and
electric engines, passenger cars, sleepers, and boxcars. But they were stopped at
the west end of the Cascade Tunnel due to slides and waited near the tiny railroad
town of Wellington for six days while a blizzard dumped snow on the tracks and avalanches added more.

The late winter storm had dropped several feet of snow on top of an unstable snow-
pack, so huge avalanches were likely.

The first warning was a crescendo of sounds "that might have been the crashing of
ten thousand freight trains," one witness said.

Tons of railroad engines and cars and cabins disappeared down the mountain, some
disintegrating, others crushed. Sleeping men and women were taken for a ride and then
buried under up to 40 feet of snow; many were dug out alive. The snow turned red.

Bodies of the dead, including 35 passengers, came down the west side of the
Cascades in toboggan-style sleds and a rope-and-pulley system over the next few
months; their route was called Dead Man's Slide.

Three weeks later, track repair was finished and trains could cross Stevens Pass. But
the town of Wellington was so linked to the disaster that residents changed the name
to Tye.

Three years later, the Great Northern completed snow sheds over 9 miles of track
between Tye and Scenic; later a new tunnel was built. The Iron Goat Trail is now on
the old grade.

Leavenworth is the city of festivals. January brings Icefest and Nordic ski events. Springtime blossoms with the **Leavenworth Spring Bird Festival** and traditional German Maifest. Choose from the **International Accordion Festival,** Leavenworth Wine Walk, or the children's Kinderfest, plus numerous productions by Icicle Creek Music Center, and the Leavenworth Summer Theater production of *The Sound of Music*, which is outdoors with the Enchantments as a backdrop. In the fall, festivals include Wenatchee River Salmon Festival, Washington State Autumn Leaf Festival, and Oktoberfest. Thanksgiving weekend features the traditional German Christkindlmarkt, and December brings three weekends of the award-winning Lighting Festival.

The outdoor recreation opportunities are endless in this area, with some of the best white-water rafting in the state, plus kayaking, canoeing, miles of incredibly scenic hiking trails, rock climbing, and hay wagon horse rides. For additional information about the area, contact the Leavenworth Visitor Information Center at (509) 548-5807.

In Everett, tour the world's largest building

If Everett is your destination, put the Future of Flight Aviation Center and the Boeing Company tour on your list. Everett, about 25 miles north of Seattle, is home to the world's largest building by volume, Boeing's 472-million-cubic-foot jet-assembly plant at 8415 Paine Field Boulevard (888-467-4777). It covers 98 acres and has six doors each 300 to 350 feet long and 82 feet high. One door has the world's largest digital graphic.

You'll feel very small in this space that houses airplanes in various stages of complex testing and manufacturing for customers around the world. The 90-minute tour tickets are a hot item, so reservations are recommended although non-reserved same-day tickets are on sale at 8:30 a.m. until all tickets are gone. Children must be 48 inches (122 cm) tall to join the tour. No personal items are allowed on the tour.

The excellent Future of Flight Aviation Center and the tour are available from 8:30 a.m. to 5:00 p.m. daily (last tour at 3:00 p.m.) except for Thanksgiving, Christmas, and New Year's Day. The recently built aviation center has exhibits, videos, graphics, and interactive stations that involve the whole family. Look up and see the futuristic-looking aircraft overhead and down at the 200-foot-long runway painted on the floor of the gallery that ends in the nose section of Boeing 727. Digitally design and test your own jet, ride the XJ5 flight simulator, try out the next generation of in-flight entertainment systems, and touch the high-tech skin of the new Boeing 787 Dreamliner.

US 2 west up to **Stevens Pass** is spectacular, with colorful fall foliage and scenic views but not nearly as dramatic as it must have been for travelers in the late nineteenth century, when the first railroad line crossed the Cascade Mountains here. The original route included 13 miles of switchbacks cut into the mountainside that required the train to stop on spur tracks, change the track switch, then reverse up the next leg. Folks now drive the mountainous route with ease.

For another Cascades summertime adventure, detour west across Stevens Pass and walk at least part of the **Iron Goat Trail** (www.irongoat.org), built by volunteers on the old Great Northern railroad bed. From US 2 at milepost 55, 9 miles west of Stevens Pass summit, follow the signs to Martin Creek trailhead and parking area. For great mountain views, waves of blooming wild-flowers, and interpretive signs, do the 3-mile round-trip hike along the lower grade to the Twin Tunnels and back. The trail is wheelchair accessible. From here continue west on US 2 through the small towns of Skykomish (there's a Forest Service ranger station on the highway), Index, Gold Bar, and Startup toward Snohomish and Everett to the west.

Back east of the mountains and heading south from Leavenworth, US 97 takes you through the southeastern section of the Wenatchee National Forest and toward **Cle Elum,** Roslyn, **Thorp,** and **Ellensburg.** The route over Swauk Pass is scenic enough, but for a special treat take the old winding highway over **Bluest Pass.** Except for occasional logging trucks, you're likely to have the road to yourself. It's also a popular route with bicyclists. For an alternate adventure take Liberty Road 2 miles east from US 97 to the town of **Liberty,** the oldest mining town site in Washington State.

The Kittitas Valley pushes into the eastern slope of the Cascade Mountains in the center of the state, and here you'll find the old coal-mining town of **Roslyn,** which has settled back into relative quiet after its starring role in the mid-1980s as Cicely, Alaska, on the *Northern Exposure* television series. The entire town is on the National Register of Historic Places. Stop by the Roslyn Café at 201 West Pennsylvania (509-649-2763).

lumpofcoal

Roslyn was so fiercely proud of its mining prowess that it shipped a twenty-two-ton lump of coal to the 1893 Chicago World's Fair as an exhibit.

Nearby, in the small community of **South Cle Elum,** railroad buffs will enjoy a pilgrimage to **Iron Horse Inn Bed and Breakfast** at 526 Marie Avenue (800-228-9246). The renovated railroad workers' bunkhouse offers cozy rooms, and on the grounds four comfortable cabooses are cozy accommodations,

Iron Horse Inn Bed and Breakfast

including the 1928 wood-sided caboose that sleeps two. Railroad memorabilia at this pleasant inn include tools, switch lights, toy trains, and conductors' uniforms. A major renovation of the 1908 Milwaukee Rail Depot and grounds located behind the inn has opened the 12-acre railyard to the public, including a path through the yard, a café, and a museum. For more information, go to www.milwelectric.org.

Iron Horse Trail State Park on I-90, with a 25-mile section of the *John Wayne Pioneer Trail,* runs adjacent to the inn. Ride mountain bikes, enjoy pleasant riverside walks, or try cross-country skiing. In nearby Cle Elum visit the 1914 Craftsman-style *Carpenter House Museum* at 301 West Third (509-674-9766), open weekends from noon to 4:00 p.m. Ask about the *Telephone Museum* at 221 East First Street (509-674-5702), and the *Roslyn Historic Mining Museum* at 203 Pennsylvania Avenue in nearby Roslyn (509-964-9640). Cle Elum was one of the last towns in the United States to use manual switchboards, and is the oldest complete telephone museum west of the Mississippi. For more information, go to www.nkc museums.org.

Find good Italian fare at *Mama Vallone's Pasta & Steak House* at 302 West First Street (509-674-5174) and an extensive specialty menu at *Spacone's* at 212 West Railroad Street (509-674-9609), both located in Cle Elum's small downtown area. Two new eateries to check out include *Diamondback's Restaurant* at 200 East First Street (509-674-9669) and *Pioneer Coffee Roasting Company* and café at 121 Pennsylvania Street (509-674-3864).

For a bit of history, turn off I-90 at the Thorp exit (milepost 101), then travel west 3 miles through the village of Thorp, past the schools, to the *Thorp Gristmill.* The mill operated from 1883 until 1946, initially powered by a waterwheel. Local citizens have worked to preserve all three stories of the sprawling structure and its fifteen antique machines. The mill is open for tours on weekends from Memorial Day weekend to the end of September and by appointment the rest of the year. Call (509) 964-9640 before you go.

The city of Ellensburg's downtown historic district is ideal for strolling. Contact the Ellensburg Visitor Information Center (888-925-2204; www.ellens burg-chamber.com) for a walking-tour guide. You'll discover more than two dozen ornate brick buildings constructed between the 1880s and 1910, most of which have been renovated and now house small businesses and shops. The **Clymer Museum of Art,** in the 1901 Ramsey Building at 416 North Pearl Street (509-962-6416; www.clymermuseum.com), highlights the Western wild-life work of artist John Clymer. You'll also see fanciful public art along the streets, including a life-size bronze bull relaxing on a downtown bench located at the Rotary Pavilion.

The **Chimpanzee and Human Communication Institute** offers semi-nars called **Chimposiums** at its pleasant facility on the campus of Central Washington University. The one-hour, educational workshops explore scien-tists' personal observations of chimps that communicate using American sign language, as well as discuss chimpanzee culture and conversations. Tuition is $10.00 for adults and $7.50 for students. The workshops are offered Saturday morning and Sunday afternoon. Call 509-963-2244 for reservations that are strongly recommended.

Within walking distance of historic downtown and the campus, travel-ers can enjoy warm and hospitable accommodations at **Wren's Nest Bed & Breakfast** at 300 East Manitoba Avenue (509-925-9061; www.wrensnest .com). Guest rooms have antique beds, sumptuous coverlets, and fresh flowers from the inn's perennial gardens. Rich wood floors and woodwork remain in the 1912 Craftsman-style home. Other welcoming inns in the Ellensburg area include **Westside Loft** at 4500 Hanson Road (888-543-6777) with skylights and cozy built-in beds; and **4W Ranch & Guest Cabins** at 11670 Manastash Road (866-497-2624; www.4ranch.net), tucked away in Manastash Canyon. The Victorian Guest House Ellensburg at 606 North Main Street (509-962-3706; www.guesthouseellensburg.com) offers a delightful stay above Ellensburg Wine Works.

Dining in Ellensburg could include the **Dakota Cafe** at 319 North Pearl Street (509-925-4783); **Pearl's on Pearl** at 311 North Pearl Street (509-962-8899); **Valley Cafe** at 105 West Third Avenue (509-925-3050); and **Yellow Church Cafe** at 111 South Pearl Street (509-933-2233). For pastries, coffee, espresso, and fresh-roasted beans, stop at **D&M Coffee Cafe,** 301 North Pine Street (509-962-6333). For classic hamburgers with names such as Rumble Seat and Dead Man's Curve, and vintage gasoline-pump memorabilia, stop by *Red Horse Diner,* 1518 W. University Way (509-925-1956).

Then plan a brisk walk or bike ride on a section of the John Wayne Pioneer Trail (Iron Horse State Park; www.parks.wa.gov/activities), which follows the former roadbed of the Chicago–Milwaukee–St. Paul Pacific Railroad two-thirds of the way across the state. From downtown Ellensburg, access the lightly graveled trail on North Water Street or just off University Way near the Kittitas County Fairgrounds. The old road between Ellensburg and Yakima, Highway 821, follows the scenic *Lower Yakima River Canyon* for approximately 25 miles. The drive offers outstanding views of the wide valley nestled between sheer basalt cliffs and the river. Raptors and songbirds live in the canyon, as well as herds of bighorn sheep. The river is famous among anglers as a catch-and-release trout stream.

The Vantage Highway from Ellensburg east to the Columbia River is a great alternative route that misses the traffic of I-90 and offers views of rich farmlands that give way to rolling sagebrush meadows. The highway passes by the *Quilomene Wildlife Area,* a 45,000-acre preserve popular with hunters. Watch for signs of the Ginkgo-Wanapum State Park (509-856-2700; www.parks.wa.gov) as you descend toward the Columbia River. Formerly the Ginkgo Petrified Forest State Park, it has two short trails highlighting exposed "trees of stone." Fifteen to twenty million years ago this land was covered with tropical swamps and thick forests. When layers of lava from volcanic eruptions covered the area, many logs that had sunk to the bottom of shallow lakes were entombed and eventually turned to stone, after minerals replaced organic materials.

The park also has rock carvings of early peoples dated from 200 to 10,000 years old at the interpretive center (call 509-856-2700) for days and hours. The center features more than 200 petrified wood displays as well as a twelve-minute film that tells the petrification story.

Picking up I-90 east, cross the Columbia, turn left and drive for a few miles and a surprise. Look right and up to see fifteen life-sized metal horses run free on a desert hilltop. Chewelah sculptor Dave Govedare's *Grandfather Cuts Loose the Ponies* symbolically re-creates the Great Spirit giving the land its first horses. Govedare wants to add a 36-foot diameter metal basket with symbols of sky, land, water, and the human spirit. Park in the rest area. You can scramble up the hill to the horses but be mindful of the rattlesnakes and keep your children close at hand.

Reverse directions and head south to where you crossed the Columbia but keep going on the east side of the river, picking up Highway 243 to the *Wanapum Dam Visitors Center,* which is open April through October. The center offers a detailed description of the people who inhabited the region for thousands of years and explains the impact of European culture on this population. The dam flooded the tribe's historic village site and ended their traditional livelihood of salmon fishing. From here you can head south on US 97 to explore Yakima and the Yakima Valley, then continue south to the scenic Columbia River Gorge. Or, you could head east on I-90 toward Spokane and the Palouse region.

Places to Stay in North Central Washington

CHELAN

Best Western Lakeside Motor Lodge
2312 West Woodin Avenue
(800) 468-2781

Chelan House Bed & Breakfast
311 South First Street
(509) 888-4000

Wild Rose Bed & Breakfast
427 South Third Street
(509) 682-2974

CLE ELUM

Iron Horse Inn Bed and Breakfast
526 Marie Street
(800) 228-9246

CONCONULLY

Shady Pines Cabins, RV Park
125 West Fort Salmon Creek Road
(800) 552-2287

CONCRETE

Cascade Mountain Lodge
44618 Highway 20
(360) 853-8870

Ovenell's Heritage Inn and Log Cabins
46276 Concrete–Sauk Valley Road
(888) 464-3414

ELLENSBURG

Wren's Nest Bed & Breakfast
300 East Manitoba Avenue
(509) 925-9061

LEAVENWORTH

Icicle River RV Resort
7305 Icicle Road
(509) 548-5420

Pine River Ranch Bed and Breakfast
19668 Highway 207
(800) 669-3877

Run of the River Inn and Refuge
9308 East Leavenworth Road
(800) 288-6491

MAZAMA

Mazama Country Inn
42 Lost River Road
(509) 996-2681

PATEROS

Lake Pateros Motor Inn
115 Lake Shore Drive
(886) 444-1985

ROCKPORT

Ross Lake Resort
503 Diablo Street
(206) 386-4437

Skagit River Resort and Clarks Eatery
58468 Clark Cabin Road
(360) 873-2250

ROSLYN

Huckleberry House Bed & Breakfast
301 West Pennsylvania Avenue
(509) 649-2900

STEHEKIN

North Cascades Stehekin Lodge
(509) 682-4494

TONASKET

Bonaparte Lake Resort
695 Bonaparte Lake Road
(509) 486-2828

TWISP

Riverbend RV Park
19961 Highway 20
(800) 686-4498

SELECTED INFORMATION CENTERS AND OTHER HELPFUL WEB SITES

Cascade Loop Association
(509) 662-3888
www.cascadeloop.com

Chelan and Lake Chelan
(800) 424-3526
www.lakechelan.com
www.cascadeloop.com

Ellensburg
(888) 925-2204
www.ellensburg-chamber.com

Leavenworth
(509) 548-5807
www.leavenworth.com

Mount Baker-Snoqualmie National Forest
www.fs.fed.us/r6/mbs

North Cascades National Park
810 Highway 20, Sedro-Woolley
(360) 856-5700
www.nps.gov/noca

Okanogan Country
(888) 431-3080
www.okanogancountry.com
www.fs.fed.us/r6/oka

Outdoor Recreation Information at REI, Seattle
(206) 470-4060

Road Reports
www.wsdot.wa.gov

Wenatchee Valley
(800) 572-7753
www.wenatcheevalley.org

Winthrop-Twisp
(888) 463-8469
www.winthropwashington.com

WATERVILLE

Waterville Historic Hotel
102 East Park Street
(888) 509-8180

WENATCHEE

Apple Country Bed & Breakfast
524 Okanogan Avenue
(509) 664-0400

La Quinta Inn
1905 North Wenatchee Avenue
(800) 531-5900

Rimrock Inn Bed & Breakfast
1354 Pitcher Canyon Road
(888) 664-5113

WINTHROP

River Run Inn & Cabins
27 Rader Road
(800) 757-2709

WolfRidge Resort
412 Wolf Creek Road
(509) 996-2828

Places to Eat in North Central Washington

CHELAN

Apple Cup Cafe
804 East Woodin
(509) 682-2933

Campbell House Restaurant
104 West Woodin
(509) 682-2561

Latte Da Coffee Stop Café
303 East Wapato Avenue
(509) 682-4196

Riverwalk Books & Open Book Espresso
116 East Woodin
(509) 682-8901

CLE ELUM

Cle Elum Bakery
501 East First Street
(509) 674-2233

Pioneer Coffee Roasting Company Cafe
121 Pennsylvania Street
(509) 674-3864

CONCRETE

Perks Espresso
44586 Highway 20
(360) 853-9006

The Cajun Bar & Grill
Main and Baker Streets
(360) 853-8518

ELLENSBURG

D&M Coffee Cafe
301 North Pine Street
(509) 962-6333

Dakota Café
319 North Pearl Street
(509) 925-4783

Red Horse Diner
1518 West University Way
(509) 925-1956

LEAVENWORTH

Home Fires Bakery
11007 Highway 2
(509) 548-7362

O'Grady's Pantry
Sleeping Lady Conference Center
7375 Icicle Road
(800) 574-2123

MARBLEMOUNT

Buffalo Run Café
60084 Highway 20
(360) 873-2461

MAZAMA

Mazama Country Store & Deli
50 Lost River Road
(509) 996-2855

OMAK

The Breadline Cafe
102 South Ash Street
(509) 826-5836

OROVILLE

Fat Boy's Diner
1518 Main Street
(509) 476-4100

Trino's Mexican Restaurant
1918 Main Street
(509) 476-9151

ROSLYN

Roslyn Cafe
201 West Pennsylvania Avenue
(509) 649-2763

TONASKET

Shannon's Cafe & Ice Cream Parlor
626 South Whitcomb
(509) 486-2259

TWISP

BJ's Branding Iron Restaurant & Saloon
123 North Glover Street
(509) 997-3576

Cinnamon Twisp Bakery
116 North Glover Street
(509) 997-5030

Twisp River Brew Pub
201 North Highway 20
(509) 997-6822

ALSO WORTH SEEING

Audubon Center and Upper Valley Museum
Leavenworth
(509) 548-5807

Lake Chelan area wineries
Chelan
(800) 424-3526

Olmstead Place State Park Heritage Area and Gardens
Ellensburg
(509) 925-1943

Wenatchee Valley Museum
Wenatchee
(509) 888-6240

WAUCONDA

The Wauconda Store and Cafe
2432 Highway 20
(509) 486-4010

WENATCHEE

Cottage Inn Steak House
134 Easy Street
(509) 663-4435

Jeepers It's Bagels Cafe
619 South Mission Street
(509) 663-4594

McGlinn's Public House
111 Orondo Street
(509) 663-9073

WINTHROP

Heenan's Burnt Finger Bar-B-Q Steakhouse and Rattlesnake Saloon
716 Highway 20 South
(509) 996-8221

Winthrop Brewing Company & Pub
155 Riverside Avenue
(509) 996-3183

South Central Washington

The south-central section of Washington State offers opportunities from apple picking to windsurfing, from two snowcapped mountains each over 8,000 feet high to waterfalls that drop from basalt ledges with one narrow ribbon of water falling hundreds of feet. On the high plateau above the Yakima River, farmers tend vast orchards of apples, apricots, peaches, and cherries; vintners work hundreds of acres of grapes that will make pinot noir, chardonnay, and Riesling wines. Washington State shares the awesome scenery of the Columbia River Gorge with its southern neighbor, Oregon. Snowy **Mount St. Helens,** now about 8,000 feet high (it was 9,677 feet above sea level prior to the eruption of May 18, 1980), and **Mount Adams,** at 12,307 feet high, guard the Washington side. The watery border extends roughly 300 miles from the eastern end of the gorge at the Tri-Cities (Kennewick, **Pasco,** and Richland) to the Pacific Ocean at the Long Beach Peninsula.

Once the river roared through the gorge, making some sections impassable by canoe or raft. Now dams cross the Columbia, smoothing out the once-swift waters once navigated by Indian tribes and the first French and American trappers, British Hudson's Bay Company explorers, American explorers

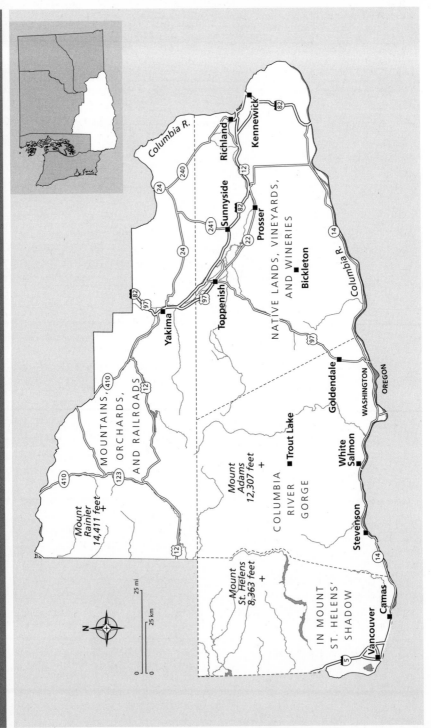

SOUTH CENTRAL WASHINGTON

and road surveyors, and the pioneers who traveled west on the Oregon Trail.

One of those early groups of explorers sent by the U.S. government, the *Lewis and Clark Corps of Discovery,* trekked along the north side of the Columbia River in the fall of 1805, reaching the Pacific Ocean around November 15.

Let's start at the 366-acre *Fort Vancouver National Historic Site,* operated by the National Park Service just east of Vancouver's downtown area. Stroll through the informative museum and visitor information area at the upper section of the complex, then walk down the grassy lawn area or drive down to the large parking area, to find the fort and the fully restored *Fort Vancouver British Gardens.* In the 1840s grapevines trailed over greenhouses for shade and the garden yielded such produce as Thomas Laxton peas, English broad beans, and yellow pear tomatoes. The flower garden section contains a walk-through arbor of hop vines, large clumps of scented lavender, old-fashioned climbing roses, and vintage perennials in large beds.

A small admission fee allows entrance to the restored fort inside the re-created stockade walls. Watch living-history vignettes in the trading house,

SOUTH CENTRAL WASHINGTON'S TOP HITS

Central Washington Agricultural Museum
Union Gap

Columbia Gorge Interpretive Center
Stevenson

Conboy Lake National Wildlife Refuge
Glenwood

Fort Simcoe State Park Heritage Site
White Swan

Fort Vancouver National Historic Site
Vancouver

Goldendale Observatory State Park
Goldendale

Hulda Klager Lilac Gardens
Woodland

Liberty Theatre
Toppenish

Maryhill Museum of Art
Goldendale

Mount St. Helens National Volcanic Monument
Castle Rock

North Front Street Historic District
Yakima

Pomeroy House Living History Farm
Yacolt

Sacajawea State Park
Kennewick

Yakama Nation Museum and Cultural Heritage Center
Toppenish

Yakima Valley Rail and Steam Museum
Toppenish

Lewis and Clark Expedition

Early in the nation's history, President Thomas Jefferson dispatched a corps of men for a discovery expedition (1804-1806) to the Pacific Ocean. It is said that Jefferson made the right choice in selecting Meriwether Lewis and William Clark to lead the expedition. Jefferson felt the two men, although different in their personalities, possessed qualities important for exploring uncharted wilderness: youth, intelligence, resourcefulness, courage, and a sense of adventure. Both men were experienced woodsmen and frontiersmen as well as seasoned army officers. The party of thirty-three explorers traveled more than 8,000 miles on foot, horseback, and dugout canoe in two years, four months, and ten days.

Where it may take today's travelers a day to leisurely drive from the Tri-Cities of Kennewick, Pasco, and Richland to the Pacific Ocean, it took Lewis and Clark one month to cover this leg of their journey. At *Sacajawea State Park,* near Kennewick, visit an interpretive center devoted to the expedition and the role of Sacajawea, the Shoshone Indian woman who served as their guide and interpreter. Interpretive material (along with panoramic views of the gorge and river also can be seen at *Hat Rock State Park* near Umatilla; Horsethief Lake State Park near The Dalles; the Columbia Gorge Interpretive Center near Stevenson; Beacon Rock State Park, west of Stevenson; and *Lewis and Clark State Park* at Ilwaco.

blacksmith shop, bakery cabin, and kitchen; staff and volunteers in period dress offer an authentic look at life in the early 1800s. Both early settlers and members of local tribes often visited the fort to socialize and trade for tobacco, candles, beads, blankets, and cotton cloth as well as vegetables, grains, and other supplies. Dr. John McLoughlin, the fort's chief factor for many years, lived in the large house that stands next to the kitchen. Visitors can tour the house, which contains furnishings and memorabilia from the McLoughlin family's time. Fort Vancouver is located at 612 East Reserve Street; for information, call (360) 816-6230. Visit the fort and its living history programs daily from 9:00 a.m. to 5:00 p.m.

You'll notice *Officer's Row,* the stately Victorian-style homes that sit in a tidy row along the boulevard just north of Fort Vancouver. These functioned as housing for military officers during World War II. The lovely houses are now preserved and open to the public during part of the year. Watch Vancouver's Heritage Players reenact tales from the past, including ghost stories around Halloween, in several of the parlors and on several of the wide verandahs. If time allows, call for lunch or dinner reservations at the *Restaurant at the Historic Reserve* (360-906-1101) located in the 1849 Grant House. For more information about the theatrical events and other public events on Officer's Row during the year, call (360) 992-1800, or check www.vnhrt.org.

Vintage-airplane buffs can also visit the ***Pearson Air Museum,*** just east of Fort Vancouver at 1115 East Fifth Street (360-694-7026; www.pearsonair museum.org). Located at the 1905 Pearson Field, the oldest continuously operating airfield on the West Coast, the museum is housed in the Jack Murdock Aviation Center. The center also includes the second oldest wooden hanger in the United States, a theater that shows full-length classic aviation-themed films, a hands-on activity center for children, and a vintage airplane-restoration section. It offers a fascinating history that dates to World War II. The grounds are open from 10:00 a.m. to 5:00 p.m. Wednesday through Saturday. There is an admission fee.

Visit nearby ***Esther Short Park,*** located off Washington Street between Sixth and Eighth Streets, which offers colorful plantings of roses, azaleas, and rhododendrons. At the southeast corner the handsome ***Salmon Run Bell Tower*** displays a historic salmon diorama; its glockenspiel's thirty-six melodious bells play several times each day. Cafes, delis, and coffee shops are located nearby. In the park next to the tower and rose gardens is the historic Slocum House, where you can find out the local theater group's current offering at the intimate ***Slocum House Theater*** (360-696-2427; www.slocumhouse.com). Consider taking in the bustling ***Vancouver Farmers' Market*** (360-737-8298; www.vancouverfarmersmarket.com) at the park on Saturday and Sunday April through October. Also browse up Main Street to find cafes, boutiques, and specialty shops such as ***Ice Cream Renaissance*** at 2108 Main Street (360-694-3892).

Travel north from Vancouver for about 20 miles to Woodland to visit the ***Hulda Klager Lilac Gardens*** at 115 South Pekin Road (360-225-8996; www

Ghosts Galore

It is said that ghosts and spirits hang around at times other than Halloween, perhaps to startle and amuse visitors. Folks claim they've heard or seen them in old theaters and hotels, vintage bed-and-breakfast inns, Victorian houses, ghost towns, and other places appropriate for denizens of the otherworld. Here are a few places to look for friendly ghosts on your travels in Washington State:

Snohomish: Blackman House Museum (ca. 1878) and also at one of the town's taverns (the ghost's name is Henry)

Spokane: Monaghan Hall (ca. 1898) at Gonzaga University

Vancouver: Marshall House Officer's Row National Historic District

Yakima: Capitol Theatre

.lilacgardens.com). Thanks to Hulda's work during most of the ninety-six years of her life, visitors can enjoy more than 150 hybrid varieties and colors of lilacs and their frothy blooms. Her family settled in this area in 1877, after emigrating from Germany via Wisconsin. She received many honors, including one for her work as a leading lilac hybridizer. To the rear of the Victorian house, volunteers have restored the old woodshed, water tower, picturesque windmill, and carriage house. The house is open selected times in April and May, when members of the Hulda Klager Lilac Garden Society don period dresses and greet visitors during the annual open house; lilac starts and plants are for sale. The arboretum is open daily and is wheelchair accessible, but call for dates and hours.

walkthetube

Explore a section of the 12,810-foot lava tube on the south side of Mount St. Helens, one of the longest continuous lava tubes in the world. It was formed about 2,000 years ago when lava poured into a creek bed and the sides and top cooled quickly, forming a crust while the lava underneath continued to flow away.

The **Cedar Creek Grist Mill National Historic Site** is located 9 miles east and north of Woodland (360-225-5832; www.cedarcreekgristmill.com). Rough-hewn and unpretentious, the mill, which dates from 1876, was for

Up Close and Personal: Mount St. Helens National Volcanic Monument

The 52-mile drive from Interstate 5 at Castle Rock (exit 49) east on Spirit Lake Highway toward Mount St. Helens offers a number of ogling possibilities, with Johnston Ridge the most spectacular at just 5½ miles from the crater. Here are a few of the highlights:

Mount St. Helens Visitor Center, milepost 5 (Washington State Parks)

Charles W. Bingham Forest Learning Center, milepost 33 (Weyerhaeuser)

Hummocks Trail, 2.4-mile trail around colorful rock formations deposited during the 1980 eruption, just east of Coldwater Ridge

Johnston Ridge Observation Center, milepost 52 (U.S. Forest Service)

For more information contact **Gifford Pinchot National Forest,** Vancouver (360-891-5001; www.fs.fed.us/gpnf/mshnvm). Ask about Ape Cave, Harmony Trail, and Windy Ridge, the last with more awesome views of the 1980 volcanic devastation; or Mount St. Helens Visitor Center, (360) 274-0962.

generations the center of local industry and the site of dances, parties, and musical shows. The mill was restored in the early 1980s and is now a working museum, with a water-powered stone flour mill and machine shop. The mill is open Saturday from 1:00 to 4:00 p.m. and Sunday from 2:00 to 4:00 p.m. Admission is free, and you may even be able to take home a small bag of fresh-milled flour; donations are always appreciated.

Continue on to Amboy, then turn south on Highway 503 through green fields and forests. In 7 miles turn east on Northeast Rock Creek Road and ignore the road's name changes; just go 4½ miles to the **Pomeroy House Living History Farm** at 20902 Northeast Lucia Falls Road, Yacolt (360-686-3537; www.pomeroyfarm.org). Browse the British specialty shop to find items such as Dewar's Scotch whiskey marmalade, Cadbury chocolates, and English teas. Enjoy a spot of tea with scones, tea sandwiches, jellies, and desserts on Wednesday through Saturday at 11:30 a.m., 1:00 p.m., and 2:30 p.m. (call for reservations). On the first full weekend of each month from June through September, watch the activities of a 1920s homestead farm during the days of candles and kerosene lamps.

For bedding down within easy driving distances from both Mount Rainier and Mount St. Helens, contact **Cowlitz River Lodge** at 13069 U.S. Highway 12

it'snotdisney

At 8:32 a.m. on Sunday, May 18, 1980, Mount St. Helens exploded in a massive outpouring of lava and ash. The eruption measured 5.1 on the Richter scale and killed 57 people, turned the top 1,200 feet of the mountain's trademark symmetrical peak into ash, and destroyed 250 homes, 47 bridges, 185 miles of road, and 230 square miles of forest. Since then, a total of 110,000 acres has been preserved for research, education, and recreation.

(888-305-2185; www.escapetothemountains.com); Crest Trail Lodge at 12729 US 12 (800-477-5339; www.cresttraillodge.com); and **Mountain View Lodge,** 13163 US 12 (877-277-7192), all in or near Packwood. For a rustic stay in a historic atmosphere, try the 1912 Hotel Packwood, a national landmark, at 104 Main Street (360-494-5431).

Good eats in the Packwood area are at the **Blue Spruce Saloon & Diner** on US 12 at Willame Street (360-494-5605) and **Peters Inn** on US 12 near Skate Creek Road (360-494-4000). Also check www.visitranier.com for vacation home rentals and mountain recreation information.

Continuing east on US 12 takes you from Randle to Packwood, then over the high mountain wilderness areas of White Pass, past the fishing resorts along Rimrock Lake, and down the Tieton River Canyon toward Yakima.

Columbia River Gorge

Heading east on Highway 14 from Vancouver, pass the small mill towns of **Camas** and Washougal. Take the highway's business loop to explore the Camas downtown area. Fourth Avenue is a pleasant walking street through the main commercial district. From here the highway climbs 1,000 feet up the Columbia plateau at Cape Horn. From the top you'll enjoy an expansive view of the **Columbia River Gorge.**

After descending back to river level, continue east to 4,650-acre **Beacon Rock State Park** (509-427-8265). **Beacon Rock** is an 850-foot basalt tower, the remains of a volcano core that served as a sign to river travelers dating back to Native Americans and Lewis and Clark (who named it) that they had passed the difficult Cascade Rapids and faced no further obstructions to the Pacific Ocean. For a breathtaking challenge, climb the steep and narrow trail, including a series of stairways with railings, to the top of Beacon Rock for panoramic views of the Columbia River and forested hills on both sides. It's worth the effort.

Just past Beacon Rock and near the town of **North Bonneville,** visit the **Fort Cascades Historic Site,** which includes a 1½-mile self-guided tour. Along the way you'll see prehistoric Indian petroglyphs, the original site of Fort Cascades (which burned during an attack in 1856), and artifacts from the territorial period, when wagons were needed to portage around the rough river waters.

Water travel is easier now. Lengthy grain and produce barges have replaced canoes and rafts on the Columbia River, passing through a network of dams and locks that begin with the **Bonneville Dam.** Visitors can tour the dam daily from either side of the river (Oregon, 541-374-8820; Washington, 509-427-4281) to see the huge electrical generators and the fish-ladder system that allows salmon and steelhead trout to continue up the river to spawn. Visitors to the Oregon side need a guide to view the generators; in Washington, visitors can see them but need a guide to get closer. On the Oregon side of the river, accessed by the **Bridge of the Gods,** you can also see the locks in action, raising and lowering pleasure boats, fishing boats, and grain barges.

savesasquatch

If you see a hairy creature between 8 and 11 feet tall and weighing 700 to 2,000 pounds, don't shoot it, at least if you're in Skamania County, where it's against the law to kill the critter. Violators can be fined $1,000 and face a five-year jail sentence.

Be sure to visit the Columbia Gorge Interpretive Center at 990 Southwest Rock Creek Drive near Stevenson (800-991-2338; www.columbiagorge.org). It's located off Highway 14 a couple of miles east of the Bridge of the Gods. This large and excellent glass-walled museum highlights the river's colorful history. Witness the geological and climatic forces that formed the gorge at the Creation Theater's twelve-minute multimedia show. Learn about the region's native Indian tribes through oral histories, a Clahclahla trading village, and dip-net fishing displays. Examine the environmental impact of dams on the river. Other highlights include a 37-foot-tall replica of a nineteenth-century fishwheel, one of many that once harvested millions of pounds of fish each year. The center is open daily (except holidays) from 10:00 a.m. to 5:00 p.m. There is a nominal admission fee.

Consider a night at nearby Bonneville Hot Springs & Spa in North Bonneville (866-459-1678; www.bonnevilleresort.com). After a long day on the road or trail, we recommend taking a room with a mineral-water-filled hot tub on your private balcony. Or try *Skamania Lodge* (800-221-7117), a large resort and conference center located on a bluff above the interpretive center. The resort offers golf, swimming, tennis, spa treatments, hiking trails on the property, road bikes, guided hikes, and more. The lodge pipes in mineral water for its pools, hot tub, and spa. On the main level at the lodge, find a well-stocked outdoor recreation information center (509-427-2528) and Forest Service staff who provide maps and information. And if you're hot-springs hopping, go north to rustic Carson Mineral Hot Springs at 1261 Wind River Road (800-607-3678; www.carsonhotspringsresort .com), open daily. The original 1892 bath house is still in use, complete with clawfoot tubs, and the 1901 St. Martin Hotel still stands; more-modern rooms are offered in nearby buildings.

sayaprayer

The Columbia Gorge Interpretive Center near Stevenson has about 4,000 rosaries from around the world, including ones from President John F. Kennedy, conductor Lawrence Welk, and football coach Lou Holtz. The oldest rosary was made in the 18th century.

Nearby *Stevenson* is a historic waterfront town and county seat for *Skamania County.* Many of its buildings date to the early 1900s, with new businesses sprouting amid the old. The *River House Art Gallery and Studio* at 115 Southwest Second Street (509-427-5930) features Columbia Gorge images and historic East Coast homes, original watercolors, local pottery, baskets, and pastels.

A number of pleasant eateries dot Stevenson, most of them easy to find along Northwest Second Street (Highway 14). Try Andrew's Pizza (509-427-

Gorge Lovers Sneak Over to Oregon

You won't be chided for taking time to visit the Oregon side of the Columbia River, crossing the bridge from White Salmon and *Bingen* to the bustling small town of Hood River. You could plan a couple of pleasant day trips:

Drive the 45-mile *Hood River Fruit Loop* into the blooming pear and apple orchards—canopies of white blooms peak around the middle of April. Take in the *Hood River Valley Blossom Festival;* visit wineries and taste local wines; see arts and crafts exhibits, find delicious baked goods and huge apple pies, sip huckleberry milkshakes; buy hardy perennials and herbs, and visit an alpaca farm and browse its country store. Pick up a Fruit Loop map at the *Hood River Visitor Information Center* (800-366-3530; www.hoodriverfruitloop.com and www.hoodriver.org).

For a second day trip and more awesome close-up views of 11,235-foot *Mount Hood,* take Highway 35 from Hood River about 25 miles south and west to U.S. Highway 26. Continue about 10 miles west on US 26 to Government Camp and take the 6-mile winding road up to the 1937 *Timberline Lodge* and its ski area at 6,000-feet elevation. Tour the second-floor lounge area with its towering fireplaces and huge windows that frame snowy Mount Hood, see the dining areas and lodge rooms, and visit the ground-floor exhibit area that details the lodge's construction during WPA days, including a vintage recording of FDR speaking at the dedication ceremony. For informal eats try the nearby Wy'East Day Lodge Deli. Retrace your route to Hood River and stay overnight or cross the Columbia River back to the Washington side.

8008), 310 Second Street for New York–style, hand-tossed pizzas. Fresh salads, calzones, and Italian sandwiches top off the main menu.

Visit *Big River Grill* at 192 Southwest Second Street (509-427-4888) for Northwest pub fare and microbrews, walls full of memorabilia, and a welcoming atmosphere. At 240 Southwest First Street, *Walking Man Brewery & Public House* (509-427-5520) offers handcrafted ales and tasty fare such as Caesar salads and clam strips on Wednesday through Sunday. In addition to ten beers on tap, the brewery makes delicious root beer, ginger ale, and cream soda. Other options include Bahma Coffee Bar & Bistro (509-427-8700) at 256 Second Street for espresso, croissant breakfast sandwiches, and great desserts; and the *Crab Shack* (509-427-4400) at 130 Southwest Cascade Street for seafood and an outside deck.

The Skamania County Chamber of Commerce, 167 Northwest Second Street in Stevenson (800-989-9178) can provide maps, information about Northwest Forest passes, and other words of wisdom about summer wildflower meadows, hiking trails, and winter cross-country ski areas in the Gifford Pinchot National Forest. Linger overnight in the area by calling *Sandhill Cottages*

at 932 Hot Springs Avenue in Carson (800-914-2178; www.sandhillcottages
.com) or stop for a friendly chat and espresso at the entry with the pet-friendly
owners of **#7 *Coffee Roasting Company Coffee Bar.***

Farther east along the Columbia is the town of ***Bingen,*** and just up the
hill is ***White Salmon.*** Until recently these were quiet riverside communities of
hardworking old-timers, but they have become recreation meccas, especially
for windsurfers. On spring and summer weekends the beaches along this
stretch of the Columbia cab be crowded with wind-surfing enthusiasts of all
ages, and the water is alive with colorful sails. The ***Inn of the White Salmon***
at 172 West Jewett Boulevard (800-972-5226; www.innofthewhitesalmon.com),
an eco-friendly boutique hotel built in 1937, features fourteen Craftsman-era-
style rooms and European-style breakfasts of meats and cheeses along with
fresh egg entrees. Down the street, ***Klickitat Pottery Shop,*** 264 East Jewett
Boulevard (509-493-4456), is a fun place to browse and observe an ancient
craft in action. The potter often works in a wide-windowed studio on one side
of the shop, creating high-quality stoneware pieces for sale in the shop.

In Bingen try ***Los Reyes*** (509-493-1017) at 120 East Steuben for delicious
Mexican fare and ***Big River Diner*** (509-493-1414) at 740 East Steuben Street
for tasty American-style eats and a good salad bar.

There is a lot to see and do in the scenic White Salmon River Valley, which
stretches from the Columbia River north to 12,307-foot-high Mount Adams.
Zoller's Outdoor Odysseys at 1248 Highway 141, just north of White Salmon
(800-366-2004; www.zooraft.com) will raft you down the river. It's an exhilarating experience and is suitable for families and beginners.

In ***Husum,*** north of White Salmon on Highway 141, plan to stay overnight in the "shadows" of ***Mount Hood*** and Mount Adams by calling ***Husum
Riverside Bed & Breakfast*** at 866 Highway 141 (509-493-8900; www.gorge-
rooms.com). It sits on the site of the Husum Hotel of the 1800s. Or arrange

Catching the Wind

You're adventurous and in excellent physical shape? The ultimate test may be learning to maneuver a windsurfing board to ply the deep waves on a windy day on the
mighty Columbia River. Although Washington has good windsurfing on its side of the
Columbia, the Big Rep is on the south side where Hood River enters the Columbia.
To learn more, contact the **Columbia Gorge Windsurfing Association** at 202 Oak
Street in Hood River (541-386-9225; www.cgwa.net). Good spots to watch and pho-
tograph are at **Port Marina Park** just west of the bridge in Hood River and farther
east at **Maryhill State Park,** south of Goldendale on the Washington side. Maryhill
also offers picnic shelters, grassy areas, and riverfront campsites.

for cozy rooms that come with a hearty farm breakfast at the Victorian Husum Highlands Bed & Breakfast (800-808-9812; www.husumhighlands.com).

Consider arranging a horseback ride on gentle steeds at ***Northwestern Lake Riding Stables*** at 126 Little Buck Creek Road (509-493-4965) near White Salmon and Trout Lake. There are horses for beginners as well as experienced riders. Children must be age eight or older. Riding lessons as well as day trips can be arranged.

treetopview

The world's largest canopy crane is used by scientists to study the ecology of the treetops. The gondola of the 190-ton Wind River crane, about 10 miles from the Columbia Gorge and north of Carson, can clear 220-foot-tall trees. It is the second tallest crane in the world and can cover a 550-foot circle.

For lunch or dinner closer to Mount Adams, locals suggest a favorite, the ***Logs Family Restaurant*** (509-493-1402), located at BZ Corner on Highway 141 about halfway between White Salmon and Trout Lake (mile marker 12). They've been serving up great fried chicken since the early 1930s.

Farther up Highway 141 near the base of Mount Adams, enjoy mountain views from the chalet cabins at ***Serenity's,*** 2291 Highway 141 (509-395-2500; www.serenitys.com), 1 mile south of Trout Lake. Each cabin has walls of glass highlighting forested scenery and comes equipped with a kitchenette, a queen-size bed, and a large bathroom. Most have whirlpool tubs, lofts, fireplaces, and TVs; one chalet is wheelchair accessible. For an additional price, the chef provides delicious dinners. The public is welcome for casual patio dining beginning at 5:00 p.m.

Folks say one of the best places to hunker down for a fresh cup of coffee, a sandwich, a slice of apple pie, and a dose of local gossip is ***KJ's Bear Creek Cafe,*** located at 2376 Highway 141 (509-395-2525), next to the service station in Trout Lake. If you travel by recreational vehicle, check with ***Elk Meadows RV Park,*** 78 Trout Lake Creek Road (509-395-2400). The RV sites come with outrageous views of Mount Adams.

For other cozy places to spend the night close to Trout Lake and snowy Mount Adams, check out several bed-and-breakfasts in the area. At the ***Farm Bed & Breakfast*** (490 Sunnyside Road; 509-395-2488; www .thefarmbnb.com), innkeepers offer two comfortable guest rooms decorated with antiques and quilts in their large 1890 farmhouse; the two rooms share a bath. Outdoors is a fine collection of scented roses, colorful perennials, four varieties of maples, graceful willows, and tall spruce. At ***Kelly's Trout Creek Inn Bed & Breakfast*** (25 Mount Adams Road; 509-395-2769; www.kellysbnb.com), innkeepers Kelly and Marilyn Enochs offer travelers a comfortable mix of old-fashioned quilts and rustic decor in three cozy guest rooms. During warm weather you can eat outdoors on the deck next to bubbling Trout Creek, where its waters rush over large rocks and low basalt ledges.

In the Mount Adams area, ancient volcanoes produced numerous lava flows, caves, lava tubes, and other natural structures. Many caves in the area were used by farmers in the days before refrigeration to store butter and cheese until they could be transported to market. These caves make the region popular with serious spelunkers (cave explorers), who approach the caverns with the same sense of challenge and caution that mountain climbers have for major peaks.

The **Ice Caves,** a series of lava tubes, are the easiest of the public caves to explore. Their name refers to columns of ice that develop naturally in the lowest chamber during the winter. A century ago the giant icicles were harvested and sold. The Forest Service has constructed a ladder leading down from the main entrance. A 120-foot tube that slopes southeastward is the most accessible part of the cave. In all there are about 650 feet of passages to explore. Be sure to bring warm clothes, boots, head protection, and dependable lights. Stop at the Mount Adams Ranger Station (509-395-3400; www.fs.fed.us/gpnf), just north of Trout Lake at 2455 Highway 141, for more information and directions.

The road east to Glenwood offers killer views of the east slope of Mount Adams (called *Pahto* by Native people) as you pass through the rich farmlands and climb hills above the White Salmon River Valley. Watch for the turnoff on your right to Conboy Lake National Wildlife Refuge (509-371-9212), which takes you to the entrance where you'll find brochures describing this wetland habitat. The Willard Springs Foot Trail, a 2½-mile loop that runs through timberland with views across the lake bed and includes interpretive signs, is a pleasant way to see carpets of spring wildflowers and learn more about the refuge's wildlife, including porcupines and wood ducks. The refuge is a nesting area for greater sandhill cranes.

Just outside the small community of Glenwood, travelers find the Mount Adams Lodge at the **Flying L Ranch** at 25 Flying L Lane (509-364-3488; www.mt-adams.com). The Lloyd family built the house in the mid-1940s, and the Lloyd sons, Darvel and Darryl, further developed the property in the 1970s and 1980s. Current owners Julee Wasserman and Tim Johnson have continued to update the facilities, twelve lodge rooms and four cabins. Guests enjoy a full breakfast served in the ranch cookhouse. You can also bring your own steaks for a cookout. The area around the ranch is perfect for hiking and biking as well as for winter cross-country skiing and snowshoeing.

Returning to Highway 14 and heading east alongside the Columbia River, consider stopping in the small community of Lyle to have dinner at the *Lyle Hotel Restaurant* at 100 Seventh Street (509-365-5953; www.lylehotel.com). The menu changes regularly and is upscale for such an out-of-the-way location, with tasty Northwest fares including salmon and, when available, organic beef. The hotel was built in 1905 to serve the town when Lyle was a railroad center linking major towns in the region. The boom ended and most folks moved on. But the hotel remains a nostalgic reminder of earlier times with its ten small guest rooms featuring early American furnishings, some with sitting areas and views of the Columbia River.

Native Lands, Vineyards, and Wineries

Some of the Columbia River Gorge's greatest wonders are now, unfortunately, flooded under the huge reservoirs behind the Bonneville and The Dalles dams. Until 1957 the Oregon side of the Columbia River cascaded over Celilo Falls. Native people had camped on this stretch of river for thousands of years, enjoying the area's abundant resources. Indians from throughout the region practiced traditional dip-net fishing from pole platforms jutting close to the swirling torrents. The area was also an important gathering place where tribes met to trade goods, enjoy festivities, and conduct peace councils. In 1805 explorer Meriwether Lewis described the Celilo Falls area as a "great emporium where all the neighboring nations assembled." Hundreds of the ancient pictographs (rock paintings) and petroglyphs (rock carvings) that once commemorated this life are now lost beneath the waters of the river.

She-Who-Watches (Tsagaglalal) is one of the most intriguing petroglyphs still visible. Legend has it that Tsagaglalal, a female chief, told Coyote, the trickster, that she wanted to guide her people to "live well and build good houses" forever. Coyote explained that the time for female chiefs would soon be over, then turned her to stone so she could watch over the river and its people unimpeded into eternity. The original petroglyph is located amid several others at Columbia Hills State Park, which includes the *Horsethief Lake* area (actually an impoundment of the Columbia River). Due to vandalism, however, the only way to see the petroglyphs is by a 10:00 a.m. guided tour on Friday and Saturday from the beginning of April to the end of October. Tours last about 90 minutes and must be booked at least two weeks ahead. For information about costs and reservations, call (509) 767-1159.

Fifteen miles east of Horsethief Lake via Highway 14 and near the junction with U.S. Highway 97 is *Maryhill Museum of Art* and a reproduction on a smaller scale of England's Stonehenge monument, two legacies of eccentric

She-Who-Watches petroglyph

millionaire road builder Sam Hill. *Maryhill,* an impressive 400-foot-long chateau-like structure, is located at 35 Maryhill Museum Drive (509-773-3733; www.maryhillmuseum.org) and is open 9:00 a.m. to 5:00 p.m. daily from March 15 through November 15; there is an admission. It is situated with a fine view of the Columbia River and is filled with an eclectic collection that includes Rodin sculptures and watercolors, nineteenth-century French artwork, Russian icons, regional Indian art, the Queen of Romania's royal memorabilia, and a collection of chess sets. Be sure to see the 1946 collection of French fashion miniatures, *Theatre de la Mode.*

Cafe Maryhill, in the museum, serves deli-style lunches and snacks with outdoor seating available overlooking the river. Outside is the museum's sculpture garden. Each year Maryhill hosts an Outdoor Sculptural Invitational to contemporary sculptors of the Northwest. There's also a permanent collection that can be viewed year-round, for free.

Stonehenge sits on a bluff a few miles from the Maryhill museum. Hill had it built as a memorial to the soldiers of Klickitat County who died in World War I. Hill is buried at the base of the bluff. There is no admission fee to walk among the stones.

The *Maryhill Winery* (877-627-9445; www.maryhillwinery.com), located just west of Maryhill Museum at 9774 Highway 14, offers outdoor entertainment and an elegant tasting room with a focus on the winery's premium reds. The intricately carved antique bar fashioned in the early 1900s of tiger oak has a back bar 12 feet high, with mirrors inset along its 12-foot length. It's one of the five most-visited tasting rooms in a state that has about 500 wineries. Hours are 10:00 a.m. to 6:00 p.m. daily. A patio offers wide-angle views of the Gorge. The 4,000-seat amphitheater includes a larger permanent stage and vistas to Mount Hood in Oregon.

Goldendale, 10 miles north via US 97, has been a commercial center for farmers since its beginning. Well-kept homes and an active downtown continue to emanate a friendly, self-sufficient atmosphere. For a historical perspective, visit the ***Presby Museum*** (509-773-4303), owned by the Klickitat County Historical Society, in the stately Presby Mansion at 127 West Broadway Street (Highway 142). Turn-of-the-twentieth-century dolls left on the antique furniture give the impression that a child has just finished playing in the parlor; the kitchen looks as if someone is cooking dinner, the dining room table is set, and period clothing is laid out in the bedrooms. The museum is open from 9:00 a.m. to 5:00 p.m. daily, April 15 to October 15, or by appointment during the off-season. There is a small admission fee.

For an exhilarating look skyward, continue down Broadway Street and turn north on Columbus, past some of Goldendale's fine old homes. Follow signs uphill to ***Goldendale Observatory State Park,*** 1602 Observatory Drive (509-773-3141), where amateur astronomers share their enthusiasm for the stars. During the day view the sun using a special telescope, perhaps catching sight of a solar prominence—arcs of light and energy thousands of miles high. At night, the 26-inch telescope brings galaxies and nebulae into view. The observatory sits on a 2,100-foot hill and has one of the nation's largest public telescopes, open to sky-watchers since 1973. Its hours are 2:00 to 5:00 p.m. and 8:00 p.m. to midnight Wednesday through Sunday, April 1 through September 30. The rest of the year, the hours are 2:00 to 5:00 p.m. and 7:00 to 10:00 p.m. Friday, Saturday, and Sunday. For more information browse www .perr.com/gosp.html for the evening star-watching schedule and links to Northwest astronomy clubs, NASA sites, and "This Week's Sky at a Glance." Since you've traveled this far off the beaten path, eat with local folks in Goldendale at ***Don's Old Homestead Restaurant*** (509-773-6006), at Quality Inn & Suites, 808 East Simcoe Drive.

Now's the time to take a little side trip, at least little by Eastern Washington's standards. Drive about 35 miles east on Goldendale-Bickleton Road to the tiny but mildly famous town of ***Bickleton,*** population under 100. From mid-February to October thousands of mountain bluebirds flock to the area, earning the small town its nickname "Bluebird Capital of the World." About 2,500 small blue-and-white nesting boxes are on posts in yards, farms, and roadsides in a 150-square-mile area around Bickleton, all made by volunteers in what is now a 40-year project by area residents.

As you come into town, look to the right and spot the tall energy-generating windmills on the southern horizon. Bickleton has the state's oldest rodeo, one of the state's oldest taverns (***Bluebird Inn Tavern,*** 509-896-2273), and a 1905 horse carousel kept in a secret-to-outsiders vault, coming out only for the annual Pioneer Picnic. The ***Bickleton Market Street Cafe*** (509-896-2671) is another food source. You won't have any problem finding them since the main drag is a country block long.

Prosser, located on the high Columbia plateau about 40 miles northeast of Bickleton on Highway 22, has more to offer than you might expect for a quiet farm town. ***Hinzerling Winery*** and the ***Vintner's Inn Restaurant*** at 1520 Sheridan Avenue (800-727-6702; www.hinzerling.com) were founded in 1976 by the Wallace family and is the oldest family owned and operated winery in the Yakima Valley. Family members share their knowledge of wine production and samples of wines, including sweet dessert wines and dry gewürztraminer. ***Pontin Del Roza*** at 35502 North Hinzerling Road (509-786-4449) is located in the scenic hill district north of Prosser. You can taste the Pontin family's special Roza sunset blush and pinot gris. They have plans to build a new winery.

Gourmet cherries, preserves, toppings, and savories are other specialties you'll find near Prosser. The ***Chukar Cherry Company*** produces this variety along with Chocolate Chukars, a pitted, ripe, partly dried cherry dipped in dark chocolate, a royal treat. Visit the gift shop just west of town at 320 Wine Country Road (800-624-9544; www.chukar.com).

The ***Benton County Historical Museum*** (509-786-3842) at 1000 Paterson Road, is open 10:00 a.m. to 4:00 p.m. Tuesday through Friday and 11:00 a.m. to 3:00 p.m. Saturday. There's a little of everything here including natural history displays, an old-time general store counter, an 1867 Chickering square grand piano that you may play, and a selection of women's clothing of yesteryear. One of the exhibits contains hand-carved and hand-painted wooden automobiles, foot-long replicas of the real thing.

The Bluebird Inn Tavern, ca. 1882, Elevation 3,000 Feet

The tavern has gone through at least fifteen owners since it opened in Bickleton in 1882. It used to double as a barbershop, and once was a social club where hats were forbidden. For a long time the place had no telephone so the women weren't able to call and check up on their card-playing menfolk. Now, the tavern sells candy to kids and serves good food, including a giant Bluebird Burger. Pull up to the small Western-style structure that looks as though it should have several horses tied up out front, just like a John Wayne movie.

Tour Columbia Gorge and Yakima Valley Vineyards and Wineries

Throw a corkscrew into the picnic basket and visit a flotilla of fine vineyards, wineries, and tasting rooms in the fertile regions of the Yakima Valley and Columbia River Valley. Some of the wineries also open by appointment.

Alexandria Nicole Cellars
(509) 786-3497
www.alexandrianicolecellars.com
Open year round Wednesday to Sunday
11:00 a.m. to 5:00 p.m.

Bookwalter Winery
(877) 667-8300
www.bookwalterwines.com
Open year round Wednesday to Saturday 10:00 a.m. to 6:00 p.m.

Chinook Wines
(509) 786-2725
www.chinookwines.com
Open May to October, Saturday and
Sunday, noon to 5:00 p.m.

Hedges Family Estate
(509) 588-3155
www.hedgesfamilyestate.com
Open year round Friday to Sunday,
12:00 p.m. to 4:00 p.m.

Piety Flats Winery
(509) 877-3115
www.pietyflatswinery.com
Open November and December, Monday to Saturday 10:00 a.m. to 5:00 p.m.

Sagelands Winery
(800) 967-8115
www.sagelandsvineyard.com
Open daily year round 10:00 a.m. to
5:00 p.m.

Yakima River Winery
(509) 786-2805
www.yakimariverwinery.com
Open daily year round 10:00 a.m. to
5:00 p.m.

For Additional Information and Maps:

Columbia Valley Winery Association
www.columbiavalleywine.com

Prosser
www.prosserchamber.org

Tri-Cities
www.visittri-cities.com

Yakima
www.visityakima.com

Yakima Valley Wineries
www.wineyakimavalley.org

Washington State
www.winecountrywashington.com

For a bite to eat in Prosser, try the ***Blue Goose Restaurant*** at 306 Seventh Street (509-786-1774), the ***Barn Restaurant*** at 490 Wine Country Road (509-786-1131), or the ***El Caporal Mexican Restaurant*** at 624 Sixth Street (503-786-4910).

For a sampling of this rich farming area's home-grown bounty, stop by the ***Prosser Farmer's Market*** next to Prosser City Park (Seventh Street and Sommers Avenue) for fresh Yakima Valley fruits and vegetables, delectable homemade baked goods, and crafts from local artisans. The market is open from 8:00 a.m. to noon Saturday from May through October.

You can reach the town of **Grandview** by heading northwest from Prosser on Wine Country Road. The **Dykstra House Restaurant** at 114 Birch Avenue (509-882-2082) is in a 1914 building. Dykstra offers delicious meals and desserts with regional wines and ales. Call for reservations.

For a pleasant spot to stay the night in this rich wine country, call the innkeepers at Sunnyside Inn Bed and Breakfast at 800 East Edison Street (800-221-4195; www.sunnysideinn.com). They offer thirteen comfortable guest rooms with private baths in a large 1919 home with all the usual comforts including restful colors, lovely window treatments, and country accessories. Families are especially welcome here. In the morning a sumptuous country breakfast is served family-style in the large dining area on the main floor.

Hungry? Try Cactus Juice Café at 632 East Decatur Avenue (509-839-4480) or **La Victoria Mexican Café** at 301 South Thirteenth Street (509-839-4772). For great ales created in small batches and tasty pub dishes, go to **Snipes Mountain Microbrewery & Restaurant** at 905 Yakima Valley Highway 12 (509-837-2739).

For more off-the-beaten-path adventures, continue west on Emerald-Granger Road, a scenic route that circles south of Snipes Mountain. Nearby, **Granger Berry Patch Farm** at 1731 Beam Road (800-346-1417) offers more than twenty varieties of U-pick berries, pumpkins, and Christmas trees in season.

Before backtracking to the northwest, go east to the cities of Kennewick, Pasco, and Richland, which form the Tri-Cities. Located at the confluence of

TOP ANNUAL EVENTS
IN SOUTH CENTRAL WASHINGTON

Country Christmas Lighted Farm Implement Parade
Sunnyside, first weekend in December
(509) 837-5939

Granger Cherry Festival
Granger, last weekend in April
(509) 854-7304

The Great Hot Air Balloon Rally
Prosser, late September
(800) 408-1517

Mural-in-a-Day
Toppenish, first weekend in June
(800) 863-6375

Prosser Wine & Food Fair
August
(800) 408-1517

Red Wine and Chocolate Festival
Yakima Valley
President's Day Weekend, February
(800) 258-7270

Thanksgiving in Wine Country
Yakima Valley, holiday weekend
(800) 258-7270

The Alphabet Houses

A 1943 spin-off of the Manhattan Project was the Hanford Engineering Works near Richland. About 300 to 350 Richland residents were evicted and the town was turned into a bedroom community for a facility on land that was half the size of Rhode Island. The goal was to produce plutonium for the bombs that were dropped on Japan during World War II.

Since speed was necessary, a Spokane architect was given precious little time to create a development plan to house an initial 6,500 people in Richland. Since managers and executives couldn't be expected to live in the same style or size of home as a janitor or an accountant, G.A. Pehrson had to design many styles of houses for hierarchical, social, practical, and visual reasons. He labeled each style with a letter.

And so Richland's alphabet houses, also called ABC houses, were built from Pehrson's plans at a rate of about 180 buildings a month for a total of 4,732 dwellings placed on streets named after famous engineers or tree species. "A" houses were three-bedroom two-story duplexes; "D," "F," and "G" were two-story single-family homes with three or four bedrooms and different exterior designs. There were also dormitories for single men.

One of the housing units, this one with 162 alphabet houses, by and large kept its original appearance and was named to the National Register of Historic Places in 2005, designated as the Gold Coast Historic District.

the Columbia, Snake, and Yakima Rivers, the area comes with 300 days of sunshine and seemingly endless recreational possibilities.

The Tri-Cities is the heart of wine country in this corner of the state, with 150 wineries within an hour's drive. The region's hot summer days and crisp evening breezes, which naturally stresses the vines, combined with the Columbia Valley's volcanic soil, creates conditions for making great wines. Visit the state's first barrel-storage caves at Terra Blanca at 34715 North DeMoss Road, Benton City (509-588-6082); the new tasting room at Kiona Vineyards Winery at 44612 North Sunset Road, Benton City (509-588-6716), the first winery built on Red Mountain; or the state's first certified organic vineyard and winery at Badger Mountain Vineyards and Powers Winery, 1106 South Jurupa Street (800-643-9463).

The area's twelve museums and interpretive centers chronicle the region's history, which includes World War II, Alphabet Houses, Oregon Trail pioneers, early cinematography, railroading, agriculture, Kennewick Man, and more. Visit the 9,200-year-old Kennewick Man at the East Benton County Historical Society Museum, 205 Keewaydin Drive (509-582-7704); to learn about Hanford's role in the Manhattan Project, World War II, and the end of the Cold War, visit the Columbia River Exhibition of History, Science and Technology,

95 Lee Boulevard, Richland (509-943-9000); view train tools and parts, early railroad signs, a 1938 gas-powered speeder used for track maintenance, and early railroad photographs at the Washington State Railroads Historical Society Museum, 122 North Tacoma Avenue, Pasco (800-465-5430).

The Hanford Reach National Monument is the last free-flowing, non-tidal stretch of the Columbia River. An abundance of wildlife can be seen along its 51 miles, including birds, elk, mule deer, coyote, river otter, and others in this natural sanctuary. Explore the Reach on a Columbia River Journeys' jet boat out of Richland (888-486-9119), which also offers a wine-and-water tour; or a Columbia Kayak Adventures tour (509-947-5901), also in Richland.

For lodging, choose from B&Bs, vacation homes, motels, and hotels. Call the Tri-Cities Visitor & Convention Bureau (800-254-5824) to learn more, or go to www.visittri-cities.com. We stayed at the reasonably priced Clover Island Inn Hotel on Clover Island in the Columbia River, 150 rooms and sweet views of the river. Built on the shoreline and connected to the mainland by a causeway, the hotel has its own dock for your boat and bikes for guests (although if the wind is blowing stiffly, you might want to reconsider the bike ride). It's next to the Cedars Restaurant and close to the Historical Downtown Kennewick District.

Many excellent restaurants offer a wide variety of food choices. From taco wagons to elegant fine dining, specialty coffee houses to ethnic bakeries, the mix is eclectic. As the world's second-leading producer of hops, the area naturally offers a selection of great craft and micro-breweries, including Atomic Ale Brew Pub and Eatery at 1015 Lee Boulevard, Richland (509-946-5465), where you can try Atomic Ale, Waynier Isotope IPA, or Oppenheimer Oatmeal Stout; or check out Ice Harbor Brewing Company at 206 North Benton Street, Kennewick (509-582-5340) and Rattlesnake Mountain Brewing Company at 2696 North Columbia Boulevard, Richland (509-783-5747).

Pause in the small town of **Granger,** population about 2,000, to visit **Worden's Lamp House** at 118 Main Street (800-541-1103). Inside, browse through a display of nearly a hundred different Tiffany-style stained-glass lampshades and learn about the stained-glass process.

Be sure to stop at Metal and Iron Artistry, 502 Sunnyside Avenue (509-854-7299; www.primoartisan.net). You might catch up with Primo Villalobos, who at age 14 started an apprenticeship with a blacksmith and dreamed about building a 24-foot-tall knight in shining armor. In 1999 his dream came true. Now the knight stands in front of Der Ritterhof in Leavenworth. For good Mexican food stop by **La Morelense** at 302 Main Street (509-854-2811).

Granger, in the heart of the Yakima Valley, logged 100 years of incorporation in 2009. Don't fear the brontosaurus, tyrannosaurus rex, triceratops and other dinosaurs as you ride down Highway 223 near Granger, though. In 1958, wooly mammoth tusks and teeth were discovered in a nearby abandoned clay mine. Now steel-wire mesh-and-concrete dinosaurs roam once more.

About 5 miles north of Granger via Highway 22 is **Toppenish**, the small community and capital of the Yakama Indian Nation and dubbed the City of Murals and Museums. Park near the historic railroad depot and enjoy a walking tour of the downtown area and its 70 giant-size murals depicting scenes from early days in the West. From May through September, hop on the horse-drawn wagon for a narrated tour. Pause for a look at the grand old **Liberty Theatre** at 211 South Toppenish Avenue. Built in 1915, the theater boasted the largest stage at the time between Seattle and Spokane and hosted stars such as Lillian Gish, Raymond Navarro, and even Tex Ritter and his horse.

When it's time to stop for nourishment, locals suggest **Pioneer Kitchen** at 227 South Toppenish Avenue (509-865-3201) for all-day breakfasts, cinnamon rolls, homemade soups, salad bar, hefty Rodeo Burgers, and great pies and cobblers. Try **Villaseñor** at 225 South Toppenish Avenue (509-865-4707) for

One Hundred Years, 1850 to 1950: the Toppenish Murals

Since 1989 folks in the **Toppenish Mural Society** have funded more than seventy gigantic murals painted outdoors on buildings all over Toppenish, from the Western Auto building and the Reid Building to Toppenish Community Hospital, Pow Wow Emporium, and Old Timers Plaza Park. We are not talking crayon and stick figures here. The historically accurate scenes represent the life and times of the Toppenish area from 1850 to 1950. Folks visit them throughout the year but on the first Saturday of June you also can watch the Mural-in-a-Day come to life and join the celebration. Stop by the Visitor Welcome Center at 504 South Elk Street (800-863-6375; www.toppenish.net); pick up a mural map and enjoy. Here are a few of the giant-size paintings of bygone days that you'll see:

Hop Museum Murals (#32), a trio of painted archways open to scenes of harvesting hops on two walls of the American Hop Museum

Lou Shattuck (#34), an original booster of the Toppenish Pow Wow Rodeo

Maud Bolin (#27), rodeo rider and early female pilot on the southwest wall of the *Toppenish Review* newspaper building

Rodeo Days (#13), on the west wall of Ferguson's Saddlery

Ruth Parton (#22), cowgirl and trick-rider on the Embarq Communications building

Western Hospitality (#36), bordello ladies of the night on the second-floor windows of the Logan Building

good Mexican fare including piping hot appetizers, fajitas, and freshly made tortillas, along with such tasty desserts as flan, sopapillas, and deep-fried ice cream. At **Gibbons Pharmacy,** 117 South Toppenish Avenue (509-865-2722), order juicy burgers and something cool and tasty at the old-fashioned soda fountain. Then, visit the **Amish Connection** at 105 South Toppenish Avenue (509-865-5300) for authentic Amish foods and handcrafted items; nearby is **Kraff's Clothing** at 111 South Toppenish Avenue (509-865-3000), which specializes in colorful Pendleton blankets.

Allow time to visit the country's only museum dedicated to the growing of hops, the **American Hop Museum** at 22 South B Street (509-865-4677; www.americanhopmuseum.org). The museum is open from 10:00 a.m. to 4:00 p.m. Wednesday through Sunday from May through September. Look at the splendid murals on the front of the large building, a series of arched windows painted on either side of the entrance. The museum focuses on the hop industry that started around 1805 in New York State.

In the 1850s hop growers took their perennial hop vines westward where the climate was sunnier with fewer mildew issues. The sunny Yakima Valley became a prime area for growing hops, which climb on tall expanses of twine strung in long rows. In the museum are artifacts, memorabilia, and old photographs collected from all over the United States, including antique hop presses, tools for cultivating hops, a horse-drawn hop duster, old picking baskets, and an early picking machine. Learn how hop cones are used to flavor and preserve beers and ales, and browse in the gift shop.

The **Yakima Valley Rail and Steam Museum** (509-865-1911), located on 10 Asotin Street in a restored railway depot built in 1911, contains interesting rail and steam artifacts, a completely restored telegraph office, and a gift shop. The third weekend of August folks can attend the **Yakima Valley Rail & Transportation Show** at the depot museum held in conjunction with the **Toppenish Western Art Show** in nearby Railroad Park. Great art, railroad memorabilia, food booths, and live country music along with tours of the museum, engine house, and grounds make for a lively day. If you travel through the area over the Fourth of July you can take in the colorful **Toppenish Pow Wow and Rodeo.**

To learn more about Native American culture, visit the well-done **Yakama Nation Museum and Cultural Heritage Center** on 100 Spiel-yi Loop, Toppenish (509-865-2800; www.yakamamuseum.com). From a distance you'll spot the colorful peaked roof of the center's Winter Lodge, modeled after the ancestral A-shaped homes of the Yakama tribes. Museum exhibits and dioramas show the tribe's history and traditions. A large, angular tule (reed) lodge at the center of the museum shows how extended families lived during the winter. Sweat lodges made from earth, branches, and animal skins illustrate sacred places of physical and spiritual purification. The museum is open daily; there is an admission fee.

At the center's gift shop adjacent to the museum, fine beadwork and other Native American art and cultural items are for sale. The center also maintains an extensive library on First Nations history and culture; it's open Monday through Saturday. The Heritage Inn Restaurant (509-865-2800; open daily, call for hours), also part of the tribal center, offers delicious meals, including Yakama and other First Nations favorites such as *waykaanish* (salmon), buffalo stew, fry bread, and huckleberry pie.

Next door to the Heritage Center, the *Yakama Nation RV Resort* (280 Buster Road; 800-874-3087) offers a luxury campground with 125 RV spaces with full hookups, a tent site, and a recreation center featuring a basketball court, hot tub, two saunas, workout room, laundry room, and swimming pool. You can also rent a tepee with room for a whole family.

Twenty-five miles west of the Yakama Indian Tribal Center in the heart of the reservation is Fort Simcoe State Park Heritage Site, a lovely park with large oak trees, a lush green lawn, and a dozen restored buildings filled with period furnishings. The former military fort is located at 5150 Fort Simcoe Road (509-874-2372; www.parks.wa.gov) near the community of White Swan and on a traditional Native village site. The ancient Mool Mool bubbling springs here have created a shady oasis of reed-filled wetlands surrounded by woods. In summer, you may catch sight of bronze-green and pink Lewis's woodpeckers, which breed in abundance in the Garry oaks. The park, a popular picnic spot for local residents, features plenty of shade trees, running water, and an adventure playground. The historical buildings and interpretive center are open Wednesday through Sunday from 9:00 a.m. to 4:30 p.m. from April through September.

Yakama Nation RV Resort

The ***Toppenish National Wildlife Refuge*** is located off US 97 south of Toppenish. The refuge's marshlands and thick riverside forests are excellent places to view the fall and spring migrations of Canada geese, grebes, and ducks such as teals, scaups, and pintails. There also are bald eagles, prairie falcons, and other wildlife.

Mountains, Orchards, and Railroads

A 10-mile, signed "Fruit Loop" route circles the orchard-covered hills above the town of ***Zillah,*** an ideal way to discover the valley's agricultural opulence. To visit Zillah take Interstate 82, exit 52 or 54, or follow the Yakima Valley Highway from Sunnyside through Granger and turn left onto Zillah's First Avenue. The Zillah Chamber of Commerce's number is (509) 829-5055. The loop starts from the downtown information office at the corner of First Avenue and Fifth Street where you can pick up a route map or just follow the colorful signs from downtown north on Roza Drive and left onto the Yakima Valley Highway. Along the way you'll enjoy grand views of the lower valley's patchwork quilt of farms, and you'll pass by several wineries.

Of course every winery claims to offer the best product, so it's up to you to determine your favorites. Each has a tasting room where visitors are offered a small sample of the vintages. Employees, and sometimes the owners, are glad to share their knowledge and offer suggestions for the best wine for various occasions. Most tasting rooms also sell nonalcoholic drinks, snacks, and gifts.

If wine tasting has given you an appetite and you forgot the picnic basket, you'll want to eat at El Portin (905 Vintage Valley Parkway; 509-829-9100). Worth a stop just a half-mile from downtown is ***Claar Cellars Winery*** at 1001 Vintage Valley Parkway (509-829-6810). The tasting room is open from 10:00 a.m. to 6:00 p.m. daily. For a nostalgic visit to an old-fashioned country store and winery, stop by ***Piety Flats Winery & Mercantile*** (509-877-3115), just east of I-82 at exit 44 on Donald-Wapato Road. The tasting room is in a fruit and mercantile store dating to 1911 and still has the old wooden floor and most of the original store fixtures.

Near Wapato you'll find ***Sagelands Winery*** (71 Gangle Road; 509-877-2112). The impressive French country–style winery, built of local stone and cedar, has a wine-tasting room and gift shop. To reach the winery take I-82 exit 40, follow the road as it curves left toward the hill, then turn right onto Gangl Road.

Just south of Yakima is the town of ***Union Gap,*** the single gap in the line of hills that divides the upper and lower Yakima Valley. Next to the gap is the

Teapot Dome Service Station

Just east of Zillah is an unmistakable landmark, a true vintage roadside attraction just off I-82 exit 54. The 15-foot-tall white teapot structure with its red handle and spout was once a gas station built in 1922. The joke here, which only old-timers or history buffs are likely to catch without explanation, is the name: the Teapot Dome Service Station, a reference to the Wyoming oil-lease scandal of the same name, big news in the early twenties; it sent Secretary of the Interior Albert Fall to prison. Zillah residents hope to move the building, on the National Register of Historic Places, to the downtown area and transform it into a visitors' information center.

Central Washington Agricultural Museum at 4508 Main Street in Fulbright Park (509-457-8735). The large collection of farm equipment is arranged inside a number of display buildings and also outdoors on spiral terraces around a windmill tower. You'll see horse-drawn plows and mowers, huge old steam tractors, antique threshers, and hop harvesters. A blacksmith shop, furnished log cabin, fruit-packing line equipment, and the Museum Grange Library are also in the 15-acre park. You might even see working horse teams plowing the museum fields or an old steam harvester in use. To get to the museum from Union Gap, follow Main Street south 2 miles and across the US 97 overpass to the Fulbright Park turnoff. If you want to picnic, there are shaded tables on the grounds at Fulbright Park, or for a bite to eat in Union Gap, check out *Old Town Station Restaurant* at 2530 Main Street (509-453-8485) and *Jean's Cottage Inn* at 3211 Main Street (509-575-9709). The food is prepared upon order.

The city of *Yakima* offers many activities little-known to outsiders. Walking or bicycling along the 10-mile *Yakima Greenway Trail* (www .yakimagreenway.org) is the perfect way to enjoy the Yakima and Naches Rivers from the quiet town of Selah at the north, past several riverfront parks, to the seventy-acre *Yakima Arboretum* at the south end. The arboretum includes hiking trails, a Japanese garden, and the new Jewett Interpretive Center. You can also access the trail and a river landing for launching kayaks and canoes at *Sarg Hubbard Park* (509-453-8280) off I-82 or off South Eighteenth Street. At the park on Saturday evenings in June, enjoy a picnic supper and at dusk take in a free movie. Folks find seating and lawn areas for blankets and folding chairs.

Railroad themes permeate Yakima. Along the old railroad line through downtown, find renovated North Front Street and browse its eclectic shops, cafes, and pubs. Check out the *Barrel House* at 22 North First Street (509-453-3769), which offers fine food, wines, and microbrews. On South Second

Street stop by Kana Winery (509-453-6611) with its quaint tasting room and multiple varietals. On Yakima Avenue between Fifth and Sixth Streets as well as on Second Street and A Avenue, browse a collection of delightful antiques shops. For a quick snack, stop by a local favorite, **Poochie's Gourmet Hot Dogs** at 301 South Third Avenue (509-452-3268) and choose from about thirty types of specialty hot dogs and sandwiches.

The 1885 Fire Station and Yakima City Hall building at 27 North Front Street now houses **Bob's Keg & Cork** (509-573-3691), serving a variety of microbrews and Yakima Valley wines Tuesday through Saturday from 3:00 p.m. The **White House Cafe** at 3602 Kern Street (509-469-2644) is in a 1929 farmhouse. It offers tasty breakfast and lunch fare as well as a gift shop and two B&B rooms.

In 1889 the Switzer Opera House was built at 5 North Front Street and housed Yakima's first performing arts and vaudeville theater. Now renovated, the building houses a variety of shops. For great baked goods find **Essencia Artisan Bakery & Chocolatiere** at 4 North Third Street (509-575-5570).

In 1898 the Lund Building was constructed on the corner of North Front Street and Yakima Avenue. In those days it housed such colorful establishments as Sam's Cafe, the Alfalfa Saloon, and the Chicago Clothing Company. The early establishments are gone; nowadays, call ahead for reservations at the splendid **Greystone Restaurant** (5 North Front Street; 509-248-9801). The dining room is open Monday through Saturday from 5:00 p.m.

The **Capitol Theatre,** at 19 South Third Street (509-853-8000; www .capitoltheatre.org), is another historic structure restored to its 1920s splendor. A resident ghost, Sparky, reportedly decided to stay on after the renovation. The theater is now home to the Yakima Symphony. Music lovers head to the Seasons Performance Hall at 101 North Naches Avenue (888-723-7660; www .seasonmusicfestival.com). The nonprofit showcases rising stars and seasoned performers playing jazz, Mexican folk, classical, and world music.

Be sure to plan a stop at the **Yakima Valley Museum** at 2105 Tieton Drive (509-248-0747; www.yakimavalleymuseum.org) for a soda, thick milkshakes, and a hot dog ordered at the old-fashioned soda fountain. A bright neon sign greets visitors at the entry to the soda fountain, the floor sports black-and-white square-tiled linoleum, and at the counter folks sit on round stools covered with bright red vinyl. In other sections of the museum you can browse a fine Native American collection, see wagons and carriages (from stagecoach to hearse), and turn the kids loose in the children's interactive center.

Located in a renovated fruit warehouse, **Glenwood Square** at 5110 Tieton Drive offers old, polished-wood floors and is home to Zesta Cucina (509-972-2000), a local restaurant open daily and offering a variety of Washington wines.

The Little Soapmaker, in downtown Yakima at 302 West Yakima Avenue (509-972-8504), sells natural handmade soaps and other natural products.

Those who get hungry for fine gourmet Mexican cooking should try the well-known *Santiago's Restaurant* (509-453-1644) at 111 East Yakima Avenue, 5 blocks west of the convention center. It's closed on Sunday. Or call for dinner reservations at the *Apple Tree Restaurant* at the *Apple Tree Golf Course,* 8804 Occidental Road (509-966-7140). The chef cooks up delicious apple-wood-smoked prime rib. The best time to go is evening in time for sunset views of the golf course and surrounding hills. The course's signature hole is number 17, a large apple-shaped island green connected to the fairway by a footbridge "stem" and with an adjacent sand trap shaped like a large leaf.

Consider staying a day or two to further explore this interesting city of railroad memorabilia and this large region of fruit orchards, vineyards, wineries, and tasting rooms. Sleep in a bed-and-breakfast inn in a cherry orchard just west of downtown Yakima. The *Orchard Inn* at 1207 Pecks Canyon Road (866-966-1283; www.orchardinnbb.com) has spacious guest rooms, private bathrooms, and gourmet breakfasts in a casual European atmosphere. Nearby, visit *Washington Fruit Place and Gift Shop at Barrett Orchards* (www.treeripened.com) for fresh cherries and other juicy fruits of the season in a big red barn located on Pecks Canyon Road. You are also invited to walk an interpretive pathway in the cherry orchard. At A *Touch of Europe Inn Bed and Breakfast* at 220 North Sixteenth Avenue (888-438-7073; www.winesnw.com/toucheuropeB&B.htm), the innkeepers offer elegant Victorian- and European-style decor in three guest rooms on the second floor. Gourmet breakfasts are served in the morning room on the main floor.

Two miles east of Yakima, *Birchfield Manor Country Inn* at 2018 Birchfield Road (800-375-3420; www.birchfieldmanor.com) offers elegant meals and overnight accommodations in a twenty-three-room Victorian-style mansion, complete with crystal chandeliers, a winding staircase, and flower garden. You'll find an abundance of genteel comforts (hot tub, pool, private baths) and a choice of eleven charming, antiques-filled guest rooms. If the notion of a sumptuous five-course gourmet dinner including decadent desserts sounds appealing, call the Birchfield staff to inquire about reservations Thursday through Saturday. Or in Selah, try the Wine Country Inn at 505 Ames (509-697-8700; www.thewinecountryinn.com) with three rooms plus a guest cottage.

US 12 west of Yakima passes through the orchard-filled Naches Valley on its way to 14,411-foot snowy Mount Rainier and the central Cascade Mountains area. Find Eschbach Park, a popular park for water-play activities and kayak

Smart Elk

This is a tale of unintended consequences. In 1913 a herd of Rocky Mountain elk were introduced into mountains near Yakima to rebuild a nearly extinct herd. Elk thrived, multiplied, and became a costly nuisance to ranchers and orchardists every winter when they migrated to the lowlands for better pickings. In 1939, when 3,000 elk were pitted against irate landowners (shots were fired), the state stepped in and created the Oak Creek Wildlife Area, now 42,000 acres.

About 100 miles of 8-foot-high fence protected landowners but the elk went hungry because their winter grazing area had been significantly reduced. Elk with their ribs showing created a new class of irate humans—hunters—who objected to prey normally weighing 400 to 900 pounds being reduced to skin and bones from lack of feed. The only solution, other than drastically reducing the herd, was to feed the elk. By 1945 the landowners were happy, the hunters' blood pressures were lowered, and the elk went on the dole, content enough to build their numbers to the current 10,000 elk in several herds.

Not every elk comes to the feeding stations but each winter the hay attracts up to 7,000. Let's see, several pounds of hay per elk times the number of elk times the number of feeding days . . . the need for hay made hay farmers happy, too. The annual feeding also attracts about 100,000 visitors, who rarely get the chance to be so close to hundreds of elk, which they do at the main Oak Creek feeding station.

That many visitors needed an interpretive center (9:00 a.m. to 4:00 p.m. daily during the winter) run by volunteers with videos, exhibits, a kids' corner, and temperatures warmer than those outside. The popular truck tour delights those who take it. Visitors can ride in the trucks that are dropping off the hay, surrounded by hungry elk. The truck experience is by reservation, (509) 653-2390, and first-come, first-serve. It's smart to call ahead.

Of course the same rationale led to the reintroduced bighorn sheep getting in line for a winter handout. They're fed mid-morning at the nearby Cleman Mountain feeding station (ask for directions). The elk are fed next to the interpretive center at 1:30 p.m., with January and February driving in the most hay-chompers.

rentals. For information, call the Yakima Greenway Foundation at (509) 453-8280.

Just past the Naches Valley, 2 miles west of the Highway 410 turnoff, is the **Oak Creek Wildlife Area** (509-653-2390), a winter feeding station for elk and mountain goats in winter and a popular spot for hunting and bird-watching. Continuing west, you'll ascend the Tieton River and climb through sagebrush-covered hills and the Gifford Pinchot National Forest up to **White Pass** at an elevation of 4,500 feet. Along the way see numerous lakes, fishing resorts, and campgrounds. This scenic route comes with dramatic geological formations and mountain areas covered with Douglas fir, western red cedar, and alpine fir. White Pass has relatively light traffic and long stretches of undeveloped forest, making it a favorite route for bicyclists and a popular destination for all-season outdoor recreation.

To find a good place to eat and sleep that's substantially farther off the beaten path, head northwest from Naches on Highway 410 toward Mount Rainier National Park. You'll find **_Whistlin' Jack Lodge_** on the Naches River at 20800 Highway 410 (800-827-2299; www.whistlinjacklodge.com). The restaurant features fresh mountain trout, prime rib, and Washington's best wines. During summer, enjoy a pleasant lunch outside on the deck. Accommodations include a lodge, riverfront motel, and streamside cottages with private hot tubs. Call for reservations or winter road conditions.

If you're traveling RV-style, you could check for sites at **_Squaw Rock Resort_** on the Naches River at 15070 Highway 410 (509-658-2926). Both the resort and Whistlin' Jack Lodge are about 40 miles northwest of Yakima and not far from 14,410-foot Mount Rainier. You can access scenic drives and campgrounds on Mount Rainier by crossing over 5,430-foot Chinook Pass. From Naches you could also travel southwest of the mountain on US 12, which winds over 4,500-foot White Pass and down toward Packwood and Randle. At Randle inquire at the Cowlitz Valley Ranger Station (360-497-1100) for backroad directions to see sections of trees blown down when Mount St. Helens erupted in May 1980 and again in 2004.

Places to Stay in South Central Washington

GRANDVIEW

Apple Valley Motel
903 West Wine
Country Road
(509) 882-3003

STEVENSON/CARSON

Columbia Gorge Riverside Lodge
200 Southwest Cascade Avenue
Stevenson
(509) 427-5650

Sandhill Cottages
932 Hot Springs Avenue
Carson
(800) 914-2178

SUNNYSIDE

Sunnyside Inn Bed and Breakfast
804 East Edison Avenue
(800) 221-4195

TOPPENISH

Toppenish Inn
515 South Elm Street
(509) 865-7444

Yakama Nation RV Resort
280 Buster Road
(800) 874-3087

TOUTLE/PACKWOOD

Cowlitz River Lodge
13069 U.S. Highway 12
(888) 305-2185

Eco Park Resort Cabins and RV Park
14000 Spirit Lake Highway
(360) 274-6542

TROUT LAKE/HUSUM

The Farm Bed & Breakfast
490 Sunnyside Road
Trout Lake
(509) 395-2488

Husum's Riverside Bed & Breakfast
866 Highway 141
Husum
(509) 493-8900

Kelly's Trout Creek Inn Bed & Breakfast
25 Mount Adams Road
Trout Lake
(509) 395-2769

VANCOUVER

Red Lion at the Quay
on the Columbia River
100 Columbia Street
(360) 694-8341

WHITE SALMON

Inn of the White Salmon
172 West Jewett Boulevard
(800) 972-5226

YAKIMA

Birchfield Manor Country Inn
2018 Birchfield Road
(800) 375-3420

Orchard Inn Bed & Breakfast
1207 Pecks Canyon Road
(866) 966-1283

Places to Eat in South Central Washington

BICKLETON

Bluebird Inn Tavern
121 Market Street
(509) 896-2273

CARSON

#7 Coffee Roasting Company at Sandhill Cottages
932 Hot Springs Avenue
(800) 914-2178

Sodbusters Cafe
1040 East Broadway
(509) 773-6160

SELECTED VISITOR INFORMATION CENTERS

Hood River
Hood River, OR
(800) 366-3530
www.hoodriver.org

Goldendale
(509) 773-3400
www.goldendalechamber.org

Greater Kelso Area
(Mount St. Helens)
(360) 577-8058

Mount Adams
(509) 493-3630
www.mtadams.com

Prosser
(800) 408-1517
www.prosserchamber.org

Skamania County
(800) 989-9178
www.skamania.org

Toppenish
(509) 865-3262
www.toppenish.net

Vancouver
(877) 600-0800
www.southwestwashington.com

Washington Road Conditions
(800) 695-7623
www.wsdot.wa.gov/traffic

Yakima Valley
(800) 221-0751
www.visityakima.com

ALSO WORTH SEEING

Barrett Orchards
Yakima
(509) 966-1275
www.treeripened.com

Cave B Estate Winery, Cave B Inn at Sagecliff and Tendrils Restaurant
Vantage area
www.cavebdirect.com

Gorge Amphitheater
Near Vantage
Info: (425) 990-0222
Lodging: (888) 925-2204

Mount Hood Railroad
Hood River, Oregon
(800) 872-4661
www.mthoodrr.com

Seasons Performance Hall
Yakima
(888) 723-7660
www.seasonsmusicfestival.com

GRANDVIEW

Dykstra House Restaurant
114 Birch Avenue
(509) 882-2082

PROSSER

The Blue Goose Restaurant
306 Seventh Street
(509) 786-1774

STEVENSON

Bahma Coffee Bar & Bistro
256 Second Street
(509) 427-8700

Walking Man Brewery & Public House
240 Southwest First Street
(509) 427-5520

SUNNYSIDE

Cactus Juice Cafe
632 East Decatur Avenue
(509) 839-4480

Snipes Mountain Microbrewery
905 Yakima Valley Highway
(509) 837-2739

TOPPENISH

Cattlemen's Restaurant
2 South Division Street
(509) 865-5885

TROUT LAKE

KJ's Bear Creek Cafe
2376 Highway 141
Trout Lake
(509) 395-2525

VANCOUVER

Dulin's Cafe
1708 Main Street
(360) 737-9907

Ice Cream Renaissance
2108 Main Street
(360) 694-3892

The Restaurant at the Historic Reserve
Officer's Row, Grant House
(360) 906-1101

YAKIMA

Ballesteri's Cafe
4001 Summitview
(509) 965-8592

El Porton Restaurant
420 South 48th Avenue
(509) 965-5422

The White House Cafe
3602 Kern Street
(509) 469-2644

Northeast Washington

Washington's northeast corner is a high desert and farming region of stark contrasts. In a few hours you can travel through steep basalt canyons with the spicy smell of sagebrush, over hills covered with wheat fields and dotted with isolated farm houses and outbuildings, and through thick pine forests. The region's geological history is dynamic and readily visible in the layered walls of coulees and steep canyons cut deep by ancient glaciers and rivers.

You meet local residents at cafe lunch counters, at small restaurants, or at bistros and brewpubs. They are aware of the seasonal changes and their relationship to the farms, ranches, forests, and rivers upon which so much of the local economy depends. They take pride in their Native American, farmer, rancher, and forestry heritages, which are very much alive.

Northeast Washington also offers a variety of all-season outdoor activities, including hiking, bicycling, fishing, hunting, boating, snowmobiling, ice fishing, and skiing. On the shores of many rivers and lakes, secluded retreats and fishing resorts beckon.

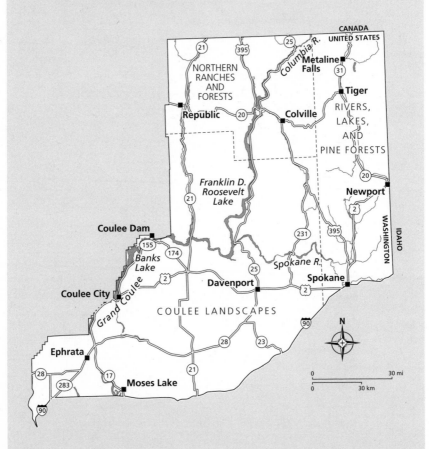

Coulee Landscapes

A good place to start your tour of the region is the town of ***Ephrata.*** From Interstate 90 take Highway 283 northeast from George or Highway 17 northwest from Moses Lake, past enormous circular fields of corn, wheat, potatoes, and legumes kept green by massive central-pivot irrigation systems. This high plain is so wide you can glimpse hills to the north but only a hint of a southern ridge.

Like many northeast Washington counties, Grant County preserves its past. The ***Grant County Historical Museum and Village*** at 742 Basin Street Northwest (509-754-3334; call for hours, closed Wednesday), located at the north end of Ephrata, offers thirty-six buildings and shops that show the region's past. Walk through carefully re-created print, camera, and blacksmith shops; saloons, a one-room schoolhouse, homesteads, a 1971 Burlington Northern caboose, laundry, the old Grant County Journal building, Saint Rosalima's Church (the first Catholic church in the county), a fire house with a 1939 fire truck, the original Krupp-Marlin jail, and a collection of the big farm machines that made Grant County a major agricultural producer, all arranged on a four-acre site. A two-hour tour with a guide begins at 3:00 p.m. Monday through Saturday. For another glimpse of local history, stop by the 1917 ***Grant County Courthouse,*** west of the highway at the corner of First Northwest and C Streets. The courthouse is heated geothermally from a nearby hot spring.

Ritzville, about 30 miles east of Moses Lake at the junction of Highway 395 and I-90, is in the heart of the rolling wheat lands and once may have been the largest wheat-receiving station in the world. A self-guided downtown walking tour is one way to be introduced to the town; printed guides are available at two museums. The large metal sculptures scattered about town represent its history.

About 50 to 60 trains a day roll by the 1910 Ritzville Railroad-Depot History Museum (201 West Railroad Avenue). "That makes this a railroad-lovers paradise. Everything from soup to nuts is shipped through here. It's the main line to Portland," said a volunteer. The women's restroom still has the original tank on the water closet. The depot collection includes a working telegrapher's office, a caboose, and the town's first horse-drawn hearse. Donations are accepted. The Burroughs Home History Museum (408 West Main Avenue) was the residence of a pioneer physician that has been restored to its original condition with household items from the 1890s to 1920s. The two museums share the same telephone number, (509) 659-1656; both are open 11:00 a.m. to 3:00 p.m. Tuesday through Saturday Memorial Day through Labor Day.

NORTHEAST WASHINGTON'S TOP HITS

Bing Crosby Memorabilia Room
Gonzaga University
Spokane

Dry Falls Interpretive Center
Coulee City

Fort Spokane
Creston

Gehrke Windmills
Grand Coulee

Grand Coulee Dam
Coulee Dam

Keller Ferry

Kettle Falls Historical Center
Kettle Falls

Lake Lenore Caves
Soap Lake

Lake Roosevelt
Kettle Falls

Lincoln County Historical Museum
Davenport

Manito Park Gardens
Spokane

North Pend Oreille Scenic Byway and
Selkirk International Loop
Ione

Northwest Museum of Arts and
Culture and Historic Campbell House
Spokane

Pend Oreille County Historical
Museum
Pend Oreille

Sherman Pass Scenic Byway
Sherman Pass

Soap Lake
Soap Lake

Spokane River Centennial Trail
Spokane

Steamboat Rock
Electric City

Stevens County Historical Museum
Colville

Stonerose Interpretive Center
Republic

Ritzville has several inns and motels; or consider the Nelson H. Greene Portico B&B at 502 South Adams (509-659-0800), a 1902 Victorian built for the town's first mayor. For dining, check out Greenside Café overlooking the Ritzville Municipal Golf Course (104 East 10th Avenue; 509-659-9868) or sample the deli and pizza at Spike's Deli and Pizza at 1611 Smitty's Boulevard (509-659-0490). Head to Sharon's Drive-in, 402 East First Avenue (509-659-0208) or eat at the Circle T Inn at 214 West Main (509-659-0922). Find good choices at the Blue Bike Café at 408 West First Avenue (509-659-0402).

Another option out of Moses Lake is to follow Highway 17 north to *Soap Lake*. Cherished by local tribes and early settlers for its healing properties, Soap Lake continues to draw people seeking physical rejuvenation. Seventeen minerals, with sodium bicarbonate the most common, give the water its soapy texture.

Soap Lake's popularity is nothing like its heyday at the turn of the twentieth century, but the crowds still come. Experience the water's effects with daily soaks at one of the town's two beaches or in baths piped from mineral waters deep in the lake to several of the motels. East Beach, located near the highway and motels, is the most popular with tourists. West Beach, separated by a small, rocky peninsula, is preferred by local residents.

If you'd like to linger a day or two, ask about accommodations at **Notaras Lodge** at 236 East Main Street (509-246-0462; www.notaraslodge .com). Choose from fifteen different rooms in four large log structures that offer outside entrances and small sitting decks. Each room has handcrafted log walls, a comfortable sitting area, and a small kitchenette (three rooms have full kitchens). All rooms are decorated with Western and antique memorabilia. Or check out the Inn at Soap Lake at 226 Main Avenue West (800-557-8514; www .innsoaplake.com) with its fascinating stone walls and history as a stable and blacksmith turned hotel in 1915.

Don's Restaurant at 13 Canna Street (509-246-1217), just across the street from Notaras Lodge, is a local favorite for steak, pasta, and seafood. Call to see what day Greek cuisine is served. For burgers stop at **B&B Restaurant** at 115 Daisy North (509-246-1231), under one owner for more than two decades.

Soap Lake is the southernmost of the Grand Coulee's chain of mineral-rich lakes. The Grand Coulee was formed by glacial action that cut through layers of thick volcanic basalt. Highway 17, from Soap Lake to **Coulee City,** provides a scenic route through the lower end of the coulee. You'll follow secluded lake beds, cut deep into reddish brown cliffs, their shorelines often crusted white with minerals. Lake Lenore has public access, with several spots to launch a boat or to stop and watch the waterfowl in lakeside wetlands.

Off the highway opposite Lake Lenore is the turnoff to **Lake Lenore Caves State Park** (509-632-5583), 8 miles north of Soap Lake. A gravel road takes you to the trailhead for a 3-mile hike through sagebrush and up the cliff sides to the ancient caves. There, like ancient hunter-gatherers, you can find shelter from the heat in these cool, rocky overhangs. Watch graceful cliff swallows, listen to crickets, hear the dry scrub rustling in the breeze, and absorb the stark beauty of the wide coulee landscape.

Between Alkali and Blue Lakes, you may catch sight of the **Caribou Cattle Trail.** A sign marks the point where the trail crosses the road. Originally a Native path, the 500-mile trail was used in the late nineteenth century as a supply route by miners and Blue Lake homesteaders. A few miles north on Blue Lake, **Coulee Lodge Resort** at 33017 Park Lake Road (509-632-5565; www.couleelodgeresort.com) offers six cabins, nine well-equipped mobile homes, and campsites. Rent a 14-foot aluminum boat to chase trout or the scenery. The site includes a nice swimming beach. The resort is located 15 miles north of Soap Lake.

Nearby, off Highway 17, **Sun Lakes-Dry Falls State Park** (509-632-5583; www.parks.wa.gov) offers camping, horseback riding, golf, mountain biking, and wildlife viewing. The **Dry Falls Interpretive Center** (509-632-5214), open daily year-round near Coulee City at the south end of **Banks Lake,** offers spectacular views of what was once a gigantic waterfall—possibly the largest that has ever existed on Earth. It is now a dry cliff 400 feet high and 3½ miles wide. Exhibits explain the geological forces that created this massive precipice and why it is now without water. Learn of the lush environment that covered this area twenty million years ago and how the largest basaltic lava flows on Earth, up to a mile thick, eventually engulfed 200,000 square miles of the Pacific Northwest. Powerful forces buckled and warped the cooled lava plateau, followed by glaciation and massive flooding, creating the dramatic landscape before you.

U.S. Highway 2 and Highway 17 intersect near **Dry Falls Cafe,** then US 2 crosses the Dry Falls Dam at the south end of Banks Lake. Turn right off US 2 at Coulee City to explore this windblown Western town, originally a watering hole along the Caribou Trail that is now dominated by huge grain elevators. Pick up a walking-tour brochure at the **Country Mall Store** on Main Street. If you happen into Coulee City on Tuesday or Saturday between 10:00 a.m. and 3:00 p.m., you can learn about art and local history from members of the **Highlighters Art Club,** who meet at 504 West Main Street (509-632-5373), tucked between two taverns, Couleegans and Grandpa Joe's. The gallery, in a building constructed in 1905, features art produced by members, such as oil paintings, woodcarvings, and dried-flower arrangements. For dinner, try **Steamboat Rock Restaurant** (509-632-5452) at 420 West Main Street.

If you continue east, US 2 passes through a series of small farm towns at about 10-mile intervals. **Wilbur,** at the junction of US 2 and Highway 21, is worth a stop. The town's main park, located south of Main Street, is a shady oasis of mature trees and green lawns. The town displays its history at the **Big Bend Historical Society Museum** (509-647-5863), housed in a 1915-era Lutheran church 1 block north of Main Street on Wilbur's west side. The museum is open Saturday 2:00 p.m. to 4:00 p.m. June through August, as well as during Wild Goose Bill Days, named for the town's infamous founder and held the second weekend in June. The museum's collection from the late 1800s and early 1900s includes old farm machinery and an extensive photography collection. It represents the towns of Wilbur, Creston, and Almira.

Wilbur has but one thoroughfare, Main Street, and the eateries there include **Billy Burger** (you're unlikely to miss the cartoon sign on a tall post),

Doxie's Drive-In, and the ***Alibi Tavern.*** The larger Homestead Café has sit-down service and a larger menu. "You really can't get lost in Wilbur," points out a longtime resident, who recently moved back to her hometown. You could also drive 8 miles east to ***Creston*** and try the ***Corner Cafe*** on Main Street. You can't get lost in Creston, either.

For another taste of Washington's varied topography, head north from Wilbur on Highway 21 past trees and farms in distant clumps like islands in a sea of grain before the road winds abruptly down through layered coulee cliffs to the Columbia River and the Lake Roosevelt National Recreation Area. If you're traveling RV-style, plan to spend at least one night at ***Keller Ferry*** at the splendid ***River Rue RV Campground*** (509-647-2647; www.riverrue.com). Folks will find full hookups, clean restrooms, and a full-service deli here.

At Keller Ferry Marina the Colville Confederated Tribes rent out thirty houseboats from 46 to 59 feet in length that sleep up to thirteen people. For information and current rates, call the Colville Tribe's Roosevelt Recreation Enterprise at (800) 648-5253 (www .rrehouseboats.com). This is a popular Coulee Country vacation option; reservations are accepted in June for the

thegehrke windmills

Erected in North Dam Park overlooking Banks Lake and near the city of Grand Coulee, more than 650 windmills have been built by local resident Emil Gehrke. He fashioned the folk-art treasures from old cast-off iron parts and painted them in bright colors. Take a camera for good shots of you and the kids and the fanciful windmills.

following year. You could bring your own canoe or kayak to reach isolated campsites along Lake Roosevelt's pristine shoreline. For houseboat rentals at the far north end of Lake Roosevelt, contact ***Lake Roosevelt Houseboat Vacations & Marina*** in Kettle Falls (800-635-7585; www.lakeroosevelt.com). Lake Roosevelt and the ***Lake Roosevelt National Recreation Area*** extend 151 miles north from Grand Coulee Dam to the scenic Colville National Forest and to the U.S.–Canadian border into British Columbia. The lake offers 630 miles of shoreline and year-round fishing for kokanee, walleye, large- and smallmouth bass, rainbow trout, perch, crappie, and sturgeon. Some of the most scenic lakeside campgrounds are head north on Highway 25 into the northern section of the recreation area that borders the Colville National Forest. For information and maps, contact the National Park Service headquarters for the Lake Roosevelt National Recreation Area (509-633-9441) in the town of Grand Coulee, or the district park service office in Kettle Falls (509-738-6266).

The Colville Confederated Tribes

Named for an Englishman who was in the rum and molasses business and who never set foot in America, the Colville Confederated Tribes is made up of twelve different bands: Chelan, Entiat, Lake, Nez Percé (from Northeast Oregon), Methow, Moses-Columbia, Nespelem, Palus, San Poil, Colville, Okanogan, and Wenatchee. Prior to 1826 these separate nomadic bands fished, hunted, and traded furs and goods with each other in the area of Kettle Falls before European settlers and business interests established the Fort Colville trading post. From 1826 to 1887 the Indians traded the lush pelts and hides of beaver, brown and black bear, grizzly, muskrat, fisher, fox, lynx, martin, mink, otter, raccoon, wolverine, badger, and wolf at the post.

St. Paul's Mission near Kettle Falls includes the original site of Fort Colville and a rustic log missionary church. In 1872 the Colville Indian Reservation was formed; today it contains about 1.4 million acres. Travelers are invited to visit the tribal headquarters located near Nespelem about 20 miles north of Grand Coulee Dam. Here you can learn about the enterprises owned and operated by the tribes, including a timber and wood products operation; a tree replanting program; a fish hatchery that provides fish for the lakes and streams in the region; and a fleet of thirty *houseboats on Lake Roosevelt* (800-648-5253). To enjoy fishing on the reservation, contact the Tribal Fish and Wildlife Department in Nespelem (509-634-2110). For a historical look, visit the Colville Confederated Tribal Museum at 512 Mead Way (509-633-0751), which in 2008 was being renovated.

The Keller Ferry offers a free ten-minute crossing with runs every fifteen minutes between 6:00 a.m. and 11:00 p.m. We're talking very small ferry here; yours may be the only car on the ferry's small deck. Many of the large houseboats are launched nearby. The river is often so placid you can see the dry sage-covered cliffs and hills reflected in the water. From the landing on the north side, you can turn left on Swawilla Basin Road to Grand Coulee Dam or continue north on scenic Highway 21 up the Sanpoil River to the old mining town of Republic.

The 24-mile Swawilla Basin Road west toward Grand Coulee Dam is a hilly one, surrounded by ponderosa pine, wild roses, purple lupine, and woolly mullein, with occasional old barns and glacial erratic along the way. *Grand Coulee Dam* is located 4 miles south of the junction with Highway 155.

Stop by the Grand Coulee Dam Interpretive Center (509-633-9265) across the bridge to learn the story of one of the world's largest concrete structures, celebrated in Woody Guthrie's famous song "Roll on, Columbia," and the largest component of the Pacific Northwest's extensive hydroelectric system. Exhibits explain the dam's history and engineering. Inquire about tours. The forty-minute laser light show of animated graphics projected on the dam's surface runs every night Memorial Day weekend through September.

Or enjoy the extensive *Community Trail System* that connects all four towns (West and East *Coulee Dam,* Grand Coulee, and Electric City) and offers exercise and spectacular views. The *Down River Trail,* a 6½-mile hiking, biking, wheelchair-accessible path, follows the Columbia River north from the dam. With gentle grades and landscaped rest stops, these trails offer relaxing strolls.

For an overnight option that offers expansive views of Grand Coulee Dam, including its grand evening Laser Light Show, call *Columbia River Inn* (800-633-6421; www.columbiariverinn.com) at 10 Lincoln Avenue in Coulee Dam. For information on other lodging, call the Grand Coulee Dam Area Chamber of Commerce at (800) 268-5332 (www.grandcouleedam.org).

Highway 155 follows the eastern shore of Banks Lake back to Coulee City. It is preferable to drive south on this road so that you can easily pull over at viewpoints and appreciate the awesome geology and the varied wildlife. Steamboat Rock, a former island in an ancient riverbed, rises like a solidified wave from the lake's north end. Picturesque *Northrup Canyon Trail* begins at the end of a ½-mile road across the highway from the rest stop near Steamboat Rock's north end. This moderately difficult trail stretches from a sheltered

Grand Coulee Dam

One of the most popular tourist attractions in Washington and one of the most impressive feats of engineering in the country, the Grand Coulee Dam attracts superlatives, comparisons, and illustrative examples to convey its sheer magnitude. Here are a few:

- The dam is the largest concrete dam in North America with enough concrete to build a standard 6-foot-wide sidewalk around the world at the equator.

- The dam is 500 feet wide at its base, 5,223 feet long, and stands 550 feet above bedrock—five feet shorter than the Washington Monument.

- It is the country's largest hydroelectric producer and the world's third-largest, generating 6,494,000 kilowatts in a single instant—more power than a million locomotives.

- Each of the six conventional pumps in Grand Coulee's Pump-Generator Plant is powered by a 65,000-horsepower motor that can pump 1,600 cubic feet of water per second, or 781,128 gallons per minute. In addition, six pump-generators, each having a 67,500-horsepower rating, can pump 1,948 cubic feet of water per second. One of these twelve units can fill the water needs of a city the size of Chicago.

canyon, through pine forests, and up a steep path to Northrup Lake atop the gorge. You'll see signs of pioneers having preceded you and perhaps spot eagles soaring overhead.

Steamboat Rock State Park (509-633-1304) offers campsites with full hookups and day-use facilities on the shore of Banks Lake just south of Grand Coulee and Electric City. Reservations are recommended because this is one of the state's more popular campgrounds (888-226-7688; www.parks.wa.gov). A hiking trail to the summit offers excellent views. Bring water for everyone in your group, and wear good walking shoes. Keep your distance from the edge of the cliff since basalt breaks easily; rattlesnakes in the area aren't considered particularly aggressive or lethal but a bite is still painful and dangerous. On scenic Banks Lake near Electric City, find beach and picnic areas, year-round fishing, immaculate grounds, cozy cabins, large villas, and RV spaces with hookups at **Sun Banks Lake Resort** (888-822-7195; sunbanksresort.com).

The town of Creston, east of Wilbur on US 2, begins and ends in wheat fields near the crest of the Columbia Plateau. Take the left fork 2 miles east of Creston to reach **Seven Bays** and **Fort Spokane.** Bachelor Drive (Miles Creston Road) zigzags through a narrow, wooded valley back to rolling wheat fields before it descends into pine forests near Lake Roosevelt and the Lake Roosevelt National Recreation Area. Located about 15 miles north of Creston, Seven Bays Campground, run by the Colville Confederated Tribes, offers a hilltop campground with RV hookup sites as well as a marina (509-725-7229) and store.

You can also visit and camp at nearby Lake Roosevelt National Recreation Area's (509-633-3830; www.nps.gov/laro) Fort Spokane and Fort Spokane Campground (509-725-2715). The campground has sixty-two sites, thirty under the reservation system (877-444-6777). Built in 1880 after the wars against Native Americans ceased, Fort Spokane was designed to maintain a truce between settlers and semi-nomadic tribes. Park volunteers and staff show what life was like back then through living-history programs at 11:00 a.m. on summer Sundays. The visitor center is located in the former guardhouse, one of the original fort buildings. An interpretive trail leads through the grounds, and the camping and RV sites are rimmed by forest-covered hills.

Continue north on scenic Highway 25 to Kettle Falls, about 40 miles south of the Canadian border, to reach the scenic Colville National Forest area (509-738-7700) and the far north section of Lake Roosevelt. Houseboat vacations are a strong draw in the northern lake area. Contact Lake Roosevelt Houseboat Vacations in Kettle Falls (800-635-7585; www.lakeroosevelt.com) to explore the world of luxurious 62-foot-long houseboats, eleven of which have hot tubs on the top deck. The houseboats accommodate up to thirteen people and contain full kitchen facilities, baths, common areas, sleeping areas, and outside and topside decks. Bring your own bedding, bath linens, food, and beverages. Cruise the upper section of the lake and pull into a secluded cove and enjoy. Houseboats are rented by the week, midweek, or weekends.

From Highway 25 you can head south, away from the Lake Roosevelt National Recreation Area, and plunge back into rolling grain country on the way to **Davenport.** This large agricultural town 33 miles west of Spokane is vibrant with farm life, sitting as it does in Lincoln County, which claims to be the second largest wheat-producing county in the world.

The Davenport City Park, south of the highway, surrounds a natural spring where huge cottonwoods have grown for centuries. The sweet water made this an important campsite for Native tribes and, in the late nineteenth century, for settlers and miners traveling along the White Bluffs Road. It is a pleasant spot for a picnic, with playground equipment, tables, and shade.

Nearby, at Seventh and Park, is the **Lincoln County Historical Museum** and Visitor Information Center (509-725-6711), chock-full of items and images collected over the past century, including a general store and a blacksmith shop. The museum is open Monday through Saturday from 9:00 a.m. to 5:00 p.m., May 1 to September 30. To satisfy an afternoon sweet tooth, try the old-fashioned soda fountain in Lincoln County Pharmacy at 621 Morgan Street (509-725-7091). Davenport has motels, or consider the Morgan Street B&B at 1001 Morgan Street (509-725-2079), a multi-roof home built in 1896 that also has a restaurant.

The rolling landscape continues east along US 2. At the town of Reardan, continue to Spokane or turn north toward Colville on Highway 231 for a scenic 70-mile drive up Spring Creek Canyon. Along this road is a scattering of old farms, many of which still use windmills to pump water for irrigation. By the time you reach the Spokane River at Long Lake Dam, the wheat fields and farms have given way to ponderosa pine forests and meadows. Find a friendly pit stop at the **Ford Trading Post** in tiny Ford with a post office, general store, rest stop, and gas station all jumbled together in a log building.

Continue on Highway 231 as the road curves west through Springdale. Nine miles north at the town of Valley, turn left on a 3-mile spur road to reach **Waitts Lake,** a spring-fed lake surrounded by wetlands and pine forests. Farms and fields dot its western shore, summer cabins and resorts hug the northeast shore, and public fishing spots offer recreation at the south end. The resorts are informal, catering to local families as well as visitors. **Silver Beach Resort** (3323 Waitts Lake Road, Valley; 509-937-2811) is open April 15-Sept. 15 and offers travelers five cabins, a general store, boat rentals, swimming and picnic sites, and a pleasant restaurant with a patio overlooking the lake.

Rivers, Lakes, and Pine Forests

Spokane, the largest city in the inland Northwest, started along the Spokane River near an ancient Indian campsite where members of the Spo-kan-ee tribe gathered for centuries to fish at the rapids. Although Spokane has grown into a major urban center, it retains much of its frontier identity. You'll see plenty of cowboy hats and pickup trucks even in downtown, and you don't have to go far past the city's suburban developments to find ranches and farms.

The Spokane River is still a dominant feature in the city. The *Spokane River Centennial Trail,* which follows the river, offers an ideal path for walking, bicycling, running, or skating. The Washington portion of the Centennial Trail runs 37 miles—22 from the Idaho border to Spokane's *Riverfront Park* in the center of downtown, where you can see the churning rapids where the tribe fished for salmon. Nearby you'll find espresso and hot dog stands as well as many pleasant eateries.

The recently renovated *Northwest Museum of Arts and Culture* and 1898 *Campbell House,* located in the city's historic Browne's Addition at 2316 West First Avenue (509-456-3931; www.northwestmuseum.org), display the region's Native American and pioneer past and current culture. The thirty-room English Tudor–revival mansion showcases the opulent lifestyle of one of the region's mining barons. Both museum and house are open 11:00 a.m. to 5:00 p.m. Tuesday through Sunday.

Consider staying at the E.J. Roberts Mansion at West 1923 First Avenue (509-456-8839; www.ejrobertsmansion .com), which involves sharing an 1889 Queen Anne–style mansion that has been restored with the Roberts' descendants' memorabilia, china, gowns, pictures, and other items for the public to view on tour. It has been featured in *Victorian Homes* magazine and on HGTV's *If Walls Could Talk.*

At the *Marianna Stoltz House Bed & Breakfast,* located in a shady residential neighborhood at 427 East Indiana Avenue (509-483-4316; www

honorthyfather

Father's Day was "invented" in Spokane in 1910 by a local housewife, Mrs. John Bruce Dodd. Mrs. Dodd wanted a special day to honor her father, William Smart, a Civil War veteran who had raised her and her five brothers after his wife's early death. The new Downtown Spokane historic walk brochure pinpoints the church where Sonora Smart Dodd heard the sermon that inspired her to create Father's Day. She contacted the local YMCA and the Spokane Ministerial Association, who persuaded the city government to set aside the third Sunday in June to "honor thy father." Father's Day was signed into national law by President Richard Nixon in 1972.

.mariannastoltzhouse.com), innkeeper Phyllis Maguire will offer visitors four comfortable guest rooms on the second floor of her large, 1908 Craftsman-style home. The living room, dining room, and parlor come with leaded-glass windows, high ceilings, and fine woodwork of polished fir. Antique light fixtures and fringed lampshades mix well with the other period furnishings. The inn is just 5 blocks from *Gonzaga University* (502 East Boone Avenue), where the *Bing Crosby Memorabilia Room* (509-328-4097), located in Crosby Student Center and open to the public, is filled with photographs, letters, and musical memorabilia from the crooner's life. Crosby lived in Spokane as a boy.

Waverly Place Bed & Breakfast is located in the Corbin Park Historic District at 709 West Waverly Place (509-328-1856; www.waverlyplace.com). Four guest rooms on the second floor have views of the park and grounds, along with dormer window seats or turret sitting areas, stained-glass windows, gleaming fir floors, antique queen beds with down comforters and quilts, and baths with claw-footed soaking tubs and tiled showers. A delicious breakfast prepares you for a fine day of exploring the Spokane area.

In the early 1900s *Corbin Park,* then the regional fairgrounds, housed a ½-mile racing track, and the Gentlemen's Riding Club was soon established nearby. Sulky and harness racing were popular sports, with many prominent gentlemen of Spokane and their ladies attending regularly. Enjoy the park and its shady walking paths that pass by many vintage homes built in the early 1900s.

TOP ANNUAL EVENTS
IN NORTHEAST WASHINGTON

City of Lights
Grand Coulee area, all of December
(800) 268-5332

Colville PRCA Rodeo
Colville, mid-June
(509) 684-5973

Curlew Barrel Derby
Curlew, early June
(509) 779-4842

Laser Light Show on the Grand Coulee Dam
May–September
(800) 268-5332

Lilac Festival
Spokane, May
(509) 535-4554

Pend Oreille Poker Paddle
Newport, mid-July
(509) 447-5812

Pioneer Days
Davenport, mid-July
(509) 725-6711

Washington Open
Fiddle Contest
Republic, early August
(509) 775-3387

Good eateries abound in the Spokane area. In the downtown and near Riverfront Park check out the **Onion Family Restaurant** at 302 West Riverside (509-747-3852) for pastas, fajitas, chicken, gourmet salads, and a variety of hamburgers; **Rock City Italian Grill** (509-455-4400) at 808 West Main inside River Park Square for serious Italian food lovers; **Sawtooth Grill** at 801 West Main Street (509-363-1100) near River Park Square downtown for great burgers in a rustic mountain-cabin setting; and **Steam Plant Grill and Brew Pub,** located in historic Steam Plant Square at 159 South Lincoln Street (509-777-3900). Near Manito Park, **Lindaman's Café** at 1235 South Grand Boulevard (509-838-3000) shouldn't be missed for freshly made entrees, great salads and sandwiches, and tempting desserts (if possible take a picnic along to the park).

To get acquainted with the natural history of the area, go hiking at **Dishman Hills Natural Area** (509-477-4730), a 518-acre sanctuary just outside Spokane with an easy 2½-mile loop walk in the southeast hills. Check out additional outings in the Spokane area through the Inland Northwest Trails Coalition (www.inlandnorthwesttrails.org) for information on mountain biking, hiking, and road biking, or call (509) 487-7366. Take a walk in the splendid **John A. Finch Arboretum,** at 3404 West Woodland Boulevard (509-625-6200, part of Spokane City Parks) with its stands of rhododendron, azaleas, and lilacs. A mile-long natural area covers about sixty-five acres along the banks of Garden Springs Creek west of downtown Spokane.

One of the best outdoor experiences is to visit **Manito Park Gardens,** South Grand at Eighteenth Avenue (509-625-6200; www.spokaneparks.org), surrounded by historic homes and offering an extensively diverse horticultural display. Start your tour at Rose Hill, situated on a four-acre slope that overlooks the other garden sections. Formal beds of about 1,500 roses represent more than 150 varieties. Walk down to the Joel E. Ferris Perennial Garden, a three-acre oasis' of lawns and large perennial beds. Next visit the splendid Duncan Formal Gardens, just opposite Gaiser Conservatory, which houses collections of begonias, fuchsias, and tropical plantings. Follow a meandering path beyond the Lilac garden to find the secluded **Nishinomiya Tsutakawa Japanese Garden.** The graceful curved bridge over the reflecting pond, called a ceremony bridge, is borrowed from the Asian tradition. A small waterfall flows from the rising sun toward the setting sun; the three vertical stones in the central pond suggest cranes or ships at sea.

Spokane's garden-in-progress is the Corbin Moore-Turner Historical Garden adjacent to the Corbin Art Center (509-625-6677) in **Pioneer Park** at Seventh and Stevens Streets. The gardens offer examples of private residential landscapes that were adapted to the country garden look of the Arts & Crafts

Crafts style. For more information on area activities, contact the Spokane Area Visitor Information Center at 201 West Main Avenue (888-776-5263; www.visit spokane.com).

Before heading north from Spokane, gas up and fill your picnic cooler. Take US 2 north or first detour onto U.S. Highway 395 and visit the *Fire Lookout Museum,* 123 West Westview, 7 miles north of downtown Spokane. It's open only by appointment (509-466-9171; www.firelookouts.com). Inspect a replica of the type of lookout used to house volunteers in the high mountain areas during summer and fall fire seasons. Continue north to the community of *Deer Park* but call ahead to make an appointment to visit the *North Spokane Farm Museum* (509-466-2744), which has a collection of vintage farm machinery and household items dating from the 1890s to the 1950s, mostly in the 5,000-square-foot Red Shed.

From Deer Park head east a few miles to US 2 and north on this route through lush farmlands to the gentle Pend Oreille (pond-er-RAY) River Valley. On the banks of the Pend Oreille River is the town of *Newport,* 8 miles south of the Canadian border, and its Idaho neighbor, Oldtown. As you enter Newport from the southwest, you'll see *Centennial Plaza* to your right with its huge steam-engine wheel. The *Pend Oreille County Historical Museum* (509-447-5388) is in the 1908 brick I&WN Railroad depot, but there are outbuildings that create a two-block-long "village" with a settler's cabin and a one-room schoolhouse. It is open daily from 10:00 a.m. to 4:00 p.m. mid-May through September. Located nearby, at 337 Washington Street, is Owen's Grocery & Deli (509-447-3525), a great spot for snacks, espresso, and a cool treat at the old-fashioned soda fountain.

Steam-engine wheel in Centennial Plaza

The Newport-Oldtown Visitor Center (509-447-5812) is right behind the Big Wheel that powered the Diamond Match Lumber Mill. It is open 8:00 a.m. to 4:00 p.m. weekdays and 10:00 a.m. to 2:00 p.m. on summer Saturdays. Newport's Centennial Plaza has a three-level drinking fountain "serving man, beast, and dog" since 1911. Across the street is Newport's oldest building, Kelly's Tavern at 324 West Fourth Street (509-447-3267), a watering hole for miners, loggers, settlers, railway workers, visitors, and town folk since 1894. The tavern's impressive lead-glass bar was shipped around Cape Horn to San Francisco and then carried by wagon train to Newport.

Lodging options include motels as well as the Walden House B&B at 631 North Warren Avenue (509-447-5771; www.waldenhouse.com) and the luxurious *Inn at the Lake* at 581 South Shore Diamond Lake Road (509-447-5772; www.innatthelake.com). The Italian-style villa, built in 1993, offers water views, and the largest suite has a four-poster bed and a whirlpool tub.

You can travel north on either side of the Pend Oreille River, but Le Clerc Road on the east bank is quieter and more scenic. A half-mile north from the Newport/Oldtown bridge, visit an ancient Indian campsite at Pioneer Park. Recent archaeological studies have uncovered artifacts, earth ovens, and house pits that indicate use by the Kalispel Tribe for at least 800 years and by prehistoric hunter-gatherers for possibly 2,000 to 4,000 years. The park offers forested camping, picnic spots, and views of herons and waterfowl in nearby wetlands and on river islands. As you continue north, watch for osprey that catch fish by diving into the water. They build large nests on river pilings and snags.

A few miles north of the Usk bridge on Le Clerc Road, keep an eye out for a herd of buffalo in pastures by the river on the *Kalispel Indian Reservation,* the smallest reservation in Washington. The Kalispel people once numbered more than a thousand; now in the hundreds, the tribe has consolidated its small holdings and developed community buildings, a bison herd raised for meat, and an aluminum plant in Cusick.

At the *Manresa Grotto* on the Kalispel Reservation, a tribal holy site located a few miles north and on the east side of the river near Usk, take a short climb up a winding pathway and through boulders to the dome-shaped grotto, theoretically formed by the waves of an ancient glacial lake. Rows of flat stone pews are before an altar of mortared rock, a site of religious ceremonies for more than a century. The view is enchanting—the peaceful river valley surrounded by forested hills, all framed by the gray stone arch of the grotto entrance. The grotto's name was provided by a missionary priest who named it after a famous Spanish cave.

Le Clerc Road ends across the bridge from the town of *Ione,* once the site of the most successful lumber mill in northeast Washington. From the

Old Railroad Depot, built in 1909, take in breathtaking scenery on the historic **North Pend Oreille Valley Lion's Club Excursion Train** from Ione to Metaline Falls and back. Two-hour rides through forests, two tunnels, and over the Box Canyon trestle high above the Pend Oreille River are scheduled during selected summer and fall weekends. Call (509) 442-5466 (www.povn .com/npovlions) for information and reservations, which must be made at least two weeks in advance.

For more scenery, continue northeast of Sullivan Lake Road on the east side of the Pend Oreille River. **Sullivan Lake,** created by a dam in 1910 to run the cement plant at Metaline Falls, is situated at the foot of snowcapped peaks. There are forested campsites at Noisy Creek at the lake's south end and near Colville National Forest's Sullivan Lake Ranger District office at 12641 Sullivan Lake Road (509-446-7500) at the north end. The 4.2-mile **Lakeshore Trail** connects the two campgrounds and offers great views, especially during autumn, as well as lakeshore access. The **Mill Pond Historic Site** includes a barrier-free interpretive trail from the western edge of Mill Pond, a small lake created in 1910 located northwest on Sullivan Lake Road. The path follows a wooden flume that once ran between Sullivan Lake and Metaline Falls.

Continue west on Sullivan Lake Road to reach **Metaline Falls,** a small town nestled on the east bank of the Pend Oreille River that has attracted a lively artist community that has been voted one of the "100 Best Small Art Towns in America." The town's block-long main street (Fifth Street) ends at the city park and visitor center, a brightly painted railway car above terraced flower beds. To the left of the park is the **Washington Hotel** at 225 East Fifth Avenue (509-446-4415). Built in 1910, the hotel has been restored to its former status as the centerpiece of a bustling turn-of-the-twentieth-century mining town. "It was never an elegant hotel. It was a working man's hotel," said owner Lee McGowan, Metaline Falls artist and former mayor. McGowan decorated the eighteen rooms and maintains a deli and art gallery on the hotel's first floor. Nearby, at 221 East Fifth Avenue, you can meet the locals over breakfast, lunch, or dinner at **Cathy's Café** (509-446-2447).

The building that is now a performing arts center, the Cutter Theater at 302 Park Street (509-446-4108) was built early in the century as a school and named for talented Spokane architect Kirtland Cutter. Browse the permanent history and traveling art exhibits. A mile away is the town of Metaline, started during a gold strike and named for the many metals found in the area.

For a spectacular view, follow Highway 31 north about 12 miles, then turn left on the ¾-mile access road to **Boundary Vista House** with a platform suspended directly over the Boundary Dam for the best views of the dam, roaring river, and valley. Cross back over the river west of Metaline Falls and take the

Boundary Road turnoff to Boundary Dam and Gardner Cave. Along the way, try to spot beaver dams in the wetlands next to this scenic woodland road.

Boundary Road divides after 11½ miles. Take the left fork to reach the 1,055-foot-long *Gardner Cave* at Crawford State Park (summer, 509-446-4065; other times, 509-238-4258). The cave's limestone walls were formed from the bodies of ancient sea creatures that settled into ooze on the floor of an ancient ocean 500 million years ago. Groundwater seepage cut away the stone over the past 70 million years, creating the passage with its fantastic stalagmites and stalactites. Visitors must be accompanied by a ranger to enter the cave. Hour-long tours are conducted Thursday through Monday from Memorial Day through Labor Day. The cave is always cool (40 degrees) and lighted; cameras with flashes are OK.

Northern Ranches and Forests

Three miles south of Ione, Highway 20 turns west from the riverbank and heads over the Selkirk Mountains. As you drive through the small community of *Tiger,* stop at the *Tiger Historical Center/Museum.* The original store and post office were constructed in 1912 and served the community until 1975, when the post office was moved to Cusick. The Tiger Store was restored in 1999 and converted to a visitor center, museum, and gateway to the North Pend Oreille Scenic Byway and *Selkirk International Loop.* It also has a gift shop carrying creations of local artists. The center is open 10:00 a.m. to 5:00 p.m. Thursday to Monday from Memorial Day through September and the first three weekends in October. Bless them, they have a 24-hour restroom.

The road climbs and descends through evergreen forests and past a chain of glacial lakes cradled between the peaks. Among the biggest trees are Douglas fir, spruce, grand fir, and tamarack (aka mountain larch), all giant conifers. The aspen, birch, and tamarack turn vibrant colors of yellow, orange, and lime green in late September and October. The highway follows the Little Pend Oreille River through the Colville National Forest and past the *Little Pend Oreille Wildlife Area.* Leo, Thomas, Gillette, and Twin Lakes have campsites. The *Springboard Trail* from East Gillette Campground offers an easy 2.4-mile loop with interpretive highlights on the area's history and ecology as well as a platform with a view of the lakes.

The pine forest begins to thin as you move west on Highway 20 and descend into the pastoral Colville River Valley. *Colville* is a large, bustling town at the junction of Highway 20 and US 395. In town follow signs from the highway (Fifth Street) leading 2 blocks uphill on Wynne Street to reach the *Keller Heritage Center* and *Stevens County Historical Museum* (509-684-

5968; call for hours). A short trail leads up from the museum to the Graves Mountain Fire Lookout, moved from its original location to the top of a small hill. Enjoy a panoramic view of the valley, town, and mountains. Keller House Museum tells the area's story in chronological order from geological, Native American, and European perspectives.

If you've worked up an appetite during your travels, several pleasant restaurants are in Colville. Try Lovitt's Restaurant at 149 Highway 395 South (509-684-5444) one-half mile south of town for regional, Slow Food, and seasonal cuisine; ***Ronnie Dee's Drive-In*** at 505 North Lincoln (509-684-2642) for good burgers; or one of the locals' favorites, Courthouse Café (509-684-4404) at Astor and Elm, for homemade soups and sandwiches. If you're heading north from Colville toward the Canadian border and southern British Columbia, try the very casual Whitebird Saloon in Northport at 304 Center Avenue (509-732-6638).

For another adventure, drive about 45 miles north of Colville into the ***Colville National Forest,*** past Aladdin, Spirit, Northport, and Deep Lake, bringing you within 3 miles of the Canadian border surrounded by classic scenery and hiking opportunities.

The original site of ***Kettle Falls,*** northwest of Colville, is believed to be one of the oldest continuously occupied spots in the Northwest. As long as 9,000 years ago, an ancient tribe known as the Shonitkwa fished the steep falls. Over the centuries Indians established permanent communities near the falls that existed until European settlement eroded traditional lifestyles. The falls and historic sites are now submerged under Lake Roosevelt. During the early spring drawdown in March or April, remnants of flooded islands and historic towns like Old Marcus (located about 5 miles north on Highway 25) are revealed.

You can learn more about the "People of the Falls" at the impressive ***Kettle Falls Historical Center,*** 1188 St. Paul's Mission Road on a spur road north of Highway 20 and 3½ miles west of Kettle Falls, just before the bridge over Lake Roosevelt. The center features murals and models for each season that tell the ancient story of tribal life near the falls.

Family owned farms and fruit orchards in the area offer berries, cherries, apricots, peaches, pears, apples, and grapes in season from June through September. Look for signs along nearby Peach Crest Road. Contact Kettle Falls Area Chamber of Commerce (509-738-2300; www.kettlefalls.com) for an orchard directory and map of fruit-picking spots.

The annual Garlic Faire at ***China Bend Winery,*** about 23 miles north of Kettle Falls at 3596 Northport Flat Road (800-700-6123; www.chinabend .com), occurs each August. From roasted garlic and garlic corn to garlic soup and pizza, garlic lovers indulge in a festive day of tasting and buying garlic products. The winery produces delicious table and dessert wines that don't contain sulfites. China Bend also offers a bed-and-breakfast for one party at a time.

If you are traveling in winter when Lake Roosevelt is at its fullest, the best bald eagle viewing area is along Highway 25. Take the turnoff south before Kettle Falls Bridge and head toward the Gifford ferry. The concentration of eagles reaches a peak in mid-February, when they're perched on top of gnarled snags and rocky outcroppings while on the lookout for fish.

Take the toll-free ferry to *Inchelium.* If you're tent camping, traveling by RV, or want a lakeside cabin, contact *Rainbow Beach Resort,* located on Twin Lakes (509-722-5901). Call well ahead for reservations because it's a popular spot during summer months. For a quiet retreat on Twin Lakes try *Log Cabin Resort* (509-722-3543; www.hartmanslogcabinresort.com) for cozy cabins and a homey family-style restaurant. After crossing the Kettle River Range and intersecting with Highway 21, head north along the picturesque Sanpoil River for about 30 miles to the community of Republic. You can also reach Republic from Kettle Falls by continuing west on Highway 20, the *Sherman Pass Scenic Byway,* winding up and over 5,575-foot Sherman Pass.

If you've ever hankered for wide-open spaces, Western hospitality, and delicious family-style meals, try a dude ranch, in this case the *K-Diamond-K Guest Ranch* five minutes south of Republic at 15661 Highway 21 South (888-345-5355; www.kdiamondk.com). A new 16-room guest lodge opened in 2007; four more guest rooms are in the Konz family's large log-style home. Activities include horseback riding, mountain biking, fishing, wildlife watching, stargazing, hunting, winter snowmobiling, cross-country skiing, and, in season, riding along on a cattle drive.

A loop around *Curlew Lake* to the north of Republic makes a pleasant bike ride or drive. The 7-mile-long lake, named after the bird, is surrounded by mountains and rolling hills. *Curlew Lake State Park* (509-775-3592; www .parks.wa.gov) offers a swimming area, boat launches, and campsites. Several small resorts are scattered along the lakeshore. *Fisherman's Cove Resort,* 11 miles north of Republic at 15 Fisherman's Cove Road (509-775-3641; http:// fishermanscove.us) welcomes families and offers rustic cabins in a quiet, lakeside setting. *Tiffany's Resort* at 1058 Tiffany Road (509-775-3152; www .tiffanysresort.com) on the opposite shore has been in business since 1939 and has comparable amenities.

The Kettle River History Club's *Car and Truck Museum* is located at 1865 North Highway 21 (509-779-4808) between the towns of Malo and *Curlew.* This is an old-car aficionado's dream: dozens of carefully preserved and restored cars, including vintage Model T Fords, Buicks, actor Walter Brennan's 1928 Phaeton, the only 1917 Chevrolet Royal Mail Roadster still running, and one of the only three 1920 Howard Cooper fire trucks ever made, all in operating condition. The museum is open from 10:00 a.m. to 5:00 p.m. daily June 1 through Labor Day weekend.

Kettle River History Club's
Car and Truck Museum

When is a ghost town not a ghost town? When it's Curlew, nestled between dry hills on the east bank of the Kettle River with a population of about 1,600. A popular Web site lists Curlew and ninety-three other Washington communities as ghost towns, although many of those designations fly in the face of any number of dictionaries' definitions. Maybe they're semi–ghost towns.

But back to the living . . . Follow signs to the right off Highway 21 into town. Curlew's main street, lined with dark-wood buildings with Western false fronts, overlooks the river through tall cottonwoods. Enter the time warp of the 1903 ***Ansorge Hotel Museum*** at 13 River Street (509-779-4823). It's a relic with clothes left in the bureau drawers and rope ladders on the second floor windows; guests are dissuaded from going into furnished rooms. A main town hub is the Second Time Around Country Store (509) 779-4808, which also serves as the phone number for the Ferry County Chamber of Commerce (www.ferrycounty.com).

Tradition says that moonshiners used to drop off barrels of illegal whiskey into the Kettle River in British Columbia and let them float across the border past customs officials. They'd be reclaimed when they reached Curlew. Since 1950 (with the exception of a few years in the 1970s), residents and visitors have placed their bets on the first Sunday in June during Barrel Derby Days. A barrel of water is dropped off the Job Corps Civilian Conservation Corps Bridge near Ferry, Wash., and the bets reflect what time and day people think the barrel will arrive in front of the Second Time Around store. Proceeds support Curlew's civic hall, built in the 1930s.

The ***Curlew Riverside Cafe*** at 813 River Street (509-779-4813) offers

Mexican and American food prepared from fresh ingredients. The dining room, with its wood-burning stove and rustic wood furniture, overlooks the Kettle River.

On your way back south on Highway 21 toward Republic, take the West Curlew Lake Road turnoff (west) at Curlew Lake's north end for a less-traveled route along the western shore. Klondike Road veers right about a mile south of the lake and then descends past pine trees and houses hugging the steep hillside into Republic.

Clark Avenue, the town's main street, was named for Republic Gold Mining and Milling Company president "Patsy" Clark. While most buildings' false fronts are recent additions to boost the town's already rustic feel, the **Republic Drug Store** (ca. 1906; 509-775-3352) at Six North Clark Avenue boasts an original storefront with hand-cranked awnings and pressed tin ceiling.

To participate in a paleontology treasure hunt, follow Sixth Avenue west to the **Stonerose Interpretive Center** at 15 North Kean Street (509-775-2295; www.stonerosefossil.org).The curator and assistants can introduce you to the fascinating world of fifty million years ago, when an ancient lake covered the future site of Republic. Fossil-hunting tours are permitted when the center is open (call for hours). Bring along a hammer and chisel, or rent some there, to use at the dig site north of town. The fossils you discover will be identified for you to take home, or, if you are lucky enough to find a new or rare species, you will be applauded as a paleontology hero, and your fossil will be kept for further study.

For tasty eats in the Republic area, try Esther's Mexican Restaurant at 90 North Clark Street (509-775-2088) for super burritos, shredded beef taco salads, and homebaked pies; and Mel's Diner at 30277 Highway 20 (509-775-0830). For coffees, espresso, and homemade pastries, stop by **Java Joy's Espresso** in Republic at 1015 South Clark Street (509-775-2025) and River Street Espresso in Curlew at 9 River Street (509-779-4937).

Places to Stay in Northeast Washington

COLVILLE/KETTLE FALLS

Beaver Lodge Resort
2430 Highway 20 East
Colville
(509) 684-5657

LAKE ROOSEVELT

Houseboat Vacations
Kettle Falls
(800) 635-7875

Lazy Bee Wilderness Retreat
3651 Deep Lake Boundary Road
Colville
(509) 732-8917

COULEE CITY

Coulee Lodge Resort
33017 Park Lake Road NE
(509) 632-5565

COULEE DAM

Columbia River Inn
10 Lincoln Street
(800) 633-6421

ELECTRIC CITY

Sky Deck Motel
138 Miller Avenue
(509) 633-0290

Sunbanks RV Resort & Marina
Banks Lake
South Highway 155
(509) 633-3786

INCHELIUM

Hartman's Log Cabin Resort
South Twin Lake
(509) 722-3543

METALINE FALLS

Washington Hotel
225 East Fifth Avenue
(509) 446-4415

REPUBLIC/CURLEW

Fisherman's Cove Resort
115 Fisherman's Cove Road
Republic
(509) 775-3641

K-Diamond-K Guest Ranch
15661 Highway 21 South
Republic
(509) 775-3536

Northern Inn
852 South Clark Street
Republic
(888) 801-1068

Wolfgang's Riverview Inn
2320 Highway 21 North
Curlew
(509) 779-4252

SOAP LAKE

Notaras Lodge
236 East Main Street
(509) 246-0462

SPOKANE

Marianna Stoltz House Bed & Breakfast
427 East Indiana Avenue
(509) 483-4316

Red Lion River Inn
700 North Division
(509) 326-5577

Waverly Place Bed & Breakfast
709 West Waverly Place
(509) 328-1856

VALLEY

Silver Beach Resort
3323 Waitts Lake Road
(509) 937-2811

ALSO WORTH SEEING

Discovery Loop

Highland Heritage Loop

North Pend Oreille County

Selkirk International Loop

Sherman Pass Scenic Byway

Places to Eat in Northeast Washington

COLVILLE/KETTLE FALLS

Whitebird Saloon & Eatery
304 Center Avenue
Northport
(509) 732-6638

COULEE CITY

Steamboat Rock Restaurant
420 West Main Street
(509) 632-5452

COULEE DAM

Melody's Restaurant & Lounge
512 River Drive
(509) 633-1151
Metaline Falls

Cathy's Cafe
221 East Fifth Avenue
(509) 446-2447

Western Star Restaurant
202 North Highway 31
(509) 446-2105

DAVENPORT

Edna's Drive In
302 Morgan
(509) 725-1071

GRAND COULEE

Sandwich Gardens & Pizza
211 Main Street
(509) 633-3367

REPUBLIC/CURLEW

Curlew Riverside Cafe
813 River Street
Curlew
(509) 779-4813

Java Joy's Espresso
1015 South Clark Street
Republic
(509) 775-2025

SOAP LAKE

Don's Restaurant
14 Canna Street
(509) 246-1217

SPOKANE

The Onion Family Restaurant
302 West Riverside
(509) 747-3852

The Shop Coffeehouse
924 South Perry Street
(509) 534-1647

Steam Plant Grill and Brew Pub
159 South Lincoln Street
(509) 777-3900

VALLEY

Silver Beach Resort Restaurant
3323 Waitts Lake Road
(509) 937-2811

WILBUR

Alibi Tavern
4 Southwest Main Street
(509) 647-2649

Southeast Washington

Southeast Washington is a region of rolling hills and wide blue skies. Much of the terrain is covered with fields of dry-land (unirrigated) wheat that casts a blanket of waving, textured green, then brown. The best way to explore this area is to get off the major highways and drive or bicycle along miles of farm roads that connect small communities. Walking, bicycling, or sitting in a grassy park or meadow, you often will hear the melodious trill of a western meadowlark, catch sight of a soaring hawk, and smell the soil warmed in the sun.

Few corners of this fertile region have been left untouched by human enterprise, although the seasonal crops still depend on natural cycles of snow, rain, and sun. Tens of thousands of acres burst with new green shoots following spring rains or undulate with tall golden grains in the late summer sun. The lives of farm and ranch families are integrated with their land and the seasons. In early spring, huge eight-wheel-drive tractors comb the terrain for planting, pulling 20-foot-wide plows that raise spires of dust. In late summer, giant combines harvest wheat, lentils, and peas. Farmhouses and big old barns nestle in valleys surrounded by tall shade trees planted by previous generations.

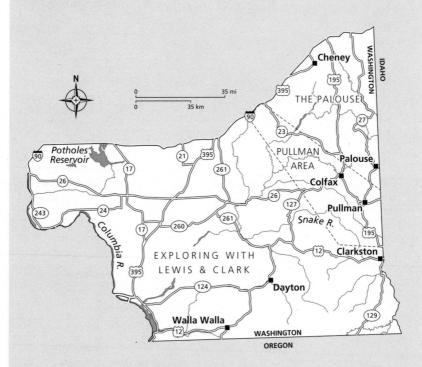

The quiet towns of this region, devoted to serving hardworking farm families, also welcome travelers. Walk any main street to see old brick buildings that once housed banks, stores, and fraternal organizations, many now in the process of being renovated for new enterprises such as coffeehouses, bakeries, cafes, and tasting rooms for the many new wineries in the region. Tall grain elevators stand like sentinels next to rail depots. Many abandoned depots have been, or are in the process of being, preserved and are coming to life again as local museums and vibrant community art centers.

Stop at the local cafe (many small towns have only one), where for the price of a cup of coffee and a piece of homemade pie you might hear stories of local history and gossip from fellow patrons eager to swap tales.

The Palouse

Palouse is derived from the French word *pelouse,* meaning "green lawn," an appropriate name for one of the most fertile grain-growing regions in the world. The Appaloosa, a breed of horses distinguished by its spotted coat and

SOUTHEAST WASHINGTON'S TOP HITS

Appaloosa Museum and Heritage Center
Moscow, Idaho

The Bank Left Gallery and Green Frog Cafe
Palouse

Bishop's U-Pick Orchard
Garfield

Dayton Depot
Dayton

Ferdinand's Ice Cream Shoppe
Washington State University
Pullman

Fort Walla Walla Museum Complex
Walla Walla

Heritage Square
Walla Walla

Palouse Falls
Starbuck

Perkins House
Pullman

Ray Chatters Newspaper and Printing Museum
Palouse

Steptoe Butte
Colfax

Three Forks Pioneer Village
Pullman

Turnbull National Wildlife Refuge
Cheney

Weinhard Hotel
Dayton

Whitman Mission National Historic Site
Walla Walla

Appaloosa Horse Museum

For history surrounding the Palouse's namesake horse, head east from Pullman on Highway 270 to the **Appaloosa Museum & Heritage Center** at 2720 West Pullman Road, Moscow (208-882-5578, press five; www.appaloosa.com). Straddling the state line but technically in Moscow, Idaho, the museum explores the Nez Percé, excellent breeders of horses whose spotted horses became known as Appaloosas. Exhibits include Native American artifacts, the Appaloosa's roots, saddles, Western art, and Western tack and clothing. During the summer, you can see Appaloosas in their fenced pasture. The museum is open 10:00 a.m. to 5:00 p.m. Monday through Friday and 10:00 a.m. to 4:00 p.m. Saturday.

gentle disposition, is a descendant of early horses used by the Native people of the Palouse.

Although most of this region is now farmed, there are still areas where the original Palouse environment is preserved. Chief of these is the **Turnbull National Wildlife Refuge** located at South 26010 Smith Road (509-235-4723; www.fws.gov/turnbull) south of Spokane near Cheney. The 16,000-acre refuge includes lakes and marshes that attract a wide variety of wildlife including elk, deer, coyotes, beaver, and muskrat. More than 50,000 ducks, geese, and other migratory birds cruise in for rest stops along the Pacific Flyway.

Generations before pioneers arrived, the Spokane tribe cherished this natural garden for its abundant roots and herbs, such as blue camas, wild onion, and kinnikinnick. Early farmers tried to drain these marsh areas but found that the resulting soil was poor. Rescued from development in the 1920s, the area was set aside as a wildlife preserve in 1937. Now visitors to Turnbull can bicycle, walk, or drive on a 5-mile gravel loop road to experience the area's original beauty. Signs along the Pine Creek Trail help acquaint you with the area's background and natural history. A wooden boardwalk over shallow Black Horse Lake allows close-up viewing.

Heading south on Rock Lake Road, watch the landscape change from rocky pine-covered meadows to rolling wheat farms. The terrain changes again around Rock Lake, a quiet expanse of water surrounded by basalt outcroppings. This area was the home of Chief Kamiaken of the Yakama Indian Nation. Along the lake's southeast shore is the **Milwaukee Road Corridor,** a railroad line until 1980 but converted to a public trail. This 100-mile-long trail system, known as the Iron Horse Trail State Park (www.parks.wa.gov), stretches from Cedar Falls near North Bend on the fringes of Seattle's suburbia east across the Cascade Mountains and to the Columbia River. The popular trail is used by hikers, bicyclists, equestrians, and even wagon trains, and there are many access points.

After traveling through the rolling hills of the Palouse, head for panoramic views from two towering buttes. *Kamiak Butte County Park,* named for Chief Kamiaken, is a 3,360-foot-tall "island" of pine, fir, and larch surrounded by wheat fields. The butte is 5 miles southeast of the town of Palouse near the Idaho border. The 3½-mile Pine Ridge Trail through the forest takes you on a self-guided nature walk to the top of the butte and back.

whataworm

If you happen to find a 3-foot-long pinkish-white wiggler, please don't bait your hook. It could be the endangered giant Palouse earthworm. They were thought to be confined to what was left of the native prairie's deep soils until 2008, when one was found in the wooded slope above Leavenworth. Only about thirty have been found in the last 30 years.

The park has nine campsites, with campfire pits and cooking grills. Picnic tables and three shelters with electricity, water, and barbecue make this a great spot for an impromptu outdoor feast. There is also an amphitheater for evening programs on local and natural history presented by volunteers from late June through August. For information contact Whitman County Parks in *Colfax,* (509) 397-6238.

Steptoe Butte, 15 miles north of Colfax, is, at 3,612 feet, the highest point in the region and a National Natural Landmark. Drive the road that spirals four times around the butte to the top to enjoy panoramic views of the Palouse's rolling fields and low hills as well as the distant Blue and Bitterroot Mountains. At the base you'll find a pleasant picnic area in an old apple orchard planted by one of the area's early homesteaders. In the 1880s another entrepreneur

Palouse fields

operated a roadhouse at the bottom of the butte and a hotel at the top, which burned down in 1896.

Oakesdale, located a few miles north of Steptoe Butte, is home to *Barron's Flour Mill,* a huge timber-frame structure, which was moved piece by piece from Illinois in 1889, and which still contains the original milling and sifting equipment. The mill was used to produce flour until 1939 and continued as a grain cleaning and storage facility until the 1960s. You can stop to take a gander at the historic structure by parking off Highway 271 as you enter Oakesdale.

Travel northeast on Highway 27 from Oakesdale to reach the village of *Tekoa,* population 826, and then Garfield (population 641) to the south. Garfield's *R.C. McCroskey House* at 803 North Fourth Street (509-635-1459) is a classical revival–style Victorian mansion constructed in 1898. Call ahead for tour information.

Bishop's U-Pick Orchard (509-635-1276; www.bishop-orchard.com), in Garfield at Eighth and Adams Streets offers a wealth of apples from September through the end of October. People come from miles around to make fresh juice on Steven Bishop's five handmade oak cider presses, patterned after the ones his great-grandfather used when he homesteaded in Garfield. Bring a picnic lunch and make it a real outing.

South of Garfield is the town of Palouse, once a bustling commercial center supplying gold-mining and logging camps in Idaho. Despite its size, it has three vehicle bridges and a foot bridge across the Palouse River. The town's main street is lined with splendid old brick buildings, many now in the process of being renovated. Palouse's historic district on Main Street is listed on the National Register of Historic Places. One old storefront now houses *Ray Chatters Newspaper and Printing Museum,* a half-block east of the town's only streetlight at 110 East Main Street. In some guide books it's called the Boomerang Museum, probably because the paper founded in the 1890s was called the *Boomerang.* The museum features newspapers from the area as well as an impressive collection of old presses and other printing equipment dating from the late 1800s. It's open 8:00 a.m. to noon on Saturday; or call Janet Barstow at (509) 878-1742 or Jack Rupe at (208) 882-3771 for an appointment. Stop in at 110 South Bridge Street in the 1889 Bank Building in Palouse that houses the *Bank Left Gallery* (509-878-8425) and a tea-and-chocolate shop behind a colorful front. Nearby is the *Green Frog Cafe* at 100 East Main Street (509-878-1490), a favorite gathering place for locals. It has an open mic on the first Friday of every month, no surprise since one of the owners once toured with rocker Joan Jett.

Browse at *Small Town Quilts* at 124 East Main Street (509-878-1253); *Open Eye Antiques* (509-878-1210) at 119 East Main Street for retro and

Bagels, Lentil or Split Pea Soup, Anyone?

Wheat, lentils, and peas are major crops grown in the Palouse region. After harvest they are barged about 200 miles down the Snake River from the Clarkston-Lewiston area to Pasco, passing through the scenic 2,000-foot-deep Snake River Canyon and negotiating through locks at Lower Granite Dam, Little Goose Dam, Lower Monumental Dam, and Ice Harbor Dam. At Pasco the large barges, pushed by fat tugboats, enter the wide Columbia River and travel another 200 miles downriver, passing The Dalles, Maryhill, Hood River, Cascade Locks, North Bonneville, Washougal, and Camas and detouring onto the Willamette River at Portland-Vancouver. Here the wheat, lentils, and peas are loaded onto huge transport ships at the Port of Portland. These vessels travel another 100 miles downriver on the Columbia River to Astoria and then out onto the Pacific Ocean for journeys to ports far and wide.

country antiques and collectibles; and *Linda's Whimseys* at 215 East Main Street (509-878-1678) for a splendid selection of Victorian gift items. Then pop into nearby *St. Elmo's Antiques* at 130 East Main Street (509-878-1471) in the 1888 St. Elmo's Hotel. Cap off your tour of Palouse by stopping at the *Family Cafe,* 126 West Main Street (509-878-1716). It's open daily except Monday and Tuesday. Note: The best days to visit small towns in the Palouse area are Wednesday through Saturday, when most establishments are open.

Pullman

Pullman is the Palouse region's largest city and a bustling mixture of agricultural businesses and student life. Washington State University (WSU, affectionately called Wazzu) is this city's Center of the Galaxy. Founded in 1890, WSU emphasizes agricultural sciences. The main number for the university is 509-335-3564. Or contact the Pullman Visitor Information Center (800-365-6948; www.pullmanchamber.com) for the current sports schedules and information about lodgings, tours of the scenic campus and its historic buildings, and a campus map.

WSU has a splendid *Museum of Anthropology* (509-335-3414) featuring displays on human evolution and the development of language and culture—and on the Northwest's mysterious Sasquatch. The museum is open 9:00 a.m. to 4:00 p.m. weekdays during the academic year. Art lovers can enjoy the University's Museum of Art (509-335-1910). The gallery has changing exhibitions featuring past and contemporary international, regional, and student artists

walkoffame

Although WSU students are often ribbed (particularly by University of Washington students) about attending a small school focused on agricultural than more (supposedly) cerebral occupations, the Cougars can point to the downtown Pullman Walk of Fame to show the bright minds of their graduates, including Phil (Class of '33) and Neva ('34) Abelson. He helped develop the first nuclear submarine and was long-time editor of *Science* magazine; she co-developed the Rh blood test that saved the lives of countless babies. Others who have risen to the top of their professions include CBS radio and TV broadcaster Edward R. Murrow ('33), TV sports commentator Keith Jackson ('54), "The Far Side" cartoonist Gary Larson ('72), and Orville Vogel ('39), a wheat breeder whose findings sparked the Green Revolution.

working in painting, sculpture, photography, and architecture. The gallery is open daily from 10:00 a.m. to 4:00 p.m. and on Thursday until 7:00 p.m.

After you've worked up an appetite from museum touring, stop at *Ferdinand's Ice Cream Shoppe* (509-335-2141), a campus ice-cream parlor named after the friendly, flower-sniffing bull from the Disney short *Ferdinand the Bull*. On the walls are quotations by author Munro Leaf and illustrations by Robert Lawson from the classic book about Ferdinand, which has been beloved by generations of children. Ferdinand's sells WSU Creamery's own Cougar brand of high-quality dairy products (such as the award-winning Cougar Gold cheese), produced on campus.

Although it's a busy college town servicing Washington State University and its thousands of Cougar fans, Pullman offers a variety of pleasant reasons for lingering in your travels to the far southeast corner of the state. Take an invigorating walk in a splendid city park or along a rails-to-trails pathway, stroll in a lovely garden, play a round of golf, put together an impromptu picnic, or stop at a friendly cafe.

Reaney Park at 609 Reaney Way is home of the Reaney Park Summer Concert Series (509-338-3227) and the National Lentil Festival in late August. Find outdoor pools, a gazebo, playground area, picnic tables, and barbecue area.

Lawson Gardens, located at Derby Street near Dilke Street, offers thirteen acres of formal gardens including a reflecting pool, gazebo, seasonal annuals and perennials, and splendid rose gardens. The Bill Chipman Palouse Trail, reclaimed from a former railroad bed near the Pullman-Moscow Highway (Highway 270), offers 7 miles of bicycle- and pedestrian-friendly trails between Pullman and Moscow, Idaho, the home of the University of Idaho.

In downtown Pullman you can find a jolt of java, tasty sandwiches, decadent baked goods, and local conversation at Swilly's at 200 Northeast Kamiaken Street (509-334-3395), *Café Moro Coffee Shop* at 100 East Main Street

(509-338-3892), and *Daily Grind Downtown Coffee House* at 230 East Main Street (509-334-3380). Caution: If the notion of enduring pep rallies, marching bands, and being trampled by some 40,000 WSU Cougar sports fans doesn't appeal, plan your trips to the Pullman area on weekends sans football. Also best to avoid Dad's Weekend and Mom's Weekend. Check www.pullman chamber.com (800-365-6948) and www.football-weekends.wsu.edu for current schedules and information.

For a step back in time to the Old West, visit the *Three Forks Pioneer Village Museum,* located about 4 miles north of Pullman at 952 Banner Road on the Roger Rossebo Farm. This re-created town, assembled during the past three decades by Rossebo, has the Wawawai General Store, barber shop, blacksmith's shop, jail, and hardware store, displaying thousands of antiques dating from the 1800s, including a piano shipped around Cape Horn, a pioneer kitchen, and a schoolhouse. The museum is open by appointment from May to September. There is a small fee. Call (509) 332-3889 for reservations and directions.

TOP ANNUAL EVENTS
IN SOUTHEAST WASHINGTON

Asotin County Fair
Asotin, April
(509) 243-4411

Autumn Harvest Hullabaloo & Arts and Antiques Fair
Colfax, mid-October
(509) 397-3712

Balloon Stampede
Walla Walla, early May
(877) 998-4748

Dayton Days
Dayton, Memorial Day weekend
(800) 882-6299

Dayton Depot Festival
Dayton, mid-September
(800) 882-6299

Dogwood Festival
Clarkston, throughout April
(800) 933-2128

Historic Homes Tour
Dayton, mid-October
(509) 382-2026

National Lentil Festival
Pullman, mid-August
(800) 365-6948

Slippery Gulch Days & Rodeo
Tekoa, late June
(509) 284-3861

The Sun Festival
Clarkston, late June
(800) 933-2128

Sweet Onion Festival
Walla Walla, mid-July
(509) 525-0850

One option after leaving Pullman is to head northwest on Highway 195 about 15 miles to Colfax. The highway runs right through town so keep a lookout on the right for Colfax's most unusual attraction, the 65-foot-tall Codger Pole, possibly the world's tallest chainsaw carving and, if not, probably the world's tallest chainsaw carving of faces, or if not that, certainly the world's tallest chainsaw carving of football players. The pole commemorates a grudge match in 1988 played between former football players (then in their late 60s) of Colfax and St. John. The Colfax team of elders attained the victory that was snatched from it 50 years earlier. The bundle of five cedar logs has the likeness of 51 players with a generic Old Codger standing on the top.

The Whitman County seat sits along the banks of the Palouse River. Stop to see the splendid Victorian **Perkins House** at 623 North Perkins Street, built by city founder James Perkins, who made his fortune with the region's first sawmill, in 1886. The oldest standing house in Whitman County is listed on the National Register of Historic Places, and was once the center of Colfax's society. It is open for tours from 1:00 to 4:00 p.m. Thursday and Sunday, from Memorial Day to Labor Day. An old-fashioned ice-cream social is held at the mansion the last Sunday in June. For current information contact the Colfax Visitor Information Center at (509) 397-3712.

Meet the local folks at **Top Notch Cafe,** 210 North Main Street (509-397-4569), or just head for a good night's sleep at the Pottingshed Guesthouse at 911 South East Street (509-397-2014; www.thepottingshedguesthouse.com. On the property of a historic home, this retreat has been a stable, a playhouse, a mother-in-law residence, and a glorified potting shed until it was completely remodeled, complete with flat panel TV, kitchen, and laundry.

To bed down in the ponderosa pine-and-farm country near Colfax, call the Gilchrest family at **Union Creek Guest Ranch,** located a few miles southwest via U.S. Highway 195 at 2501 Upper Union Flat Road (509-397-3292; www.unioncreekranch.com). Guests are welcomed to this 2,200-acre ranch nestled in the hills. The working farm and cattle ranch offers horseback and hayrides as well as hunting and fishing opportunities and stalls for your horses. Penny Gilchrest serves a hearty country breakfast of bacon, ham, eggs, and hash browns along with fresh fruit, juices, homemade cinnamon rolls, and, often, her delicious apple crisp tortillas.

Another option is to leave Pullman and head south on US 195 toward **Uniontown.** Check at Premier Alpacas of the Palouse at 401 South Railroad Avenue (509-229-3655; www.premieralpacas.com). The remodeled bunkhouse contains sleeping quarters for four, with cozy quilts and comforters, and comes with a spiral staircase to the sleeping loft. There's also a guest room and an indoor lap pool in the turn-of-the-century farmhouse. Another splendid option in Uniontown is the ***Churchyard Inn Bed & Breakfast*** at 206 Saint Boniface Street (509-229-3200; www.churchyardinn.com). Guests find comfy bed-and-breakfast accommodations in the 1905 European Flemish–style parish-turned-convent. The house and its interior were completely renovated in 1995, including the fine hand-detailed woodwork, moldings, doors of red fir, the impressive staircases, seven bedrooms, and several balconies. The inn is located next to the 1904 Saint Boniface Catholic Church, which has an interior beauty worth your time.

Since 1948 the men of Uniontown have made sausage from a secret recipe for the annual Sausage Feed on the first Sunday in March. For other good eats, check out ***Eleanor's Place*** at 101 North Montgomery (509-229-3389), a local saloon on the very short main drag that offers a good selection of microbrews and possibly "the best burgers on the Palouse." Stop at the splendid ***Sage Baking Company*** (509-229-3716), which offers crusty rustic breads as well as tasty pastries, coffee drinks, and deli fare on Friday and Saturday.

Another option going southwest from Pullman is to stay at the Eaton Season Ranch (509-334-6406) at 11601 Wawawai Road, at least in part for

Miracle on the Palouse

It could be called a miracle, a deteriorating 1935 dairy barn used until 1952 that was brought back to life by a volunteer-run non-profit with grants and donations after Steve and Junette Dahmen donated the Uniontown property. The town of 300 residents pulled together and volunteers donated more than 3,000 hours.

Fifty years of pigeon droppings were taken out of the loft; a beam-and-cable system pulled the tilting barn into plumb; an interior support structure was built; and amenities, including an elevator and the hot-water radiant-heat system in the ground floor's concrete slab, were added. Much credit goes to Jennifer Anthony of Fearless Engineers of Missoula, a specialist in log and timber-frame construction.

After giving the barn new physical life, the spirit was added with working artists in ten small studios as well as a name: *Artisans at the Dahmen Barn.* They use their spaces to show their creations; each works there eight hours a week (Thursday through Sunday). An excellent gift shop sells work on consignment from nearly 100 regional artists. The Hayloft Hall is used for dances, exhibits, classes, and concerts.

You won't miss the barn at 419 North Park Way (509-229-3414; www.artisanbarn .org) because of the eye-catching wheel fence. Steve Dahmen had a folk-art gate-building project and friends started donating wheels, including those from various machines and an antique baby buggy. Eventually more than 1,000 wheels of up to 60 inches in diameter created the landmark fence line off the main road. The Adopt-a-Wheel program raises money that helps maintain the barn and fence. Select a wheel or have one chosen for you for $25 to $100, based on size.

the scenic drive. The street number may sound like suburbia but it's not even close although it's only about 25 minutes from Pullman. Nicole or Joe Eaton's Web site, www.eatonseasonranch.com, will provide directions that end with a 4½-mile winding, descending route through Wawawai Canyon to your cabin.

Joe is the fifth generation of Eatons to own the 3,000-acre ranch; the cattle part is at lower elevations, the alfalfa and wheat on top of the canyon. In addition to ranching and farming, the Eatons recently entered agri-tourism with a cozy one-room, two-loft cabin with a matching heated outhouse (heated toilet seat, shower) across the driveway, but will involve guests in ranch activities or arrange for a lesson in roping or a guide for a horseback ride.

A short descent below the cabin is the delightful little Wawawai County Park with a ¾-mile trail (a mile if you take the loop) and shoreline, a good place for birdwatching in the spring. The phrase "wa-wa-wai" means "council grounds" in the native language; three "wa" together essentially means talk-talk-talk together.

The Snake River is but another quick descent beyond the park. Turn left. WaWaWai Landing on Lower Granite Lake, part of the Snake, is home to the Washington State University crew teams and boathouse; you might catch them training on the water.

From there, follow the road that hugs the Snake all the way to Clarkston.

Exploring with Lewis and Clark

South of Pullman at the confluence of the Snake and Clearwater Rivers, the twin cities of **Clarkston** and, across the Snake River, **Lewiston, Idaho,** have become the embarking point for adventures at Hells Gate State Park, the Nez Percé Reservation, and boat or raft trips through Hells Canyon National Recreation Area, the deepest river gorge in North America. Contact the Clarkston Visitor Information Center at 502 Bridge Street (800-933-2128; www.clarkston chamber.org) or the Hells Canyon Visitor Association at 504 Bridge Street (877-774-7248; www.www.hellscayonvisitor.com) for information on river trips, bike and walking paths, and lodgings.

Captain William Clark, Meriwether Lewis, and their original **Corps of Discovery** camped for nine October days on the Snake River at present-day Clarkston in 1805. Visit the Lewis and Clark Expedition Timeline, etched and painted in the pavement at Hells Canyon Marina, 1550 Port Drive. The nearly blocklong timeline illustrates key events from the Corps of Discovery's journey across the western half of the United States, including canoeing down sections of the nearby Snake River and the Columbia River on their way to the Pacific

Ocean. U.S. Highway 12 from Lewiston and Clarkston west toward **Pomeroy** and **Dayton** roughly parallels the party's return journey in 1806.

After all this busy history-browsing you may be ready for some vittles. Check out Sun Bean Coffeehouse Cafe at 720 Sixth Street in Clarkston (509-751-8887) for great breads, soups, and sandwiches; find tasty homemade pie and cool libations at the old-fashioned soda fountain at Wasem's Drugstore, 800 Sixth Street (509-758-2565); and for waterside dining with great views, call Rooster's Landing on the Snake River (1550 Port Drive; 509-751-0155).

Heading west on US 12, you many want to stop and explore Pomeroy. Park 1 block over on Columbia Street, where you'll see colorful flower beds

From flour mill to Bugs Bunny cartoons

One of the bonuses to traveling off the beaten path is the number and quality of surprises that pop up out in the country. Do you remember the XXX Flour seen in some of the early Bugs Bunny cartoons? That brand was produced in the 1878 **Pataha Flour Mill** in Pomeroy and was the first patented flour, known across the nation for its high protein content. High in gluten, it was often used to make macaroni.

Also known as the Houser Mill, it closed in 1943 when the owners were unable to meet federal regulations. They walked away and left all the milling equipment behind. Jon VanVogt bought the mill in 1998 and, after clearing some of the interior and painting the exterior, opened the building to the public in August 1998 with a Hometown Revival of gospel music.

Most important, he left the milling equipment. Start in the basement to see the coal-burning furnace and a 6-foot bull wheel and wide leather belts. The first floor has grinders used to process 100,000 bushels of wheat each year, or 80 barrels of flour a day. Now there's also a restaurant.

Bran, used for animal feed, was sacked on the second floor, which still has various milling machines as well as the being-constructed Houser Room that will someday be used for special events. The third floor houses a plane sifter with wooden augers suspended by wooden dowels, and a fan separator, in which the wheat went first. All the floors have huge timbers from the nearby Blue Mountains and tongue-and-groove floors and siding.

At Pataha, there are surprises within surprises. In one small room check out Delbert Niebel's branding iron collection that includes the brands Duck Foot, Goose Egg, Hoof & Nail, One Pipe and Rocking A. Another room, one of five cribs for wheat, has a large train garden, all lit up. Another room has Neil Keatts' collection of more than 400 antique cameras, including a No. 4 Folding Pocket Kodak Model A 4x5 from about 1915.

The Pataha Flour Mill & Museum is at 50 Hutchens Hill Road, Pomeroy (509-843-3799). Renovation work continues; the restaurant is open for lunch Wednesday through Saturday and dinner on Saturday.

planted down the center of the street where the train tracks once ran. Browse along Main Street and poke into inviting shops such as Three Forks Art Gallery at 807 Main Street (509-843-1600) and Victorian Rose at 741 Main Street (509-843-1989), where the collectibles include figurines from the Trail of Painted Ponies. Admire the 16-foot-high ceilings in the 1900 building that houses Meyer's at 796 Main Street (509-843-3721) and its eclectic collection of hardware items, gifts, and the Bean Counter Espresso Bar.

Check out the 1916 Seeley Building at 67 Seventh Street, which housed an early vaudeville theater; the historic Hotel Revere, currently being renovated by Beverly and John Gordon, owners of Castlemoyle Books (509-843-5009); and *Garfield County Museum* at 708 Street (509-843-3925).

You can also bed down in Pomeroy in a comfy style by checking on guest rooms at Maggie's Garden B&B, 714 Arlington Street (509-843-2495). If you're traveling RV-style and want hookups, call the *Last Resort Store & Blue Mountains KOA* at 2005 Tucannon Road (509-843-1556), about 10 miles south of Pomeroy in the Umatilla National Forest. The Pomeroy ranger station at 71 West Main Street (509-843-1891) can supply information about camping, hiking, and fishing (including flyfishing) along the Tucannon River.

The town of Dayton is another well-preserved historic community. When Lewis and Clark explored the region on their return trip in 1806, what is now Dayton's main street served as a racetrack for American Indian tribes who camped in the area. Although this land was first homesteaded by cattle ranchers in 1859, grain farming took over within a few years. Dayton was also a stagecoach stop between Walla Walla and Lewiston. Logs from the Blue Mountains traveled down to the town mill by an 18-mile flume.

Its one claim to fame for about 70 years was the world's largest asparagus cannery, run by Senaca Foods, which moved its operations to Peru after the 2005 season. For a couple of decades, a farmer would fertilize the huge shape of the iconic Jolly Green Giant high on a hillside. The giant got greener and more visible as the season progressed. In 1991, locals decided on a more permanent approach that used white patio blocks along the 300-foot-tall, 40-foot-wide outline, which can be seen about a mile west of Dayton.

To see the 1881 *Dayton Depot* (509-382-2026), the oldest surviving railway station in the state, turn west from Main Street onto Commercial. Call for hours or check with www.daytonhistoricdepot.com. For information about self-guided historic walking tours and the lively Dayton's Depot Days Festival in mid-September, contact the Dayton Visitor Information Center at (509) 382-4825 or go to www.historicdayton.com. Dayton's Columbia County Courthouse, across from the depot, is the oldest operating courthouse in the state.

The **Purple House B&B** (415 East Clay Street; 509-382-3159), built in 1882 by a pioneer physician and philanthropist, is one of Dayton's finest homes with four guest rooms, a guest library, a lovely parlor, and an outdoor pool. Just for fun stop by Dingles of Dayton at 179 East Main Street (509-382-2581). In this old-fashioned general store, you'll find everything from nuts and bolts, nails and screws, and plumbing supplies to teddy bears, coloring books, crystal glassware, and fishing rods. "If you can't find it at Dingles, you don't need it," is the store motto.

If exploring makes you thirsty, stop at the Elk Drug Store at 176 East Main Street to order milkshakes and sodas from an old-fashioned soda fountain. Step back in time in grand style at the 1889 **Weinhard Hotel** at 235 East Main Street (509-382-4032; www.weinhard.com), restored in a Victorian motif with 14-foot-high ceilings, elaborate antiques, and a rooftop garden. All fifteen rooms have private baths and antique furniture. Enjoy fine Italian specialties at Weinhard's Café at 258 East Main Street (509-382-1681). The cafe is open Tuesday through Saturday for lunch and dinner. For gourmet fare and great desserts in a comfortable setting, try the popular **Patit Creek Restaurant** at 725 East Dayton Avenue, on US 12 at the east end of town (509-382-2625). Dinner reservations are recommended. Another local favorite, **Skye Book & Brew** (148 East Main Street; 509-382-4677) offers good reads along with microbrews, espresso, and casual fare. Panhandlers Restaurant, 400 West Main Street (509-382-4160), serves good breakfasts as well as steaks, burgers, salads, and tasty desserts.

About 15 miles from Dayton, towering wind turbines generate electricity. Puget Sound Energy offers Wind Tours of the Hopkins Ridge Wind Facility. Call the Dayton office, (509) 382-2043.

Dayton is the access point for the Blue Mountains in the Umatilla National Forest, which includes the **Wenaha-Tucannon Wilderness,** an area of steep ridges, talus slopes, and tablelands accessible only by backcountry trails. Wildlife includes Rocky Mountain elk, white-tailed and mule deer, bighorn

Patit Creek Campsite: Camping Lewis and Clark Style

On May 2, 1806, the Lewis and Clark Corps of Discovery camped near Dayton for one night on their return trip home. Eighty life-size metal silhouette sculptures produced and arranged on the site by Dayton artists and community members show the entire party setting up camp. The silhouettes include horses, cooking gear, and even Clark's dog, Seaman. To reach the site, turn off US 12 just north of downtown Dayton and onto Patit Creek Road.

sheep, black bear, cougar, and bobcat. For information, call the Pomeroy Ranger Station at (509) 843-1891.

Palouse Falls State Park, 30 miles north of Dayton, offers a glimpse of what some river canyons in the area looked like before they were dammed. The spectacular falls tumble 198 feet over basalt-column cliffs, surrounded by grass- and sage-covered hills. Although this 1,281-acre park offers only ten primitive campsites, nearby ***Lyons Ferry State Park*** (www.parks.wa.gov) has fifty standard campsites with no hookups. ***Lyons Ferry Marina*** (509-399-8020), on the Snake River just off Highway 261, offers RV sites, boat-launch facilities, and a cozy eatery, ***Coffees on Cafe.***

Palouse Falls

To the south, the Walla Walla Valley is known primarily for fertile fields of grain, but since the late 1980s the valley also hosts about twenty wineries and large vineyards with grapes that will produce merlot, cabernet sauvignon, and syrah each year. For lists and maps of tasting rooms, check with the Walla Walla Area Visitor Information Center at 29 East Sumach Street, Walla Walla (877-998-4748; www.wallawalla.org). Collect self-guided tour maps for the nostalgic downtown area and helpful information about the bustling arts scene in this farm and college town. The Walla Walla Foundry at 405 Woodland Avenue (509-522-2114) specializes in bronze but also produces works in gold, silver, and aluminum. You can visit more than twenty eclectic art galleries and also see twenty-four historic homes in the area.

wallawalla sweets

About 40 growers grow 39 million pounds of the jumbo-sized sweet onions. They're sweeter because of a 6 to 15 percent sugar content, well above the 3 to 5 percent sugar content of regular onions.

Downtown, after browsing the art galleries, gift shops, historic buildings, and antiques shops along Main Street, join the locals and relax in ***Heritage Square*** in the heart of town. On one side of the square is a mural of nineteenth-century downtown Walla Walla. On the opposite wall is the 1902 Odd Fellows building facade. The park also has playground equipment, a picnic area, and restrooms. For a pleasant breakfast or lunch on a sunny day, find an outdoor table under the green-and-red-striped awnings at Merchants Limited & French Bakery at 21 East Main Street (509-525-0900), which also offers a take-out deli, freshly baked pastries, and regional wines. Locals suggest *Colville Street Patisserie* at 40 South Colville Street (509-301-7289) for desserts, wines, and espresso.

Walla Walla is home to several inviting bed-and-breakfast inns and guest ranches. The 1909 Craftsman-style *Green Gables Inn Bed and Breakfast,* 922 Bonsella Street (888-525-5501; www.greengablesinn.com), once a residence for nurses, has five guest rooms, elegant and comfortable havens with private baths. A separate carriage house cottage that sleeps four has a full kitchen. Or call the *Inn at Blackberry Creek* at 1126 Pleasant Street (877-522-5233; www.innatblackberrycreek.com), a 1912 Victorian farmhouse offering travelers three guest rooms and tasty breakfasts. Other options include staying at the Fat Duck Inn, 527 Catherine Street (888-526-8718), the city's newest luxury inn with optional gourmet dinners and box lunches; and the upscale and more-modern Areus at 1903 Smith Road (509-200-9931), just outside of town. If you have four-wheel drive, call *Top of the Mountain Retreats* in the Blue Mountains at 9052 Mill Creek Road (509-529-4288; www.mountainretreats .com). Choose between the Strawberry Canyon Lodge and the cabins at 3,800 feet elevation next to the Umatilla National Forest.

exploringthe blues

The Blue Mountains run from its northern point in Washington's southeastern corner to its southern tip in extreme northeastern Oregon. The Umatilla National Forest is in the Blues. *Umatilla* is a Native American word for "water rippling over sand."

Walla Walla has many good dining options. A local favorite is *Clarette's Restaurant* at 15 South Touchet Street (509-529-3430) for all-American-style fare and all-day breakfast; and *Mill Creek Brew Pub* at 11 South Palouse Street (509-522-2440) for pub food and regional ales.

Southwest of town is the splendid *Fort Walla Walla Museum Complex* (509-525-7703; www.fortwallawallamuseum.org) at 755 Myra Road on the grounds of Fort Walla Walla Park. The museum complex includes a re-created pioneer village with fourteen historic log buildings filled with antique items; and six large museum buildings with additional displays. The historical complex is open daily from 10:00 a.m. to 5:00 p.m., from April to October. There is an admission.

Be sure to visit the ***Whitman Mission National Historic Site*** 7 miles west of town (509-522-6360; www.nps.gov/whmi). It commemorates the mission Waiilatpu, established by Marcus and Narcissa Whitman in the early 1800s. The visitor center displays and an interpretive trail on the grounds describe the history of the mission and bring to life activities in the Walla Walla Valley between 1836 and 1847, when waves of settlers stopped here on their arduous trek along the Oregon Trail. For a panoramic view of the grounds, walk through the small grove of trees, past the tepee, and up the path to the nearby hilltop monument. The visitor center is open daily from 8:00 a.m. to 6:00 p.m. in summer and 8:00 a.m. to 4:30 p.m. the rest of the year.

Places to Stay in Southeast Washington

CLARKSTON

Best Western Rivertree Inn
1257 Bridge Street
(800) 597-3621

COLFAX

Union Creek Guest Ranch
2501 Upper Union Flat Road
(509) 397-3292

DAYTON

Mill House Cottage
504 North First Street
(509) 382-2393

The Weinhard Hotel
235 East Main Street
(509) 382-4032

PULLMAN

Paradise Creek Quality Inn
140 Southeast Bishop Boulevard
(509) 332-0500

UNIONTOWN

Premier Alpacas of the Palouse
401 South Railroad Avenue
(509) 229-3655

WALLA WALLA

Best Western Walla Walla Suites Inn
7 East Oak Street
(509) 525-4700

Green Gables Inn Bed & Breakfast
922 Bonsella Street
(509) 525-5501

Inn at Blackberry Creek
1126 Pleasant Street
(877) 522-5233

Places to Eat in Southeast Washington

CLARKSTON/LEWISTON

Bogey's Restaurant at Quality Inn
700 Port Drive
(509) 758-9500

Rooster's Landing
1550 Port Drive
(509) 751-0155

The Sugar Shack Candies & Gifts
923 Sixth Street
(509) 758-2090

COLFAX

Top Notch Cafe
210 North Main Street
(509) 397-4569

DAYTON

**Country Cupboard
Bakery, Deli & Espresso**
330 East Main Street
(509) 382-2215

**Patit Valley Products
Cafe**
232 Main Street
(509) 382-1998

Skye Book & Brew
148 East Main Street
(509) 382-4677

Weinhard's Cafe
229 East Main Street
(509) 382-1681

PALOUSE

The Family Café
126 West Main Street
(509) 878-1716

**Green Frog Coffee Shop
Cafe**
100 East Main Street
(509) 878-1490

PULLMAN

Café Moro Coffee House
100 East Main Street
(509) 338-3892

Daily Grind Coffee House
230 Main Street
(509) 334-3380

**Ferdinand's Ice Cream
Shoppe**
Food Quality Building
WSU Campus
(509) 335-2141

The Fireside Grille
195 SE Bishop Boulevard
(509) 334-3663

TEKOA

The Feeding Station
205 North Crosby
(509) 284-3141

UNIONTOWN

Eleanor's Place
101 North Montgomery
(509) 229-3389

WALLA WALLA

Clarette's Restaurant
15 South Touchet Street
(509) 529-3430

Coffee Connection Cafe
57 East Main Street
(509) 529-9999

Stone Soup Cafe
105 East Alder Street
(509) 525-5008

SELECTED INFORMATION CENTERS AND OTHER HELPFUL WEB SITES

Clarkston
(800) 933-2128
www.clarkstonchamber.org

Colfax
(509) 397-3712
www.visitcolfax.com

Dayton
(800) 882-6299
www.historicdayton.com

Pullman
(800) 365-6948
www.pullmanchamber.com

Walla Walla Valley
(509) 525-0850
www.wwvchamber.com

Washington Road Conditions
(800) 695-7623
www.wsdot.wa.gov/traffic

Useful Resources

Government Agency Resources

Bicycle Program
Washington State Department of Transportation
Olympia
(360) 705-7277 Bicycle Hotline
Ask for the state bicycle map.

National Park Service, U.S. Forest Service Outdoor Recreation Information Center
222 Yale Avenue North
Seattle
(206) 470-4060
www.nps.gov and www.fs.fed.us/r6/mbs
Information on camping, hiking, and trail conditions for Western Washington's national parks and national forests.

North Cascades National Park Service Complex
810 State Route 20
Sedro-Woolley
www.nps.gov/noca and www.fsfed.us/r6/mbs
The complex, about 5 miles east of Interstate 5, is open daily 8:00 a.m. to 4:30 p.m. from Memorial Day weekend through mid-October and Monday through Friday (same hours) during the rest of the year. For information about North Cascades National Park, Ross Lake, and Lake Chelan, call 360-854-7200. For information about Mount Baker, Mount Baker Ranger District, and the *North Cascades Institute,* call (360) 856-5700. For information about backcountry hiking, call the Wilderness Information Center at (360) 854-7245. Ask NCI for a catalog of year-round seminars on the state's natural and cultural history. Farther east on Highway 20 and 14 miles east of Marblemount, the North Cascades Visitor Center in Newhalem (206-386-4495) is open daily from 9:00 a.m. to 4:30 p.m.

Washington Department of Fish and Wildlife
21961 Wylie Road
Mount Vernon
(360) 445-4441
www.wdfw.wa.gov

Washington State Department of Natural Resources
111 Washington Street Southeast
P.O. Box 47016
Olympia, 98504
(360) 902-1000
www.dnr.wa.gov
DNR manages more than 135 primitive recreation sites with hiking trails, 4WD roads, and limited backcountry facilities.

Washington State Ferries
Colman Dock/Pier 52
801 Alaskan Way
Seattle
For schedule information call (206) 464-6400 in Seattle or in-state only (888) 808-7977.
www.wsdot.wa.gov/ferries

Washington State Parks
7153 Cleanwater Lane
Olympia
(360) 902-8844
www.parks.wa.gov
Information on state parks and campgrounds.

Washington Tourism Information
Bellingham
Call (800) 544-1800 and request a *Washington State Traveler's Guide.*
www.ExperienceWashington.com

U.S.–Canadian Border Crossing
(206) 553-0770
www.cbp.gov

Other Resources

BIRDS AND BIRDING

Audubon Washington: www.wa.audubon.org (Ask about *The Great Washington State Birding Trail* map.)

Seattle Audubon Society online guide: www.birdweb.org

Washington Ornithological Society: www.wos.org

PRINTED MATERIALS

Artguide Northwest
(206) 367-6831
www.artguide.com
The guide lists all galleries, museums, and antiques shops west of the Cascades.

Exploring Washington's Past: A Road Guide to History
Ruth Kirk and Carmela Alexander
University of Washington Press
This comprehensive handbook describes local history for much of Washington, including fascinating stories and insights about many of the places described in *Washington Off the Beaten Path*.

Washington Atlas & Gazeteer
This atlas provides topographical maps covering all of Washington State at approximately half an inch to the mile, making it ideal for exploring back roads.

OUTINGS

Sierra Club, Cascade Chapter
Seattle
For outings and events check
www.cascade.sierraclub.org.

Sound Experience
2310 Washington Street
Port Townsend
(360) 379-0438
www.soundexp.org
A nonprofit educational organization specializing in environmental, marine science, and sailing programs for youths and adults aboard the 136-foot-long 1913 tall ship *Adventuress*.

Washington State Scenic Byways

The Cape Flattery Tribal Scenic Byway that runs from Neah Bay to Cape Flattery is the first Tribal Scenic Byway in the state. The 36-mile loop route, designated in 2002, starts at the Makah Cultural and Resource Center. Highlights include the Makah National Salmon Hatchery, Neah Bay and marina, Olympic Coast National Marine Sanctuary, Shi Shi Beach, Tatoosh Island and lighthouse, and the Cape Flattery Trail, which leads to the most northwestern point on the U.S. mainland.

The state has six nationally designated routes: two All-American Roads—Chinook Pass Scenic Byway (S.R. 310) and International Selkirk Loop (S.R. 31, 20); and four National Scenic Byways—Mountains to Sound Greenway (I-90), Strait of Juan de Fuca Highway (S.R. 112), Coulee Corridor (S.R. 17, 155), and Stevens Pass Greenway (U.S. 2). There are also dozens of state-designated byways and scenic drives.

For more information or to obtain a Washington State Scenic Byways Map, call 800-544-1800.

Washington Trails Association

(206) 625-1367

www.wta.org

WTA is the state's most active volunteer trails-maintenance organization with an excellent Web site that includes trip notes from hikers in the field.

Washington Water Trails Association

Seattle

(206) 545-9161

www.wwta.org

Promotes preservation of marine shorelines and the creation of the Cascadia Marine Trail, a network of sites accessible to kayaks and canoes throughout Puget Sound.

Index

About the Authors

Sharon Wootton and Maggie Savage are co-authors of the Insiders' Guide, *You Know You're in Washington When . . . 101 Quintessential Places, People, Events, Customs, Lingo, and Eats of the Evergreen State.*

Sharon, a Washington resident since 1974, has more than 3 million words in print as a journalist, columnist for two daily newspapers, and full-time free-lance writer. Her stories and photographs have appeared in dozens of regional and national magazines and newspapers.

Maggie, a Washington native, is a free-lance travel writer and musician. In her past life, she toured nationally as a musician, led songwriting workshops at Northwest Folklife Festival for more than a decade, and performed regularly at Folklife for more than 20 years. Her recordings include the CD "With Whom Will You Spend the Rest of Your Life." She continues to write songs and also performs with Orcas a Capella.

The partners live on a small island (200 residents) in the San Juans and are co-owners of Song&Word, a business that offers songwriting and writing workshops and retreats.